EBS

Gupta Empire and Middle Kingdom

Gupta Empire and Middle Kingdom

Edited by

H.C. Sharma
Dharam Singh

GLOBAL PUBLICATIONS
NEW DELHI-110 002 (INDIA)

GLOBAL PUBLICATIONS
4378/4B, G-4 JMD House
Murari Lal Street, Ansari Road
Daryaganj, New Delhi - 110 002
Phone : 23278062 (Off.)
e-mail : omega_publications@yahoo.com

Head Office :
79/23, Laxmi Garden
Near Satya Jyoti School,
Gurgaon (Haryana)
Mob : 9213562438

Gupta Empire and Middle Kingdom

First Published : 2011

ISBN : 978-93-80833-26-2

PRINTED IN INDIA

Published by Ishwari Prasad Garg for Global Publications, New Delhi-110002
and Printed at Suman Printers, Delhi

Preface

The Guptas were famous rulers of ancient India, who constructed their own imperialism and introduced the Golden era in India. After the lapse of a prolonged Dark Age, it was the Guptas who initiated peace and coalesced the entire disintegrated Northern India. The Gupta rulers ascended the throne in 320 A.D. and continued to be the sovereign authority of India till 550 A.D. When the Guptas came into the political scenario of India, the condition of entire North India was pretty lawless and due to lack of any central authority the provincial governors unfurled their flag of independence after the downfall of the Kushanas. Furthermore they were at continuous strife with one another for which the socio-political condition of Northern India was extremely chaotic. During that time the Guptas and the Kshatriyas rose to power, who not only defeated the provincial kings, but also compelled them to offer their allegiance to the Guptas. In such a manner, the Guptas consolidated the entire northern India under their own supremacy.

The Gupta Empire was an Ancient Indian empire which existed approximately from 320 to 550 CE and covered much of the Indian Subcontinent. Founded by Maharaja Sri-Gupta, the dynasty began the *Classical Age* in the Middle kingdoms of India. The capital of the Guptas was Pataliputra, present day Patna, in the north Indian state of Bihar.

The peace and prosperity created under leadership of Guptas enabled the pursuit of scientific and artistic endeavors. Historians place the Gupta dynasty alongside with the Han Dynasty, Tang Dynasty and Roman Empire as a model of a classical civilization. The time of the Gupta Empire is referred to by some scholars as the Golden Age of India in science, technology, engineering, art, dialectic, literature, logic, mathematics, astronomy, religion and philosophy.

Fa Hsien was the first of the Chinese pilgrims who visited India during the reign of Chandra Gupta II. He started his journey from China in AD 399 and reached India in AD 405. During his stay in India up to AD 411, he went on a pilgrimage to Mathura, Kanauj, Kapilavastu, Kushinagar, Vaishali, Pataliputra, Kashi and Rajgriha and made careful observations about the empire's conditions. Fa Hsien was pleased with the mildness of administration. The Penal Code was mild and offences were punished by fines only. From his accounts, the Gupta Empire was a prosperous period.

The major topics dealt in this book are : *Introduction to Gupta Empire; Characteristics of Gupta Empire; History of the Gupta Dynasty; Middle Kingdoms of India; Maurya Empire; Han Dynasty; Tang Dynasty; Roman Empire; etc.*

No doubt, these will serve the purpose of trainees and trainers, professional and policy planners in the field. Since the sources of information are all secondary, we express our gratitude to the scholars whose works are cited or substantially made use of. We are thankful to all those who rendered ready help and cooperation while working on this project.

We express our gratitude to various scholars, teachers and friends for their assistance and guidance. Finally, we thank our publishers for bringing out this book in very limited time.

—*Editors*

Contents

1

Introduction to Gupta Empire

The **Gupta Empire** was an Ancient Indian empire which existed approximately from 320 to 550 CE and covered much of the Indian Subcontinent. Founded by Maharaja Sri-Gupta, the dynasty began the *Classical Age* in the Middle kingdoms of India. The capital of the Guptas was Pataliputra, present day Patna, in the north Indian state of Bihar.

The peace and prosperity created under leadership of Guptas enabled the pursuit of scientific and artistic endeavors. Historians place the Gupta dynasty alongside with the Han Dynasty, Tang Dynasty and Roman Empire as a model of a classical civilization. The time of the Gupta Empire is referred to by some scholars as the Golden Age of India in science, technology, engineering, art, dialectic, literature, logic, mathematics, astronomy, religion and philosophy.

Origin of Guptas

Fa Hsien was the first of the Chinese pilgrims who visited India during the reign of Chandra Gupta II. He started his journey from China in AD 399 and reached India in AD 405. During his stay in India up to AD 411, he went on a pilgrimage to Mathura, Kanauj, Kapilavastu, Kushinagar, Vaishali, Pataliputra, Kashi and Rajgriha and made careful observations about the empire's conditions. Fa Hsien was pleased with the mildness of administration. The Penal Code was mild and offences were punished by fines only. From his accounts, the Gupta Empire was a prosperous period.

The Chinese traveler Yijing (see also Xuanzang) provides more knowledge of the Gupta kingdom in Magadha. He came to north India in 672 CE and heard of Maharaja Sri-Gupta, who built a temple for Chinese pilgrims near Mrigasikhavana who lost their lives in epic battle.

The most likely date for the reign of Sri-Gupta is c. 240-280 CE. He was, perhaps, from a Vaishya community and a Prayag based feudatory of Kushanas. His successor Ghatotkacha ruled probably from c. 280-319 CE. In contrast to his successor, he is also referred to in inscriptions as 'Maharaja'. At the beginning of the 5th century the Guptas established and ruled a few small Hindu kingdoms in Magadha and around modern-day Bihar.

Chandra Gupta

Ghatotkacha (c. 280–319 CE), had a son named Chandra Gupta. (Not to be confused with Chandragupta Maurya (340-293 BCE), founder of the Mauryan Empire.) In a breakthrough deal, Chandra Gupta was married to Kumardevi, a Lichchhavi princess—the main power in Magadha. With a dowry of the kingdom of Magadha (capital Pataliputra) and an alliance with the Lichchhavis, Chandra Gupta set about expanding his power, conquering much of Magadha, Prayaga and Saketa. He established a realm stretching from the Ganga River (Ganges River) to Prayaga (modern-day Allahabad) by 321 CE. He assumed the imperial title of "Maharajadhiraja".

Samudragupta

Samudragupta succeeded his father in AD 335, and ruled for about 45 years, till his death in AD 380. He took the kingdoms of Shichchhatra and Padmavati early in his reign. He then attacked the Malwas, the Yaudheyas, the Arjunayanas, the Maduras and the Abhiras, all of which were tribes in the area. By his death in 380, he had incorporated over twenty kingdoms into his realm and his rule extended from the Himalayas to the river Narmada and from the Brahmaputra to the Yamuna. He gave himself the titles *King of Kings* and *World Monarch*. He is considered the *Napoleon of north India*. He performed *Ashwamedha yajna* (horse sacrifice) to underline the importance of his conquest. The stone replica of the sacrificial horse, then prepared, is in the Lucknow Museum. The Samudragupta Prashasti inscribed on the Ashokan Pillar, now in Akbar's Fort at Allahabad, is an authentic record of his exploits and his sway over most of the continent.

Samudragupta was not only a talented military leader but also a great patron of art and literature. The important scholars present in his court were Harishena, Vasubandhu and Asanga. He was a poet and musician himself. He was a firm believer in Hinduism and is known to have worshipped Lord Vishnu. He was considerate of other religions and allowed Sri Lanka's buddhist king Meghvarna to build a monastery at Bodh Gaya.He provided a gold railing around the Bodhi Tree.

Chandra Gupta II

Samudragupta was succeeded by his elder son Ram Gupta , a weak king, he agreed to surrender his wife Dhruvadevi to the Saka Chief Rudrasimha II. However, Ram Gupta's younger brother Chandra Gupta II went to the Saka camp disguised as the queen and assassinated the Saka Chief. After this he killed his brother Ram Gupta, married Dhruvadevi and ascended to the throne. Chandra Gupta II, the Sun of Power (*Vikramaditya*), ruled from 380 until 413. Chandra Gupta II also married to a Kadamba princess of Kuntala region and a Nag princess, Kubernag.His daughter Prabhavatigupta from this Nag wife was married to Rudrasena II, the Vakataka king of Deccan (this daughter was forced to be married by the father). Only marginally less successful than his father, Chandra Gupta II expanded his realm westwards, defeating the Saka Western Kshatrapas of Malwa, Gujarat and Saurashtra in a campaign lasting until 409, but with his main opponent Rudrasimha III defeated by 395, and crushing the Bengal (Vanga) chiefdoms. This extended his control from coast-to-coast, established a second (trading) capital at Ujjain and was the high point of the empire.

Despite the creation of the empire through war, the reign is remembered for its very influential style of Hindu art, literature, culture and science, especially during the reign of Chandra Gupta II. Some excellent works of Hindu art such as the panels at the Dashavatara Temple in Deogarh serve to illustrate the magnificence of Gupta art. Above all it was the synthesis of elements that gave Gupta art its distinctive flavour. During this period, the Guptas were supportive of thriving Buddhist and Jain cultures as well, and for this reason there is also a long history of non-Hindu Gupta period art. In particular, Gupta period Buddhist art was to be influential in most of East and Southeast Asia. Much of advances was recorded by the Chinese scholar and traveller Faxian (Fa-hien) in his diary and published afterwards.

The court of Chandragupta was made even more illustrious by the fact that it was graced by the *Navaratna* (Nine Jewels), a group of nine who excelled in the literary arts. Amongst these men was the immortal Kalidasa whose works dwarfed the works of many other literary geniuses, not only in his own age but in the ages to come. Kalidasa was particularly known for his fine exploitation of the *sringara* (erotic) element in his verse.

Chandra Gupta II's Campaigns against Foreign Tribes

- Fourth century AD Sanskrit poet Kalidasa, credits Chandragupta Vikramaditya with having conquered about twenty one kingdoms, both in and outside India. After finishing his campaign in the East and West India, Vikramaditya (Chandra Gupta II) proceeded northwards, subjugated the Parasikas (Persians), then the Hunas and the Kambojas tribes located in the west and east Oxus valleys respectively. Thereafter, the glorious king proceeds across the Himalaya and reduced the Kinnaras, Kiratas etc and lands into India proper .

- According to the *Brihat-Katha-Manjari* of the Kashmiri Pandit Kshmendra, king Vikramaditya (Chandra Gupta II) had *"unburdened the sacred earth of the Barbarians like the Sakas, Mlecchas, Kambojas, Yavanas, Tusharas, Parasikas, Hunas, etc. by annihilating these sinful Mlecchas completely"* .

Kumaragupta I

Chandragupta II was succeeded by his son Kumaragupta I. Known as the *Mahendraditya,* he ruled until 455. Towards the end of his reign a tribe in the Narmada valley, the Pushyamitras, rose in power to threaten the empire.

Skandagupta

Skandagupta is generally considered the last of the great ruler. He defeated the Pushyamitra threat, but then was faced with invading Hephthalites or "White Huns", known in India as the Huna, from the northwest. He repulsed a *Huna* attack c. 455, But the expense of the wars drained the empire's resources and contributed to its decline. Skandagupta died in 467 and was succeeded by his son Narasimhagupta *Baladitya.*

Military Organization

The Imperial Guptas could have achieved their successes through force of arms with an efficient martial system. Historically, the best accounts of this comes not from the Hindus themselves but from Chinese and Western observers. However, a contemporary Indian document, regarded as a military classic of the time, the *Siva-Dhanur-veda,* offers some insight into the military system of the Guptas. The Guptas seem to have relied heavily on infantry archers, and the bow was one of the dominant weapons of their army. The Hindu version of the longbow was composed of metal, or more typically bamboo, and fired a long bamboo cane arrow with a metal head. Unlike the composite bows of Western and Central Asian foes, bows of this design would be less prone to warping in the damp and moist conditions often prevalent to the region. The Indian longbow was reputedly a powerful weapon capable of great range and penetration and provided an effective counter to invading horse archers. Iron shafts were used against armored elephants, and fire arrows were also part of the bowmen's arsenal. India historically has had a prominent reputation for its steel weapons. One of these was the steel bow. Due to its high tensility, the steel bow was capable of long range and penetration of exceptionally thick armor. These were less common weapons than the bamboo design and found in the hands of noblemen rather than in the ranks. Archers were frequently protected by infantry equipped with shields, javelins, and longswords.

The Guptas also had knowledge of siegecraft, catapults, and other sophisticated war machines.

The Guptas apparently showed little predilection for using horse archers, despite the fact these warriors were a main component in the ranks of their Scythian, Parthian, and Hepthalite (*Huna*) enemies. However, the Gupta armies were probably better disciplined. Able commanders like Samudragupta and Chandragupta II would have likely understood the need for combined armed tactics and proper logistical organization. Gupta military success likely stemmed from the concerted use of elephants, armored cavalry, and foot archers in tandem against both Hindu kingdoms and foreign armies invading from the Northwest. The Guptas also maintained a navy, allowing them to control regional waters.

The collapse of the Gupta Empire in the face of the *Huna* onslaught was due not directly to the inherent defects of the Gupta army, which after all had initially defeated these people under Skandagupta. More likely, internal dissolution sapped the ability of the Guptas to resist foreign invasion, as was simultaneously occurring in Western Europe and China.

Huna Invasions and the end of Empire

Skandagupta was followed by weak rulers Puru Gupta (467-473), Kumaragupta II (473-476), Buddhagupta (476-495?), Narasimhagupta, Kumaragupta III, Vishnu Gupta, Vainya Gupta and Bhanu Gupta. In the 480's the Hephthalite King Oprah broke through the Gupta defenses in the northwest, and much of the empire was overrun by the *Huna* by 500. The empire disintegrated under the attacks of Toramana and his successor Mihirakula. The *Hunas* conquered several provinces of the empire, including Malwa, Gujarat and Thanesar and broke away under the rule of local dynasties. It appears from inscriptions that the Guptas, although their power was much diminished, continued to resist the Hunas. Narasimhagupta formed an alliance with the independent kingdoms to drive the *Huna* from most of northern India by the 530's. The succession of the sixth-century Guptas is not entirely clear, but the tail end recognized ruler of the dynasty's main line was king Vishnugupta, reigning from 540 to 550.

Legacy of the Gupta Empire

Scholars of this period include Aryabhatta, who is believed to be the first to come up with the concept of zero, postulated the theory that the Earth moves round the Sun, and studied solar and lunar eclipses. Kalidasa, who was a great playwright, who wrote plays such as Shakuntala, which is said to have inspired Goethe, and marked the highest point of Sanskrit literature is also said to have belonged to this period.

According to historian's work,

The Gupta Empire is considered by many scholars to be the "classical age" of Hindu and Buddhist art and literature. The Rulers of the Gupta Empire were strong supporters of developments in the arts, architecture, science, and literature. The Gupta Empire circulated a large number of gold coins, called dinars, and supported the Universities of Nalanda and Vikramasila.

Chess is said to have originated in this period, where its early form in the 6th century was known as *caturaEga*, which translates as "four divisions [of the military]" – infantry, cavalry, elephants, and chariotry - represented by the pieces that would evolve into the modern pawn, knight, bishop, and rook, respectively. Doctors also invented several medical instruments, and even performed operations. The Indian numerals which were the first positional base 10 numeral systems in the world originated from Gupta India. The ancient Gupta text Kạma Sutra is widely considered to be the standard work on human sexual behavior in Sanskrit literature written by the Indian scholar Vatsyayana. These ideas spread throughout the world through trade.

Gupta Dynasty Rulers

The main branch of the Gupta dynasty ruled the Gupta Empire in India, from around 320 to 550. This dyansty was founded by Srigupta. The rulers are:

- Srigupta
- Ghatotkachagupta
- Samudragupta
- Ramagupta
- Chandragupta II
- Kumaragupta I

- Skandagupta
- Purugupta
- Kumaragupta II
- Buddhagupta
- Narasimhagupta Baladitya
- Kumaragupta III
- Vishnugupta
- Vainyagupta
- Bhanugupta

Indian Subcontinent

The **Indian subcontinent**, also **Indian Subcontinent**, is a region of the Asian (and, in turn, the Eurasian) continent on the Indian tectonic plate south of the Himalayas, forming a peninsula which extends southward into the Indian Ocean. Historically forming the whole of greater India, the region now comprises the countries of India, Pakistan, and Bangladesh.

Geographically, the Indian subcontinent is a peninsular region in southern Asia, south of the Himalayas and Kuen Lun mountain ranges and east of the Indus River and the Iranian Plateau, extending southward into the Indian Ocean between the Arabian Sea (to the southwest) and the Bay of Bengal (to the southeast). It covers about 4.4 million km^2 (1.7 million mi^2), which is 10% of the Asian continent or 2.4% of the world's land surface area; however, it accounts for about 34% of Asia's population (or over 16.5% of the world's population) and is home to a vast array of peoples.

Geologically, most of this region is a subcontinent: it rests on a tectonic plate of its own, the Indian Plate (the northerly portion of the Indo-Australian Plate), and is isolated from the rest of Asia by mountain barriers. It was once a small continent before colliding with the Eurasian Plate about

50-55 million years ago and giving birth to the Himalayan range and the Tibetan plateau. In addition, it is also home to a variety of geographical features, such as glaciers, rainforests, valleys, deserts, and grasslands.

The subcontinent is washed upon on the south by the Indian Ocean and, in turn eastward, by the Arabian Sea and Bay of Bengal.

Political Boundaries

The Indian subcontinent since 1947 has included parts of various countries, in geopolitical contexts grouped under the term "South Asia". This includes those countries on the continental crust (India, Pakistan, Bangladesh, Nepal and Bhutan), an island country on the continental shelf (Sri Lanka), and an island country rising above the oceanic crust (the Maldives).

Names of India

The name **India** may refer to either the region of Greater India (the Indian subcontinent), or to the contemporary Republic of India contained therein. The term is derived from the name of the Sindhu (Indus River) and has been in use in Greek since Herodotus (4th century BC). The term appears in Old English in the 9th century, and again in Modern English since the 17th century.

The Republic of India has three principal short names, in both official and popular English usage, each of which is historically significant. All three originally designated a single entity comprising all the modern nations of the Indian subcontinent. These names are ***India, Bharat*** and **Hindustan**. The first Article of the Constitution of India states that "India, that is Bharat, shall be a union of states." Thus, *India* and *Bharat* are equally official short names for the Republic of India, while "Hindustan" is still widely used as an alternative name when Indians speak amongst themselves. "Hindustan" is also used in historical contexts (especially British India). Indians commonly refer to their country as ***Bharat, Hindustan*** or ***India*** depending on the context and language of conversation. India is also known as Âryâvarta ("abode of the Aryans") because of its Aryan heritage.

India

The English term is from Greek *India,* via Latin *India. Iindía* in Byzantine (Koine Greek) ethnography denotes the region beyond the Indus river, since Herodotus (5th century BC) "Indian land", "an Indian", from Avestan *Hinduš* (referring to Sindh, and listed as a conquered territory by Darius I in the Persepolis terrace inscription). The name is derived ultimately from *Sindhu,* the Sanskrit name of the river, but also meaning "river" generically. Latin *India* is used by Lucian (2nd century).

The name **India** was known in Old English, and was used in King Alfred's translation of Orosius. In Middle English, the name was, under French influence, replaced by *Ynde* or *Inde,* which entered Early Modern English as *Indie.* The name *India* then came back to English usage from the 17th century onwards, and may be due to the influence of Latin, or Spanish or Portuguese.

Sanskrit *indu* "drop (of Soma)", also a term for the Moon, is unrelated, but has sometimes been erroneously connected, listed by, among others, Colonel James Todd in his *Annals of Rajputana.* Todd describes ancient India as under control of tribes claiming descent from the Moon, or "Indu", (referring to Chandravanshi Rajputs), and their influence in Trans-Indian regions where they referred to the land as *Industhan.*

Bharata

The name is used for the Republic of India. *Bhârata* is the official Sanskrit name of the country, *Bhrata Ganarâjya,* and the name is derived from the ancient Indian texts, the Puranas, which refers to the land that comprises India as *Bharata varsam,* and uses this term to distinguish it from other *varcas* or continents. For example, the Vayu Purana says *he who conquers the whole of Bharata-varsa is celebrated as a samrât* (Vayu Purana 45, 86).. However in some puranas, the term 'Bharate' refers to the whole Earth as Emperor Bharat had ruled the whole Earth. Until the death of Maharaja Parikshit, the last formidable emperor of the Kuru dynasty (there were other emperors too after him but they were not as powerful as him), the whole Earth was called as Bharatvarsha.

The Sanskrit word *bhârata* is a vrddhi derivation of *bharata,* which was originally an epithet of Agni. The term is a verbal noun of the Sanskrit root bhr-, "to bear / to carry", with a literal meaning of "to be maintained" (of fire). The root *bhr* is cognate with the English verb *to bear* and Latin *ferô.* This term also means "one who is engaged in search for knowledge".

The Bhâratas were Indians mentioned in the Rigveda, notably participating in the Battle of the Ten Kings.

The realm of Bharata is known as *Bhartavarca* in the *Mahabhârata* (the core portion of which is itself known as *Bhârata*) and later texts. The term *varsa* means a division of the earth, or a continent. A version of the Bagavatha Purana says, the Name Bharatha is after Jata Bharatha who appears in the fifth canto of the Bagavatha.

From: Vishnu Purana (2.3.1)

uttaram yatsamudrasya himdrescaiva daksinam

varcam tadbhâratam nâma bhâratî yatra santatih

"The country (*varsam*) that lies north of the ocean and south of the snowy mountains is called *Bhâratam;* there dwell the descendants of Bharata."

The term in Classical Sanskrit literature is taken to comprise the territory of Republic of India, Pakistan, Nepal and Bangladesh, as well as portions of eastern Afghanistan. This corresponds to the approximate extent of the historical Maurya Empire under emperors Chandragupta Maurya and Ashoka the Great (4th to 3rd centuries BC). Later political entities unifying approximately the same region are the Mughal Empire (17th century), the Maratha Empire (18th century) , and the British Raj (19th to 20th centuries).

Akhanda Bharata ("undivided Bharat") is a term of Hindu nationalism calling for a re-unification of the region.

From the perspective of the Malayans, Indian traders were the most common ones coming from "the West", therefore the word was absorbed into the Malay language. In the Malay language, "Barat" literally means "West".

For Middle Eastern traders, particularly Arabs and Turks, spices were the most common materials coming from the East. Hence, the term "bharat" was borrowed first into Arabic *bahart,* meaning "spices;" this migrated into the Turkish "baharat" with the same meaning.

Hindustan and Hind

The name *Hind* is derived from the Iranian equivalent of Indo-Aryan *Sindh*. The Avestan *-stân* means country or land (cognate to Sanskrit *sthâna* "place, land").

India was called *Hindustan* in Persian although the term *Hind* is in current use. *al-Hind* is the term in the Arabic language (e.g. in the 11th century *Tarikh Al-Hind* "history of India"). It also occurs intermittently in usage within India, such as in the phrase *Jai Hind*.

The terms *Hind* and *Hindustân* were current in Persian and Arabic from the 11th century Islamic conquests: the rulers in the Sultanate and Mughal periods called their Indian dominion, centred around Delhi, Hindustan. -stan is a Persian suffix meaning "home of/place of".

Hindustân, as is the term Hindu itself, entered the English language in the 17th century. In the 19th century, the term as used in English referred to the northern region of India between the Indus and Brahmaputra rivers and between the Himalayas and the Vindhyas in particular, hence the term Hindustani for the Hindi-Urdu language. *Hindustan* was in use synonymously with *India* during the British Raj.

Hind remains in use in Hindi-Urdu. In contemporary Persian language, the term Hindustan has come to mean the Indian subcontinent, and the modern Indian Union is called *Hind*. The same is the case with Arabic language, where *al-Hind* is the name of the Republic of India.

Âryâvarta

Âryâvarta ("abode of the Aryans") is the ancient name for northern and central India, where the culture of the Indo-Aryans was based.The Manu Smriti (2.22) gives the name to "the tract between the Himalaya and the Vindhya ranges, from the eastern to the western sea".

Tenjiku

Tenjiku is the Japanese word commonly used in reference to pre-modern India. *Tian,* the root word for the Japanese kanji means, 'heaven,' while, *jiku,* means: 'the center of', or 'primary concentration of'. Therefore the word is known to mean: 'the heavenly center of the world" or "the spiritual axis (center)", a reference to the Indian origins of Buddhism.

Jambudvipa

There is a story in Jain mythology and in Hindu and Buddhist texts as well that describe Jambudvipa being one of the seven islands/continents of the world. It is possible that perhaps *"island"* is used to refer to India because India in one time was a separate Indian Plate. Perhaps the phrase is used in the manner that the land of India is still an island in between the Indus River and the rest of the Asian Plate. Jambudvipa is also addressed in Buddhist mythology and in some he is addresses as the ruler over entire Jambudvipa and in one, *"He reigned over a quarter of the land of Jambudvipa..."*

●●

2

Characteristics of Gupta Empire

The Guptas were famous rulers of ancient India, who constructed their own imperialism and introduced the Golden era in India. After the lapse of a prolonged Dark Age, it was the Guptas who initiated peace and coalesced the entire disintegrated Northern India. The Gupta rulers ascended the throne in 320 A.D. and continued to be the sovereign authority of India till 550 A.D. When the Guptas came into the political scenario of India, the condition of entire North India was pretty lawless and due to lack of any central authority the provincial governors unfurled their flag of independence after the downfall of the Kushanas. Furthermore they were at continuous strife with one another for which the socio-political condition of Northern India was extremely chaotic. During that time the Guptas and the Kshatriyas rose to power, who not only defeated the provincial kings, but also compelled them to offer their allegiance to the Guptas. In such a manner, the Guptas consolidated the entire northern India under their own supremacy.

The Gupta records mentioned the names of the first three rulers of the Gupta lineage who ascended the throne, namely Maharaja Sari Gupta, his son Maharaja Sri Ghatotkacha and the latter's son Maharajadhiraja Chandragupta. Though Maharaja Sri Gupta was the founder king of the Gupta dynasty and established dynastic stronghold in Northern India, yet the third ruler Maharajadhiraja

Chandragupta I was more powerful and famous than his predecessors. However historians have pointed out unanimously that the first two Gupta kings had used the title of "Maharaja", only the third king Chandragupta I initiated the status of Maharajadhiraja. From the Gupta records of 4th century it is known that the title "Maharaja" only was ascribed to subordinate kings under the Central authority during that time and the title "Maharajadhiraja" was used by an independent king. Hence from these records it was presumed by the scholars that the first two Gupta rulers appeared to be feudatories, but their authority is still unknown. Though K.P. Jaiswal has pointed out that the Guptas were feudatories under the Bharasivas, the theory was discarded due to lack of any supportive evidence. Dr. S. Chattopadhya has however pointed out that after the downfall of the Kushanas, the Saka Murandas occupied Magadha and the Guptas acted as their vassals. Finally Chandragupta I liberated Magadha from the Sakas or the Scythians and established himself as the independent king of the Gupta Dynasty and used the title "Maharajadhiraja". However the feudatory status of the Guptas and the Scythian suzerainty over them is a subject of doubt, because conclusive proofs are yet unavailable. Allan, one of the famous interpreters of ancient history has inferred that the title "maharaja" was not always ascribed to the feudatories. He also adds that the title Maharaja was used by many independent rulers belonging to the tribes like Bharasiva, Magha, Licchavi, and Vakataka. Hence it is not unlikely that the early Guptas also used the same title as independent provincial kings.

Not much is known about Maharaja Sri Gupta, the founder king of the Gupta dynasty in ancient India. Knowledge about Maharaja Sri-Gupta is limited to the accounts of the Chinese traveller I-Tsing, who visited the court of Maharaja Sri Gupta. I-Tsing in his historical documents had mentioned that the extent of the Gupta Empire was too small when the founder king of Gupta dynasty, Maharaja Sri Gupta ascended the throne. It comprised the areas of Bengal and some parts of Bihar. A patron of the Buddhist cult, Maharaja Sri Gupta, constructed a temple for the Chinese pilgrims near Mrigashikhavana, close to Varendri or Varendra bhumi in Bengal and also granted twenty-four villages for its maintenance. Maharaja Sri Gupta reigned probably from 275 to 300 A.D.

Maharaja Ghatotkacha succeeded his father, king Maharaja Sri Gupta to power. According to Vakataka records of Prabhabati Gupta, the daughter of Chandragupta II described Maharaja Ghatotkacha as the founder of Gupta Dynasty in ancient India. However there is no conclusive proofs or supportive evidences about the Vakataka records. Moreover it provided ambiguous documentations, hence in the later years historians discarded the confirmation of the Vakataka records. The Rewa inscription of Skandagupta also recorded the genealogy of the Gupta rulers, where the name of Maharaja Sri Gupta was not mentioned. However Dr. Majumdar has pointed out that one of these records is the official Gupta record, hence much importance should not be attached to the omission of the name of Maharaja Sri Gupta as the founder king of the Gupta Dynasty. However Maharaja Ghatotkacha was regarded a powerful ruler of the Gupta Dynasty. Allan has pointed out that the Gupta Dynastic inscription mentioned him as "Ghatotkacha" and not Ghatotkacha Gupta. Furthermore he adds that Ghatotkacha was also identified as "Kacha". The coins issued in the name of "Kacha" were ascribed to the second Gupta ruler, Maharaja Ghatotkacha. Historians have fixed his date between 300 and 320 A.D., after a prolonged research.

The second Gupta ruler, Ghatotkacha was succeeded by his son Chandragupta I. He not only inherited the throne of his father, one of the powerful rulers of Gupta Dynasty, but at the same time brought Gupta dynasty in the limelight of ancient history, by unveiling the obscurity, which covered the contemporary political scenario after the Dark Age. The emergence of Gupta Dynasty under him as a superior power, is evident from his adoption of the title "Maharajadhiraja". As historical records suggest, the third king of the Gupta Dynasty, Maharajadhiraja Chandragupta I was not only a powerful king, but at the same time was a shrewd diplomat. To augment the power of Gupta house he not only subdued the provincial kings, but also established marital relationship with some of the tribes, in order to strengthen the authority of the Gupta Empire. It is for this reason Chandragupta I married the Licchavi princess Mahadevi Kumaradevi. Some of the coins of Chandragupta I bore images of the Maharajadhiraja and his Licchavi queen Mahadevi Kumaradevi on one side and the figure of goddess Lakshmi on the reverse.

The matrimonial alliance of Chandragupta I with the Licchavi princess Kumaradevi, is a subject of keen controversy among the scholars. Matrimonial alliance between royal families for political purposes was prevalent in all times, in all countries, for all ages, especially in India. Therefore, historians hold that the Licchavi marriage of Chandragupta I had immensely increased his power. Since the Licchavis were extremely powerful warrior tribes, Chandragupta did not find it wise enough to wage a war against them. But he decided to establish friendly relations with the Licchavis, to enhance the strength of the Gupta Empire. But scholars differ widely about the nature and extent of power of Chandragupta I, acquired by his alliance with the Licchavis. Allan has suggested that by matrimonial alliance, the Guptas succeeded the prestige and pedigree in the ancient line of the Licchavis, but did not gain any material power. Romila Thapar supported the view of Allan and endorsed the fact by pointing that the Guptas perhaps did not have any royal origin. But Dr. Majumdar has refuted the views of Allan by saying that the Licchavis did not enjoy any status in the contemporary society. Hence the matrimonial alliance of Chandragupta I could not enhance the pedigree of the Guptas. Moreover "Manu Samhita " denoted the Licchavis as the "degraded Kshatriyas". Allan has further pointed out that after matrimonial alliance, the kingdom of Vaishali ruled by the Licchavis was annexed with the Gupta Empire. But later historians contradicted the view. This is so because the name Vaishali was not mentioned in the list of territories ruled by Samudragupta. Hence if it were included in his father`s kingdom, then unquestionably Vaishali would have been part of Samudragupta`s kingdom. Hence according to modern historians, though Chandragupta I engaged in matrimonial alliance with the Licchavis, yet, the kingdom of Vaishali was ruled by the Licchavis independently. However it is generally believed that the alliance of the Guptas with the Licchavis had strengthened the Gupta supremacy in ancient India.

Almost nothing is known about the conquest of the third Gupta ruler Maharajadhiraja Chandragupta I. Professor R.D. Bannerjee has suggested that- strengthened by the Licchavi alliance, firstly Chandragupta liberated the kingdom of Magadha from the shackles of the Sakas or the Scythians. Some scholars have also identified Chandragupta I with Chandrasena, a character of the play "Kaumudi Mahotsava". In the play, the alliance of Chandrasena with the Licchavi princess was also mentioned. From the evidence of the drama, it is known that Chandragupta I allied with the Licchavis and overthrew the legitimate king Sundaravarmana from the throne of Magadha and usurped it.

Prof. R.G. Basak has expounded the theory that Chandragupta I had conquered the province of Pundravardhana (North Bengal). The Allahabad Pillar Inscription of Samudragupta however did not mention that he had conquered the territory of Pundravardhana. It was already part of the Gupta Empire before the ascension of Samudragupta. Therefore it can be inferred that

Pundravardhana was conquered by Chandragupta I. Professor Basak has also identified a king named Chandra of Meharauli Pillar inscription, with Chandragupta I. However this theory did not have wide acceptance. Though the information available about the extent of Chandragupta I's Empire is very meagre, yet historians have presumed that probably it was a large one, which justified his title of Maharajadhiraja. Pargiter, one of the eminent historians, has suggested on the evidence of a Puranic passage that Saketa (Oudh), Prayag (Allahabad) and Magadha (South-Bihar) were included in Chandragupta's kingdom. Chandragupta I evidently had defeated the Magha kings of Kosala and Kausambhi and annexed their kingdom. Later modern historians have opined after prolonged research of the available evidences and the campaigns made by Samudragupta, that the Empire of Chandragupta I consisted of whole Bihar, portions of Bengal, except the Eastern region or Samatata and eastern territory of U.P.

The political importance of Chandragupta I lies in the fact that he had initiated the Gupta era in 320 A.D., that had commenced from February 26th. According to some other scholars, Gupta era actually dated from December 319 A.D. Again some scholars held that the son of Chandragupta I, Samudragupta initiated the Gupta era in order to commemorate his coronation. However a strong theory has been approached by another group of scholars that Chandragupta II might have started the Gupta Era, although it was calculated from 56 years previous to his reign. However Chandragupta I, the third king of Gupta lineage, was the most powerful among the early Guptas, who not only established a stronghold of the Gupta Empire in Northern India, but also had extended the boundary of his Empire.

GUPTA EMPIRE IN INDIA

It was with the destruction of the Kushana Empire due to political imbalance, the emergence of the Gupta Empire by

Sri Gupta took place in India. Gupta Empire ruled India between 3rd century and 6th century CE. Gupta Dynasty mainly covered the huge area of Northern part of India. This period was known as the golden age of India due to its remarkable achievement in astronomy, mathematics, religion, philosophy and science. They had an effective administrative and economic system and an impressive political history. In the literary circle also there were many developments enriching the cultural and social history of India.

The kings of Gupta Empire were in origin probably a family of wealthy landowners who gradually attained both economic power and political status. Unlike the founder of the Maurya Dynasty, who is described as an adventurous young man with no significant antecedents, the founder of the Gupta Empire, also called Chandra Gupta, belonged to a family which had established its power at a local level in Magadha. A judicious marriage with a Licchavi princess gave him additional prestige, the Licchavis claiming a long-established respectability. Following his coronation as king of Magadha in A.D. 319-320 Chandra Gupta took the title of 'maharajadhiraja', Great King of Kings. Chandragupta was the first of the Guptas to be referred to as 'Maharajadhiraja' or 'King of Kings', 'maharajadhiraja paramabhat taraka' Great King of Kings, the Supreme Lord.

The Gupta period is often described as a period of Hindu renaissance. Gupta Empire was patrons of sculpture, art and music, architecture, and this cultural was at its zenith during their rule. The Guptas prevailed in most of the northern India. In about A.D. 335, Samudra Gupta, the son to Chandra Gupta, inherited the kingdom of Magadha. He conquered the kingdom of Shichchhatra and Padmavati, stretching from the Himalayas to Narmada River and Brahmaputra River, and gradually included twenty kingdoms into his realm. He issued a series of beautifully executed gold coins in which he is depicted both as a conqueror and as a musician, a strange combination of interests. Fortunately for later historians a lengthy panegyric on him was composed by one of his high officials and engraved on an Ashokan pillar which has since been brought to Allahabad. The inscription refers among other things to the martial exploits of Samudra Gupta; to the kings uprooted and the territory annexed in the northern part of the subcontinent. It mentions also the long march which Samudra Gupta undertook in the south, reaching as far as Kanchipuram. Nor are the tributes from foreign kingdoms omitted. Mention is made of the Sakas, Ceylon, various Iranian rulers of the north-west and the inhabitants of all the islands. The latter may refer to Indian trading stations on the islands of South-East Asia and in the Indian Ocean.

The nucleus of the Gupta kingdom, as of the Mauryan Empire, was the Ganga heartland. This and the adjoining territory to the west were the only regions over which Samudra Gupta had absolute and unchallenged control. Gupta control of the Deccan was uncertain and had to be propped up with a matrimonial alliance, a Gupta princess marrying a prince of the Vakataka Dynasty of the Deccan, the successors to the Satavahana power. This secured a friendly southern frontier for the Guptas, which was necessary to Samudra Gupta's successor, Chandra Gupta II, when he led a campaign against the Sakas in western India.

It was during the reign of Chandra Gupta II that Gupta ascendancy was at its peak. His successful campaign against the Sakas, resulting in the annexation of western India, was, however, not his only achievement. Like his predecessor, he was a patron of poets, philosophers, scientists, musicians, and sculptors. This period saw the crystallization of what came to be the classical norm in ancient India on both the political and the cultural levels. Grammar, logic, astronomy, metaphysics, mathematics, and medicine became highly specialized during the reigning period of Gupta kings. Sanskrit literature reached at its highest glory during this period which produced works like Mrichchakatika by Shudraka, Panchatantra, along with Kalidasa, Bhasa and others. Buddhist and Jain literature also began to be produced in Sanskrit language. In architecture and art it was splendid with the Ajanta caves, Sarnath Buddha, the panels of Dashavatara Temple in Deogarh and the Udaygiri Varaha Cave. In mathematics, Aryabhata brought the concept of 'zero' or infinity. In astronomy too it was brilliantly discovered hat the earth was not flat. Several medical advancements also took place and overall the Gupta period is marked for its overall development in art and culture.

In case of administration, it has been observed that superficially Gupta administration was similar to that of the Mauryas. The king was the highest authority and the kingdom was divided into a hierarchy of administrative units like the provinces, districts, and groups of villages had their own range of officers responsible to the most senior officer in the unit. During the Gupta period there was far greater stress on local administration and far less direct control from the centre. There was an efficient administration and political unity in India under the Guptas. The vast empire was divided into provinces, which were under the control of the governors who were from the royal family. The provinces were divided into Vishayas or districts. Lowest unit of administration was the village administered by a local chief. The standing army was laced with cavalry and horse archery. The Gupta judicial system was developed with a differentiation between civil and criminal laws. There were land taxes and excise duties that was collected.

The Guptas were tolerant to any religious tradition and they continued worshipping their family deity of Lord Vishnu. They were active participants in the bhakti devotional movement centered on Vishnu. Hinduism was revived along with its components: major deities, image worship, the importance of the temple and devotionalism.

Even in urban administration, the City Boards consisted opinion and interest (such as the heads of guilds bodies) rather than officers of state. A parallel tendency was developing in the agrarian system, particularly in the sphere of land revenue. The revenue was still collected by the king's officers, but they retained a certain predetermined percentage in lieu of a regular cash salary. This procedure of payment to officers came to be adopted with increasing frequency. On occasion the king would even grant the revenue from an area of land or a village to non-officials, such as Brahmans renowned for their learning. Inscriptions recording such grants are known from the early centuries A.D. onwards. Since a major part of the state revenue came from the land, grants of revenue were gradually to cause a radical change in the agrarian system. Although it was the revenue alone which was granted, it became customary to treat the land itself as part of the grant. Technically the king could resume the grant, but in fact he seldom did so. The lessening of central control in any case weakened the authority of the king and emphasized local independence, an emphasis which increased in times of political trouble. The recipient of the grant came to be regarded as the lord of the land and the local patron, and he attracted local loyalty towards himself. The more obvious shift in emphasis from central to local power took place later, but its origin can be traced to the Gupta period. However, the more forceful of the Gupta kings still kept authority in their hands and continued to be regarded as the lords of the land par excellence.

The commercial system of the Gupta Empire was engineered in a very proper way. The steady stream of revenue from the land was augmented by income from commercial activity. Indian trading stations were dotted throughout the islands of South-East Asia, Malaysia, Cambodia, and Thailand. The gradual acceptance of many features of Indian culture in these areas must doubtless have been facilitated by activities such as commerce. Goods were transported by pack animals and ox-drawn carts and by water when rivers were navigable. The literature of the period is replete with descriptions of the marvels and wonders witnessed by sailors and merchants in distant lands. The textile guilds had a vast market, both domestic and foreign. Ivory-workers, stone-workers, metal-workers, and jewellers all prospered in the economic boom. Spices, pepper, sandalwood, pearls, precious stones, perfume, indigo, herbs, and textiles were exported in large quantities. Amongst the more lucrative imports were silk from China and horses from Central Asia and Arabia.

Some of the wealth of merchants and princes was donated to religious causes: Large endowments had made the Buddhist temples extremely powerful, and provided comfortable if not luxurious living for many Buddhist monks in the more important monasteries. These endowments enabled the monasteries to own land and to employ labour to work it. The superfluous income from such sources was invested in commercial enterprises which at times were so successful that monasteries could even act as bankers. Monastic establishments built in splendid isolation, like the one at Ajanta, were embellished with some of the most magnificent murals known to the ancient world. The growth of centres of Buddhist teaching led to devoted scholars spending many hours on theology and philosophical speculation, thus sharpening the intellectual challenge which the Buddhists presented to the Brahmans.

Some certain reasons are responsible for the demolition of Gupta dynasty. The supremacy of Gupta power in northern India did not remain unchallenged. The challenge came from the unexpected invasion of northwestern India by a distinctly barbaric people, the Hunas. The name is etymologically related to the late classical Himni or Huns, but they were probably only remotely connected with the barbarian hordes of Attila. The threat was felt during the reign of Chandra Gupta's son and successor Kumara Gupta (A.D. 415- A.D. 454) when a tribe of Hunas, branching away from the main Central Asian hordes, had settled in Bactria, and gradually moved over the mountains into north-western India. Slowly the trickles became streams as the Hunas thrust further into India. The successor of Kumara Gupta, Skanda Gupta (A.D. 454- A.D. 467) had to bear the brunt of the Huna attacks, which were by now regular invasions. Gupta power weakened rapidly. By the early sixth century the Huna rulers Toramana and Mihirakula claimed the Punjab and Kashmir as part of their kingdom.

The Gupta dynasty was the period of â€œGreater India,â€ a period of cultural activity in India, also influencing the neighboring countries. The Guptas not only enriched the Indian culture but also had a global impact. Scientific discoveries that were made were helpful not only to India but also the rest of the world. The specimens of art and architecture that flourished were an inspiration for the following dynasties and the legacy continued with more exceptional work of art in the future. The golden rule had enormous impact on religion as well and the Gupta rulers stand apart with their liberal attitude towards it.

The coming of the Hunas not only created political disorder but also put into motion new currents whose momentum was felt for centuries to come. The migration of the Hunas and other Central Asian tribes accompanying them and their settling in northern India resulted in displacements of population. This disturbance led in turn to changes in the caste structure, with the emergence of new sub-castes. The rise of many small kingdoms was also due to the general; confusion prevalent during this period.

With the decline of the Guptas the northern half of the subcontinent splintered into warring kingdoms, each seeking to establish itself as a sovereign power. The successors of the Guptas attempted to recreate an empire, but the political fabric was such that an empire was no longer practicable, a possible exception being the Pratihara kingdom in limited periods. The ability to create large kingdoms and empires moved south to the powers of the peninsula, the kingdoms of the Deccan and the Tamil country. In the centuries that followed the Gupta period it was in the kingdoms of the Chalukya Dynasty, Rashtrakutas, Pallavas, and Chola Dynasty that Indian civilization showed its greatest vitality.

CONDITION OF NORTHERN INDIA BEFORE THE RISE OF GUPTAS

Before the rise of the Gupta dynasty, northern India was divided into number of small monarchical kingdoms and republics.

Monarchical Kingdoms

It can be known from the puranas, the Nagas were very powerful in Vidisa, Kantipuri, Mathura and Padmavati. The Nagas had spread in the different parts of the country. Sisha, Bhogin and Sada-chandra Chandramsa were some of the famous rulers of the Naga dynasty of Vidisa. The inscriptions refer Bhavanag. Some coins found at Padmavati mention his name. Allahabad inscription of Samudragupta describes that Samudragupta had defeated the two Naga kings. They were king Ganpati Nag and Nagasena. Some scholars are of the view that king Virsena of Mathura was also a king of Naga dynasty. His coins have been discovered in Mathura, Punjab and district Bulandshahr, etc.

Ahichattra Kingdom

Bhadraghosa, Suryamitra, Phalgunimitra, Agnimitra, Brihatsvatimitra etc. were the kings of Ahichattra kingdom and the coins of the first three centuries of A.D. refer to these kings as well. Some of the coins refer the name of Achyuttra who was defeated by Samudragupta.

Vakataka Kingdom

Vindhyasakti is said to be the founder of Vakataka dynasty. But some scholars are of the view that it was Paravarsena who founded the Vakataka dynasty. He was a powerful king and performed four horse sacrifices and adopted the title of 'samrat'. He was succeeded by his son Rudrasena. Samudragupta defeated Rudrasena and incorporated his kingdom into his empire.

Ayodhya Kingdom

From certain coins it can be known that Dhandeva and Vishakhadeva were the ruler of Ayodhya. Dhandeva was probably the descendent or Pushyamitra. Satyamitra, Ayumitra, Sanghmitra were some of the other rulers of Ayodhya.

The Maukhari Kingdom

Sunderverman was the king of Maukhari dynasty and ruled in Oudh. The Maukhari Senapatis are given the credit of constructing sacrificial pillars.

Kaushambi Kingdom

Certain coins refer to Sudeva, Brihatsvamitra, Asvaghosa, Agnimitra, Devamitra, Varunmitra, Jyeshthmitra and Partapatimitra as the ruler of Kaushambi.

The Guptas

Before conquering the whole of northern India, the Guptas were also a local power. Srigupta is regarded the founder of the Gupta dynasty. Srigupta was succeeded by Ghatokacha. After Ghatotkacha, Chandra Gupta I succeeded him as a king. In Chandra Gupta's reign the growth of the Gupta empire begins in rapid strides.

The Arjunayans

The Arjunayans ruled in the modern Bharatpur and Alwar states in Rajasthan. They had become prominent during the reign of the indo Greek kings but after them the Sakas subdued them. Thereafter, they again rose after the decline of the Kushanas but were ultimately defeated by the Guptas as well.

The Yaudheyas

The Yaudheyas had established their rule in the east Punjab, Uttar Pradesh and parts of Rajasthan. They were the worshipper of Brahmandeva. The Sakas and the Kushanas had subdued them but after their fall they again came into prominence. They were ultimately subdued by the Guptas.

The Malavas

The Malavas ruled in Punjab at the time of Alexander's invasion but later on they settled in Rajasthan and made Malavnagar near Jaipur as their capital. The Malva coins refer to the legend 'Malavanam jayah'. They are said to be the first to use vikram era. They also used the Krita era. They had defeated the Sakas and the Mankhari Senapati was their vassal. However, they were also subdued by the Guptas.

The Lichchhavis

This was a very old republic. It existed in the time of lord Buddha and was a very strong republic before the rise of the Guptas. This is born by the fact that Chandra Gupta I had married a Lichchhavis princess.

The Sibis

They had a very big infantry and were a strong power at the time of the Alexander's invasion. Later on they settled in Rajasthan and made Madhyamika as their capital. This Madhyamika was placed near Chitod.

The republic of Kunindas

This republic was between the Yamuna and the Sutlej and the upper courses of the Bias and probably Chatra was their capital.

The Kulutas

The Kulutas lived in the valley of Kabul and were successful in overthrowing the Kunindas. Virayasas and Bhadrayasas were their famous rulers.

The Audumbaras

The Audumbaras were placed in the eastern part of Kangra, Gurdaspura and Hoshiarpura. Dharaghosa, Sivadas and Rudradasa were some of their famous rulers. Their coins have the figure of a Siva temple with a Dhavaja, a trident and a battle area. Some of the names of the Audumbara rulers can be mentioned as Agnimitra, Mahimitra, Bhumitra and Mahabumitra. Their names were mentioned in the coins.

GUPTA SCRIPT

Known to have essentially descended from the Brahmi script, Gupta script comes under the category of Northern Indian group of scripts. The script had evolved with the rise of the Gupta Empire in India in the earlier periods of 4th to 6th centuries A.D. After the invasion of the plundering Huns, Gupta script witnessed a loss in its novelty. In spite of all such drawbacks and hindrances, it continued to develop in the next few centuries and by the 8th century umpteen versions of the script emerged, two of which are Nagari and Sarada. The script involving the Gupta rulers, is written fundamentally in the direction from left to right and later gave rise to the Siddham script. Gupta script, also referred to as Gupta Brahmi, was used for writing Sanskrit and Sanskritic verses and prose. The period of ruling of Gupta Empire in India was a period of materialistic affluence and opulence, coupled with immense religious and scientific maturations.

In contemporary times, scholars and scientists have at times modified the aboriginal Gupta script to signify syllables instead of single sounds. Gupta script's popularity and spreading to common masses over extensive areas of conquered territory time and again reverberates back to Gupta dynasty and its exceedingly intelligent and gifted rulers, with the result that the Gupta alphabet was the ancestor (for the most part by means of Devanagari script) of most later Indian scripts.

The original Gupta alphabet from the aboriginal script possessed 37 letters, together with 5 vowels. Four principal subtypes of Gupta script developed from the original alphabet: eastern, western, southern and Central Asian. The Central Asian Gupta can be further divided into Central Asian Slanting Gupta and its Agnean and Kuchean variants and Central Asian Cursive Gupta, or Khotanese. A western offshoot of eastern Gupta gave rise to the Siddhamatrka script (c. A.D. 500), which, in turn, developed into the Devanagari alphabet (c. A.D. 700), the most prevalent of the modern Indian scripts. A northern form of Brahmi further evolved into the Gupta scripts, from which were descended the Tibetan and Khotanese systems. Khotanese was however also influenced by the Kharosthi script. Historic theories also state that Gupta script were the prototypes of the North Indian subdivision of the Brahmi script from the 1st centuries B.C. and A.D.

GUPTA EMPERORS OF INDIA

The fearless Gupta emperors established their dynasty in 280 A.D. and continued to rule India till 550 A.D. The earliest Gupta emperor known to Indian history is Sri Gupta. He was succeeded by Ghatatkocha. However, it was Chandragupta I who is truly recognised as the consolidator of the Gupta Empire. He extended his territory to Magadha, Prayaga and Saketa. The Gupta emperors, from the very beginning, were renowned for their military dexterity, astuteness, diplomacy and chivalry. They would guard their kingdoms and subjects with astonishing valour.

Addressed as 'Maharaja' the Gupta emperors were gallant and possessed a cultural bent of mind. This was one of the reasons why several litterateurs received royal patronage. One of the most distinguished rulers of Gupta Empire was Chandragupta II or Vikramaditya. Whilst he fought with unfathomable courage to extend his empire, he was an ardent admirer of various cultures.

The rule of the Gupta emperors led to unprecedented achievements in the fields of science, mathematics, art, astronomy, literature, religion and philosophy. While the rulers of the dynasty followed Hinduism, they practised religious tolerance. Several temples were built by the Gupta emperors which are till date remembered for their superb architectures. From Nagara style temples to rock cut caves; a variety of religious monuments were constructed during their rule. The Gupta emperors truly proved themselves to be prolific builders.

Whether it was trade, medicine, astronomy, metaphysics, martial arts or sculpture, the Gupta emperors employed every possible strategy to make their subjects happy and prosperous. This, indeed, resulted in the ushering of the Golden Rule in ancient India.

ALLAHABAD PRASASTI

The Allahabad Pillar inscription or Allahabad Prasasti is one of the most important epigraphic evidences of the Imperial Guptas. Composed by Harishena, Allahabad Pillar inscription delineates the reign of the Guptas in ancient India. Achievements of different rulers of the Gupta lineage are also mentioned in the Allahabad Pillar Inscription. Harishena, who composed the Allahabad Prasasti, was the court poet and minister of Samudragupta. Parts of Allahabad Prasasti were composed in verse and other parts, in prose. The verse portion contained eight stanzas, which is followed by the prose portion. The Allahabad Prasasti composed during Samudragupta's reign, delineates a vivid description of the reign and conquest of Samudragupta. Allahabad Prasasti, composed by Harishena, does not bear any date and for this reason, historians have presumed that it was composed probably before the Ashwamedha Yajna performed by Samudragupta. They have opined this on the basis that there is no mention of the Ashwamedha Yajna completed by Samudragupta. The Allahabad Prasasti was originally engraved on the Ashokan Pillar in Kausambhi near Allahabad. Later it was removed to the Allahabad fort.

Since the first two stanzas of the verse portion are damaged, these are considered illegible. The third stanza refers to the character of Samudragupta, his versatility and good qualities. The fourth stanza mentions the nomination of Samudragupta by his father Chandragupta I and his consecration to the throne. Though the sixth and seventh stanzas of the inscription are partly damaged, yet, from the available part it has been presumed by scholars that those stanzas referred to certain wars, probably with his kinsmen and Samudragupta's victory over them. The seventh and eighth stanzas and the prose text, narrates the conquests of Samudragupta.

Since several lines of the Allahabad Prasasti were damaged, it is not possible to describe what was mentioned in those lines. Yet historians after a prolonged study of the available part provide several details about the reign of Samudragupta. Lines 13 to 15 of the inscription refer to his conquest of the three kings of the north. They were Achyuta, Nagasena and Ganapati Naga, all belonging to the Naga dynasty.

Lines 19-20 describe Samudragupta's Deccan campaign. The names of 12 Deccan kings are mentioned in the Allahabad Prasasti, viz. -Mahendra of Kosala, Vyaghraraja of Mahakantara, Mantaraja of Kaurala, Mahendragiri of Pistapuram, Svamidatta of Kottura, Damana of Erandapalla, Vishnugopa of Kanchi, Nilaraaja of Avamukta, Hastivarmana of Vengi, Ugrasena of Palakka, Kuvera of Devarashtra, and Dhananjaya of Kushtalapuara.

Lines 21 to 23 mention the names of the nine kings of Aryavarta defeated by Samudragupta. Among these nine kings three Aryavarta kings mentioned earlier in lines 13 to 14 are also included. Apart from those three Naga kings, the rest who were defeated by Samudragupta were- Rudradeva, Matila, Nagadatta, Chandravarmana, Nandin and Balavarmana. Apart from that, Samudragupta's conquest of the Atavika kings is also mentioned in Allahabad Prasasti.

Line 22 specially describes about the five frontier kingdoms, which were occupied by the Gupta king Samudragupta. Moreover it has been inscribed in Allahabad Prasasti that those frontier kingdoms were bound to pay homage or tribute to Samudragupta. Line 22 also mentions the names of nine tribes viz: -Malavas, Arjunayas, Yaudheyas, Madrakas, Abhiras the Prarjunas, Sanakanikas, Kakas, Kharaparikas etc, who had offered allegiance and tribute to Samudragupta.

DEVELOPMENT OF SCIENCE IN GUPTA PERIOD

Not only in the traditional Sanskrit literature or in the field of other worldly literature but changes came in the over all social life in the Gupta period with the tremendous development of science during this period. With the growth and intensification in the arena of mathematics, astrology, astronomy, medicine, Chemistry, Metallurgy, Botany, Zoology and Engineering Gupta period gained a striking facet.

Mathematics: In ancient India, mathematics was treated as a handmaid to astronomy. But Aryabhata treated this as an independent subject. He wrote his work Aryabhtiyam at Pataliputra in 499 A.D. He was the first scholar to discover the decimal system of place values. He has given all his results in the form of finished formulas. Regarding geometry he discussed his work with the area of a triangle, the theorem on similarity of triangles, the area of a circle and the theorem relating to rectangles contained by the segments of chords or a circle. In algebra he discusses the rule of three and a rule for solving examples concerning interest. He has also discussed other mathematical subjects such as arithmetical progression and a formula for the sum of squares and the cubes of natural numbers.

Astronomy: In Astronomy, Aryabhata was the first to assert that the earth rotates round its axis. He was the first person to utilize sine functions in astronomy. He also calculated the increase and decrease in two consecutive days, he stated calculating accurately the angular diameter of the earth's shadow at the moon's orbit and gave a method of finding the duration of an eclipse. These were all new things for the nation as till then they believe in another world.

Varahamihira was another important astronomer of the Gupta period. Most probably he began composing his work Panchasiddhahtika in 505 A.D. He discusses in this work the principles of the five astronomical schools, which were considered as the most authoritative one in his time. Of these five schools the Romaka Siddhanta clearly betrays Western influence. This is expected to happen as a result of active trade contacts between the Roman Empire and the Gupta Empire. The Surya Siddhanta is the most important and complete astronomical work of the period. It seems that Greek astronomy served as the basis of the Surya-siddhahta. The other three schools of astronomy discussed by Varahamihira are the Paitamaha Siddhahta, the Vasistha Siddhahta, and the Paulish Siddhanta. In his work Varahamihira has preserved the essential teachings of these five schools of astronomy, which is a great collection of work.

Astrology: The Vriddha Garga Samhita is the only work on astrology prior to Varahamihira's Brihatsamhita, which is a collection of ancient Indian learning and sciences. Besides the sections on astrology in the Brihatsamhita, Varahamihira also composed four other works on astrology, which deal with auspicious muhurtas for marriage, auspicious portents for the expeditions of kings and the time of man's birth, and its influence on his future.

Medicine: The Bower manuscript was discovered by Lt. H. Bower in a Buddhist stupa in Kashgar in 1890. Out of the seven works discovered by Bower three deal with medicine. The manuscript on the basis of palaeographical grounds has been dated to the second half of the fourth century A.D. The manuscript deals with such subjects as the use of garlic in curing diseases, digestion, and eye diseases. A book named Navanitaka deals with different kinds of powders, decoctions, oils, elixirs and children's diseases. The only familiar name of a medical authority referred to in the Bower manuscript is that of Susruta.

Chemistry, Metallurgy, Botany, Zoology, Engineering and Meteorology

Nagarjuna was the great Mahayana Buddhist philosopher of ancient time. He is believed to have been the real father of scientific chemistry. But there is no evidence or work on chemistry composed by Nagarjuna. The Meharauli iron pillar will forever remain a living monument to the progress in metallurgy achieved in the age of the imperial Guptas. In spite of exposure to the open air for over 1500 years the pillar has not rusted hence it has become an object of research for eminent metallurgists of the world as well.

Varahamihira was a scientist of encyclopedic interests. Besides being an astronomer, mathematician and astrologer he was also a student of metallurgy. He was a good jeweller and has supplied useful information for ascertaining the nature and value of gold, emerald, pearls, diamonds etc. He was also a student of botany as he has discussed various topics of gardening in the Brihatsamhita. He has also discussed the nature of good as well as bad horses, elephants and dogs. His work contains valuable information about the nature and structure of temples, palaces, mansions and houses. This shows that; he had good knowledge of civil engineering as well. He had studied the science of meteorology as he states in his work what kind of clouds will bring us rain etc. It is a pity that Varahamihira could not succeed in founding a school of his own to continue a systematic study of these different branches of science.

Homeland of Gupta Empire

The Gupta dynasty ascended the throne around 320 A.D. and continued upto 550 A.D., with magnificence and splendour. They consolidated the entire Northern India by subjugating the local and provincial powers that became independent after the downfall of the Kushanas. The period during the Gupta Empire is referred as the Golden Age in all fields, embracing art, architecture, literature, sculpture and education. However the origin of the Guptas is still shrouded in obscurity. This is so because the sources of Gupta History, which have been unearthed till date, do not throw enough light on the ancestry of the Guptas and also their original homeland. The Shunga and the Sattavahana referred to many officials bearing the surname Gupta. But their relationship with the Imperial Guptas is not yet determined. Furthermore it is not yet discovered whether the term Gupta indicated any surname of a family or referred to any clan. However the Gupta records itself and the Chinese records provided by I-Tsing, furnished the names of the first three rulers of the Gupta Dynasty, viz. Maharaja Sri Gupta, Maharaja Sri Ghatotkacha and Maharajadhiraja Sri Chandragupta. K.P. Jaiswal has suggested that the Guptas belonged to the Jat tribe of Punjab. But since the theory of Jaiswal lacked conclusive proofs, it was discarded. Dr. H.C. Roychowdhury, however holds that the majestic Guptas belonged to the

Dharana Gotra. According to Roychowdhury, the Guptas were related to queen Dharini of Agnimitra, son of famous king Pushyamitra Shunga. Roychowdhury drew his theory about the pedigree of the Guptas based on the records of Prabhabati Gupta, daughter of Chandragupta II. In her records she claimed herself to be a descendant of the Dharana Gotra. Again Dr. S. Chattopadhya has put forth a different theory about the ancestry of the Guptas. According to him, in the Panchobh Copper Plate, some kings bearing the title Guptas and related to the imperial Gupta Dynasty, claimed themselves as Kshatriyas. The theory of S.Chattopadhya has been widely accepted, after a prolonged research by scholars.

The identification of the Guptas as Kshatriyas though has been supported by facts, the controversy whether the term "Gupta" was a family surname or a full name is still unresolved. This is so because the name of the first king was Sri Gupta, where the term "Gupta" seemed to be a title, but the second Gupta did not use the title like that. Hence, here lies enough dubiousness about the term "Gupta". However the expression "Gupta" had been systematically used by all the Gupta rulers from Chandragupta I onwards, which had led to the acceptance of the term `Imperial Gupta dynasty`.

There is a keen controversy among the scholars about the original homeland of the Guptas. K.P Jaiswal has pointed out that the Guptas were originally inhabitants of Prayag (Allahabad), as the feudatories of the Nagas or Bharsivas.Thereafter they rose in prominence. Dr. Gayal also supported the theory of Jaiswal, suggesting that the original home of the Guptas was Antarvedi in eastern U.P, embracing the regions of Oudh and Prayag. These historians have derived their theory based on the fact that several coins belonging to the Gupta Dynasty have been found in those regions and the study of those numismatics evidences lead to the conclusion that the Guptas were the original inhabitants of that region. However Dr. D.C Ganguli has provided a different view about the original homeland of the Guptas. According to him the Guptas were inhabitants of the Murshidabad region of Bengal and not of Magadha in Bihar. He based his theory on the statement of I -Tsing, who had visited India during 675 and 695 A.D. Fleet and other historians however criticise the above theory because of the fact that Sri Gupta ruled during the end of the third century, but I-Tsing placed him at the end of the second century. Hence the theory of historians, who have provided their views based on the accounts of I-Tsing, can be refuted without much difficulty.

Not only the ancestry and homeland of the Guptas, the extent of the Gupta Empire, when they ascended the throne after the lapse of the prolonged Dark Age, is a also subject of intense controversy among the scholars. Dr. R.C. Majumdar has pointed out that the picture of a stupa has been found in Nepal with the label "Mrigasthapana" Stupa of Varendri. This "Mrigasthapana" is the same as "Mrigashivana" of I-Tsing. As Sri Gupta built a temple in Mrigashivana and as the place was in Varendri, so historians have pointed out that Varendri might have been under the sway of the Guptas, when they ascended the throne. According to Dr.Ganguli, Bengal and parts of Bihar was also included in the Gupta Empire, when they were ruling from the seat of power.

From these theories, several conflicting opinions about the original homeland and the Empire of the Guptas are available. According to Allan and some other scholars, the Guptas were originally concentrated in the region of Magadha and from there they extended their sway upto Bengal. According to other groups, the original homeland of the Guptas was Varendri or the Varendra Bhumi in Bengal, wherefrom they extended their Empire upto Magadha. Whatever the theory is, the Imperial fabric of the Guptas initiated the Golden Age in history of ancient India and with passage of time they became the sole authority of entire Northern India.

RELIGIOUS MOVEMENTS IN GUPTA PERIOD

The Gupta Period was marked by great transformation in Hinduism and Buddhism. Gupta rulers themselves were very sophisticated and benevolent. Though they were patrons of Brahmanism, yet the Guptas were highly tolerant towards the other creeds.

The Gupta period had witnessed the synthesis of Brahmanical Hinduism with heterodox creeds. The integration of various heterodox creeds like Saivism, Vaishnavism and Shakti cult with Brahmanical Hinduism, had marked the culmination of the Gupta period. The synthesis of heterodox creeds gave rise to neo-Hinduism or Puranic Hinduism, the flavour of which is still found in contemporary Hinduism. The ideal of Neo-Hinduism had almost changed the concept of Vedic Brahmanism, but the form however remained unchanged. Neo-Hinduism had shed its concept of multi-cult creators. The concept of three gods connected with life, death and destruction united together as "Trinity" or "Trayi" had first materialised during the Gupta Period. According to neo-Hinduism, the three gods Brahma-Vishnu-Maheswar were united in the trinity concept or Trayi. According to scholars, due to religious admixture of heterodox creeds, the concept of "monism" or the doctrine of different schools of thought had evolved during the Gupta period. Gradually Brahma, considered the God of creation, passed into oblivion. Only Siva and Vishnu dominated the neo-Hindu doctrine of the Gupta period. The Puranas were rewritten in order to accommodate Siva and Vishnu as the chief Gods. Not only they were considered the chief Gods, but were also attributed with extraordinary powers. Most of the Vedic Gods passed into oblivion and were replaced by new Gods according to the concept of neo-Hinduism. Gods like Siva, Vishnu, Kartikeya, and Ganesha who belonged to the heterodox creeds formerly replaced all the Vedic Gods. Thus due to religious movements during the Gupta Period, Hinduism became the vast mosaic of various religious patterns, combining religious ideas of both the old and the new.

One of the interesting features of religious development during the Gupta Period was the wide prevalence of worship of 'Shakti' or mother goddess. 'Tantricism', or the cult of Tantra that preached the worship of female deities, had initiated the fertility cult. Hinduism, prevalent in the contemporary Gupta Period could not escape the influence of the Shakti cult. Henceforth it gave rise to worship of several female gods, who themselves were considered the wives of the chief gods. The cult of mother Goddess became very popular. Originally "Shakti" was worshipped as the goddess of force in the form of Kali, Chamunda and Bhima. In the "Markandeya Purana" Chandi is described as a destroyer of Mahishasura, the symbol of evil. Gradually the character and concept mellowed down into goddess Shakti, who was considered the wife of Siva and mother of Kartikeya, Ganesha etc. The concept of Siva and Durga was very popular. Durga was the new form of Shakti. Two opposite cults were ascribed to the concept of Shiva-Shakti. Their violent aspect came to be known as Rudra or Ghora or Chamunda respectively. In their graceful manifestation they came to be known as Aghora Mahadeva and Uma. Uma, Haimavati, Durga, Kali were worshipped as the various manifestations of the wife of Shiva. Lakshmi was worshipped as the wife of Vishnu. Puranas were re-written to accommodate the new Gods and Goddesses in Hindu temples. The Puranas described the cult of neo-Hinduism and narrated the mutual relationship of various gods and goddesses, worshipped according to the concept of neo-Hinduism.

Prevalence of idol worship was another feature of Puranic Hinduism of the Gupta period. Specification of images of different gods and goddesses were incorporated from Puranas. The cult of Kartikeya and Ganesha was also very prominent during that period. The Kartikeya cult was popular among the Kushanas is evident from the figure of Kartikeya on the coins of Hubiskha, a Kushana chief. Kartikeya was originally considered the war God. Later he was included in the family of Shiva-Parvati. Ganesha was also unknown before the 300 A.D. In the Gupta period he became a popular God. Many images of Ganesha made of stone and terracotta, belonging to the Gupta period has been found. The concept of Goddess Lakshmi underwent an evolutionary change during the Gupta Period. Lakshmi was originally Gaja-Lakshmi and a solitary goddess. Later, according to the concept of neo-Hinduism, goddess Lakshmi was considered the wife of Lord Vishnu and the Puranas delineated the story of her birth from the ocean. Various virtues were added to her character and she was popularised as the goddess of wealth.

In the Gupta era, the Vedic form of worship by performance of yajna did not survive much. In order to make a synthesis with Vedic Hinduism, 'yajna' or sacrifice was retained along with idol worship. Yajna lost its prominence in the form of image worship. Bhakti or the devotion of the worshipper became more important. Still priests were needed to perform the worship, but the concept of priesthood lost its dominance due to the emergence of Bhakti cult. Worship of god henceforth became personal matter of the worshipper. Priests became irrelevant due to the decline of yajna or sacrifice. Therefore Almighty became a much more concern for the individual. Men started believing that he had four fold objects in life- Dharma, Artha, Kama and Moksha.

Apart from Hinduism, Buddhism also underwent transformation during the Gupta Period. Since Gupta rulers were tolerant towards other religious creeds, all religions flourished during that period. Nalanda received patronage from the Guptas. However the typical change that entered the folds of Buddhism, was the rise of Vajrayana or Tantric Buddhism. Buddhism adopted worship of mother goddesses like Tara. Buddhism also accepted the theory of incarnation of Buddha and thus prepared the way for assimilation by Hinduism. Jainism however remained much original in its creed. It received the patronage of the merchant community of western India. Jainism continued to flourish in south and western India, while neo-Hinduism became a dominating creed of north India.

The religious movement in India during the Guptas therefore is a synthesis and integration of different heterodox creeds with Brahmanical Hinduism, which ultimately led to a complete transformation of Brahmanical Hinduism prevalent in ancient India.

RELIGIOUS MOVEMENTS IN GUPTA PERIOD

The Gupta Period was marked by great transformation in Hinduism and Buddhism. Gupta rulers themselves were very sophisticated and benevolent. Though they were patrons of Brahmanism, yet the Guptas were highly tolerant towards the other creeds.

The Gupta period had witnessed the synthesis of Brahmanical Hinduism with heterodox creeds. The integration of various heterodox creeds like Saivism, Vaishnavism and Shakti cult with Brahmanical Hinduism, had marked the culmination of the Gupta period. The synthesis of heterodox creeds gave rise to neo-Hinduism or Puranic Hinduism, the flavour of which is still found in contemporary Hinduism. The ideal of Neo-Hinduism had almost changed the concept of Vedic Brahmanism, but the form however remained unchanged. Neo-Hinduism had shed its concept of multi-cult creators. The concept of three gods connected with life, death and destruction united together as "Trinity" or "Trayi" had first materialised during the Gupta Period. According to neo-Hinduism, the three gods Brahma-Vishnu-Maheswar were united in the trinity concept or Trayi. According to scholars, due to religious admixture of heterodox creeds, the concept of "monism" or the doctrine of different schools of thought had evolved during the Gupta period. Gradually Brahma, considered the God of creation, passed into oblivion. Only Siva and Vishnu dominated the neo-Hindu doctrine of the Gupta period. The Puranas were rewritten in order to accommodate Siva and Vishnu as the chief Gods. Not only they were considered the chief Gods, but were also attributed with extraordinary powers. Most of the Vedic Gods passed into oblivion and were replaced by new Gods according to the concept of neo-Hinduism. Gods like Siva, Vishnu, Kartikeya, and Ganesha who belonged to the heterodox creeds formerly replaced all the Vedic Gods. Thus due to religious movements during the Gupta Period, Hinduism became the vast mosaic of various religious patterns, combining religious ideas of both the old and the new.

One of the interesting features of religious development during the Gupta Period was the wide prevalence of worship of 'Shakti' or mother goddess. 'Tantricism', or the cult of Tantra that preached the worship of female deities, had initiated the fertility cult. Hinduism, prevalent in the contemporary Gupta Period could not escape the influence of the Shakti cult. Henceforth it gave rise to worship of several female gods, who themselves were considered the wives of the chief gods. The cult of mother Goddess became very popular. Originally "Shakti" was worshipped as the goddess of force in the form of Kali, Chamunda and Bhima. In the "Markandeya Purana" Chandi is described as a destroyer of Mahishasura, the symbol of evil. Gradually the character and concept mellowed down into goddess Shakti, who was considered the wife of Siva and mother of Kartikeya, Ganesha etc. The concept of Siva and Durga was very popular. Durga was the new form of Shakti. Two opposite cults were ascribed to the concept of Shiva-Shakti. Their violent aspect came to be known as Rudra or Ghora or Chamunda respectively. In their graceful manifestation they came to be known as Aghora Mahadeva and Uma. Uma, Haimavati, Durga, Kali were worshipped as the various manifestations of the wife of Shiva. Lakshmi was worshipped as the wife of Vishnu. Puranas were re-written to accommodate the new Gods and Goddesses in Hindu temples. The Puranas described the cult of neo-Hinduism and narrated the mutual relationship of various gods and goddesses, worshipped according to the concept of neo-Hinduism.

Prevalence of idol worship was another feature of Puranic Hinduism of the Gupta period. Specification of images of different gods and goddesses were incorporated from Puranas. The cult of Kartikeya and Ganesha was also very prominent during that period. The Kartikeya cult was popular among the Kushanas is evident from the figure of Kartikeya on the coins of Hubiskha, a Kushana chief. Kartikeya was originally considered the war God. Later he was included in the family of Shiva-Parvati. Ganesha was also unknown before the 300 A.D. In the Gupta period he became a popular God. Many images of Ganesha made of stone and terracotta, belonging to the Gupta period has been found. The concept of Goddess Lakshmi underwent an evolutionary change during the Gupta Period. Lakshmi was originally Gaja-Lakshmi and a solitary goddess. Later, according to the concept of neo-Hinduism, goddess Lakshmi was considered the wife of Lord Vishnu and the Puranas delineated the story of her birth from the ocean. Various virtues were added to her character and she was popularised as the goddess of wealth.

In the Gupta era, the Vedic form of worship by performance of yajna did not survive much. In order to make a synthesis with Vedic Hinduism, 'yajna' or sacrifice was retained along with idol worship. Yajna lost its prominence in the form of image worship. Bhakti or the devotion of the worshipper became more important. Still priests were needed to perform the worship, but the concept of priesthood lost its dominance due to the emergence of Bhakti cult. Worship of god henceforth became personal matter of the worshipper. Priests became irrelevant due to the decline of yajna or sacrifice.

Therefore Almighty became a much more concern for the individual. Men started believing that he had four fold objects in life- Dharma, Artha, Kama and Moksha.

Apart from Hinduism, Buddhism also underwent transformation during the Gupta Period. Since Gupta rulers were tolerant towards other religious creeds, all religions flourished during that period. Nalanda received patronage from the Guptas. However the typical change that entered the folds of Buddhism, was the rise of Vajrayana or Tantric Buddhism. Buddhism adopted worship of mother goddesses like Tara. Buddhism also accepted the theory of incarnation of Buddha and thus prepared the way for assimilation by Hinduism. Jainism however remained much original in its creed. It received the patronage of the merchant community of western India. Jainism continued to flourish in south and western India, while neo-Hinduism became a dominating creed of north India.

The religious movement in India during the Guptas therefore is a synthesis and integration of different heterodox creeds with Brahmanical Hinduism, which ultimately led to a complete transformation of Brahmanical Hinduism prevalent in ancient India.

THE HUN INVASION AND ITS EFFECTS

The Huns were violent tribes, who invaded the Gupta Empire during the reign of Skandagupta. They were originally the inhabitants of Central Asia and were divided in two tribes- the Epthalites or the White Huns, who invaded India and the Huns who invaded Europe. The Huns were notorious warlike tribes, who were famous for their barbarism and cruelty. The dominion of the Huns was extended from the border of Persia to Khotan in Central Asia.

The Epthalite branch of the Huns entered through the northwestern gate of India in fifth century A.D. Consolidating their base in Afghanistan and the capital in Bamiyan, they tried to invade India. About 458 A.D., they entered Punjab and the failure of the Guptas to guard the northeast frontier of the Empire led the Huns to an unopposed entrance in the Gangetic valley, the heart of the Gupta Empire. However the invasion by Toraman was completely unsuccessful against the Guptas because the Gupta Emperor Skandagupta inflicted a crushing defeat upon them and pushed them out of their frontier. The Huns suffered a great loss. According to some scholars, it was due the tough resistance against the Huns by the Guptas and the Chinese kings that the main tide of the Hun invasion turned back towards the European countries.

However, the Hun invasion suppressed by Skandagupta did not completely perish the tribe. These notorious warlike tribes renewed their invasion against the strong foundation of the Gupta Empire. But the later Gupta emperors were not powerful enough to protect the northeastern frontier of the Gupta Empire from fresh incursions of the Huns. The Huns under Toraman poured in once again through the Hindukush passes. During this phase of invasion, Toraman conquered Punjab, Rajputana and Malwa. He concentrated his base in Punjab and from there controlled his operation in the interiors of India. He reduced a number of local kings as his vassals and he assumed the title of "Maharajadhiraja". His coins and inscriptions are found in extensive regions of Sutlej and Yamuna. It is known from numismatics and epigraphic evidences that Toraman had his sway over the regions of Punjab, Rajputana, Malwa, Kashmir and parts of Doab. Some of the Gupta provincial governors also joined Toraman during the course of his invasion in India. However Toraman`s ascendency in India did not last long. He ruled from 510 to 511 A.D. Bhanu Gupta, a scion of the Gupta House and his feudatory Gopalachandra, challenged Toraman`s dominance in India. They inflicted a humiliating defeat upon him, which forced him to retreat to the other side of India.

Toraman was succeeded by his son Mihirkula. He was a Hinduised Hun and from his coins it is evident that he was a Saiva. Mihirkula was a notorious warrior like his father and killed people, demolished Buddhist temples and also devastated towns and cities. From Punjab Mihirkula tried to dominate on Rajputana and Malwa. In this course of his victorious march, he came in conflict with the Guptas and their feudatories. From the inscription of Mihirkula belonging to his 15th reigning year, it is known that Yasodharmana, a feudatory of the Guptas had imposed a severe crush on Mihirkula. At that time Mihirkula was engaged in terrible warfare with Baladitya. It is presumed by historians that perhaps after the death of Yasodharmana, Mihirkula had started a fresh attack on the Gupta territory. Hiuen Tsang had identified Baladitya as Narasimha Gupta and also suggested that Narasimha Gupta successfully had defeated the Hun chief and permitted him to leave the Gupta Territory. According to historians, the struggle between Mihirkula and the Gupta chief Baladitya was not merely political, it has a religious shade also. It is suggested that the anti-Buddhist activities of Mihirkula had magnified the dimension of his conflict with Mihirkula.

Perhaps after this defeat Mihirkula had concentrated his authority in the regions of Punjab. The inscription of Mihirkula states that he had built the Sun temple and the Buddhist monastery. There is keen controversy among the scholars regarding the facts provided by the inscription of Mihirkula. This is because, a group of historians have suggested that Mihirkula was prejudiced against Buddhism, which had led him to war against Narasimha Gupta. But according to another group of writers, a destroyer of Buddhism could not establish Buddhist monasteries in the latter part of his career. Henceforth there is still a keen controversy over the subject that whether Mihirkula was a destroyer of Buddhism or not.

However the significance of Hun invasion in India had far reaching effects. The Huns had destroyed the precarious hold of the Gupta sovereign on their feudatories. As the Guptas were busy in their resistance against the Huns, their hold on the semi-independent feudatories was weak. Petty kingdoms began to flourish on the ruins of the Gupta Empire. Hence the political unity established by the early Guptas was completely shattered during the time of the later Guptas. Moreover the Hun inroads in western and central India had upset the trade of the Guptas in India with the Roman Empire, which led to the devastation of the Gupta economy. As a result the economic and cultural cities like Ujjaini or Pataliputra lost their significance and glory. There was total dislocation of the socio-political and economic life during the later Guptas caused by the Hun invasion. The debased Gupta coins bear testimony to this fact. But the Hun invasion in India had positive effects also. With the decline of trade relations with the Roman Empire through West Indian ports, trade with South East Asia and China was vastly prospered through ports like Kaveri Pattanam, Tamralipta etc.

The more significant effect of the Hun invasion was the racial admixture. When the Huns had appeared in India, there was an elaborate racial movement. The Huns had thrown open the gates of northwest, through which various other tribes apart from the Huns had also poured into the land. They adopted the Hindu religion and completely merged with the bulk of the Indian population. The Huns and other martial cultures introduced the Indian society to their vigour and warlike culture. Thus the Hun invasion led to socio-economic and cultural transformation of the Indian society as a whole.

HUN INVASION AND ITS EFFECTS

The Huns were violent tribes, who invaded the Gupta Empire during the reign of Skandagupta. They were originally the inhabitants of Central Asia and were divided in two tribes- the Epthalites or the White Huns, who invaded India and the Huns who invaded Europe. The Huns were notorious warlike tribes, who were famous for their barbarism and cruelty. The dominion of the Huns was extended from the border of Persia to Khotan in Central Asia.

The Epthalite branch of the Huns entered through the northwestern gate of India in fifth century A.D. Consolidating their base in Afghanistan and the capital in Bamiyan, they tried to invade India. About 458 A.D., they entered Punjab and the failure of the Guptas to guard the northeast frontier of the Empire led the Huns to an unopposed entrance in the Gangetic valley, the heart of the Gupta Empire. However the invasion by Toraman was completely unsuccessful against the Guptas because the Gupta Emperor Skandagupta inflicted a crushing defeat upon them and pushed them out of their frontier. The Huns suffered a great loss. According to some scholars, it was due the tough resistance against the Huns by the Guptas and the Chinese kings that the main tide of the Hun invasion turned back towards the European countries.

However, the Hun invasion suppressed by Skandagupta did not completely perish the tribe. These notorious warlike tribes renewed their invasion against the strong foundation of the Gupta Empire. But the later Gupta emperors were not powerful enough to protect the northeastern frontier of the Gupta Empire from fresh incursions of the Huns. The Huns under Toraman poured in once again through the Hindukush passes. During this phase of invasion, Toraman conquered Punjab, Rajputana and Malwa. He concentrated his base in Punjab and from there controlled his operation in the interiors of India. He reduced a number of local kings as his vassals and he assumed the title of "Maharajadhiraja". His coins and inscriptions are found in extensive regions of Sutlej and Yamuna. It is known from numismatics and epigraphic evidences that Toraman had his sway over the regions of

Punjab, Rajputana, Malwa, Kashmir and parts of Doab. Some of the Gupta provincial governors also joined Toraman during the course of his invasion in India. However Toraman`s ascendency in India did not last long. He ruled from 510 to 511 A.D. Bhanu Gupta, a scion of the Gupta House and his feudatory Gopalachandra, challenged Toraman`s dominance in India. They inflicted a humiliating defeat upon him, which forced him to retreat to the other side of India.

Toraman was succeeded by his son Mihirkula. He was a Hinduised Hun and from his coins it is evident that he was a Saiva. Mihirkula was a notorious warrior like his father and killed people, demolished Buddhist temples and also devastated towns and cities. From Punjab Mihirkula tried to dominate on Rajputana and Malwa. In this course of his victorious march, he came in conflict with the Guptas and their feudatories. From the inscription of Mihirkula belonging to his 15th reigning year, it is known that Yasodharmana, a feudatory of the Guptas had imposed a severe crush on Mihirkula. At that time Mihirkula was engaged in terrible warfare with Baladitya. It is presumed by historians that perhaps after the death of Yasodharmana, Mihirkula had started a fresh attack on the Gupta territory. Hiuen Tsang had identified Baladitya as Narasimha Gupta and also suggested that Narasimha Gupta successfully had defeated the Hun chief and permitted him to leave the Gupta Territory. According to historians, the struggle between Mihirkula and the Gupta chief Baladitya was not merely political, it has a religious shade also. It is suggested that the anti-Buddhist activities of Mihirkula had magnified the dimension of his conflict with Mihirkula.

Perhaps after this defeat Mihirkula had concentrated his authority in the regions of Punjab. The inscription of Mihirkula states that he had built the Sun temple and the Buddhist monastery. There is keen controversy among the scholars regarding the facts provided by the inscription of

Mihirkula. This is because, a group of historians have suggested that Mihirkula was prejudiced against Buddhism, which had led him to war against Narasimha Gupta. But according to another group of writers, a destroyer of Buddhism could not establish Buddhist monasteries in the latter part of his career. Henceforth there is still a keen controversy over the subject that whether Mihirkula was a destroyer of Buddhism or not.

However the significance of Hun invasion in India had far reaching effects. The Huns had destroyed the precarious hold of the Gupta sovereign on their feudatories. As the Guptas were busy in their resistance against the Huns, their hold on the semi-independent feudatories was weak. Petty kingdoms began to flourish on the ruins of the Gupta Empire. Hence the political unity established by the early Guptas was completely shattered during the time of the later Guptas. Moreover the Hun inroads in western and central India had upset the trade of the Guptas in India with the Roman Empire, which led to the devastation of the Gupta economy. As a result the economic and cultural cities like Ujjaini or Pataliputra lost their significance and glory. There was total dislocation of the socio-political and economic life during the later Guptas caused by the Hun invasion. The debased Gupta coins bear testimony to this fact. But the Hun invasion in India had positive effects also. With the decline of trade relations with the Roman Empire through West Indian ports, trade with South East Asia and China was vastly prospered through ports like Kaveri Pattanam, Tamralipta etc.

The more significant effect of the Hun invasion was the racial admixture. When the Huns had appeared in India, there was an elaborate racial movement. The Huns had thrown open the gates of northwest, through which various other tribes apart from the Huns had also poured into the land. They adopted the Hindu religion and completely merged with the bulk of the Indian population. The Huns and other martial cultures introduced the Indian society to their vigour and warlike culture. Thus the Hun invasion led to socio-economic and cultural transformation of the Indian society as a whole.

CAUSES AND DOWNFALL OF THE GUPTA EMPIRE

After the downfall of the Kushanas in north and Sattavahanas in south, no great power had arisen in India. For more than a hundred years, India was divided into many independent states that continuously struggled for power. It was the Guptas who established a strong foundation of their Empire by coalescing the disintegrated republics. The Gupta period constituted the "Golden era" in history of ancient India. However, such a vast and strong foundation like the Guptas also declined due to the weak successors of Skandagupta. According to scholars there were several natural and local causes, which contributed to the collapse of the Guptas. Internal dissension, rebellion of the provincial governors, growth and feeling of the local independence and impact of foreign invasions, had chiefly worked behind the gradual decline and downfall of the Guptas.

The reign of Skandagupta marked the beginning of the decline of the Gupta Empire. In spite of the sweeping military success against the Pushyamitras and the Huns, the strain of constant war depleted the resources of the realm. The debased coinage and the lack of variety of coins during Skandagupta testified the financial drain of the royal exchequer of the Guptas. The death of Skandagupta and the short reign of Puru Gupta hastened the pace of decline. The latter rulers could not hold back the administration of the vast Gupta Empire. Buddha Gupta was the last great ruler who tried to halt the process of decline for sometime, but his hold over the western part of the Gupta Empire was very weak. The feudatories of Kathiawar and Bundelkhand region had assumed a semi-independent status during his reign. The

Maitrakas of Valabhi became the hereditary rulers and unfurled the flag of their independence. The other provincial governors of Bundelkhand, Uchchakalpa etc. also declared their independence, defying the dominion of Buddha Gupta. In Jaipur, in Uttar Pradesh and in Narmada valley, the local governors became the de-facto sovereign. Brahmadatta, the governor of Pundravardhana in North Bengal had assumed the high-sounding title of 'Uparika Maharaja' and thus declared his independence. All these factors led to the decline of the Gupta authority in the outlying provinces during the reign of Buddhagupta. The Vakataka invasion in Malwa reduced the authority of Buddhagupta in that region also. As a result, forces of disintegration set within the Gupta Empire and it augmented after the death of Buddhagupta.

The discord within the imperial family was supposed to be the primary cause for the decline of the Gupta Empire. After the death of Kumaragupta I there was probably a struggle for succession among the successors. However Skandagupta did ascend the throne. But the family feud initiated by the successors of Kumaragupta continued even in the following generations, which weakened the family integrity of the Gupta Dynasty. Since the latter Guptas were busy in civil war over the accession to the throne, they could not pay attention towards the administrative maintenance of the vast Empire. Thus the struggle for throne inside the family substantially weakened the central authority in the provinces and feudatories. Thus family grudges continued to be the primary reason for the downfall of the Guptas.

The Vakatakas in Deccan were powerful neighbours of the Guptas. Since Samudragupta projected his campaign in eastern Deccan, the Vakatakas in western Deccan were left unscathed. Chandragupta II had established matrimonial relations with them, by accepting Rudrasena II, the Vakataka king, as the husband of his daughter, Prabhabati Gupta. But the successors of Chandragupta II did not maintain peaceful relations with the Vakatakas. During the reign of Buddha Gupta, the Vakataka king Narendrasena had invaded Malwa, Kosala and Mekala. His invasion considerably had weakened the Gupta authority over the regions of central India and Bundelkhand. Later the Vakatakas ousted the Gupta supremacy from the regions of Malwa and Gujarat.

Since the later Guptas could not check the forces of disintegration, hence, there absence of strong centralised administration. Thus, lack of a centralised management contributed to a steady downfall of the Guptas. Provincial administration was extremely weak and consequently the regional governors enjoyed a great deal of authority and freedom. Again due to exhaustion of the royal exchequer, the Guptas were suffering from shortage of money and accordingly could not spend enough money for provincial administration. Finally the local chiefs or the governors, who were working under the supremacy of the central authority, unfurled the flag of independence. Thus the vast Gupta Empire was disintegrated into provinces and was ruled by local governors, who were originally feudatories of the Gupta suzerain.

The final and perhaps the most important cause for the downfall of the Guptas were the repeated Hun invasions. Though Dr. R.C. Majumdar is of the opinion that Skandagupta successfully had delayed the violent Hun invasion by Toraman and Narasimha Gupta had suppressed the forthcoming invasions, yet most of the historians are inclined to suggest that the Hun incursion had brought about the immediate downfall of the Guptas. Internal dissension already had decomposed the base of the Gupta family and the Hun invasion was just adding of fuel to fire. The Hun plunderings not only exhausted the royal exchequer but also weakened the military organisation of the Guptas. The Hun inroads in western India completely had destroyed the lucrative trade of the Guptas with Rome. The ports and markets of western India were completely devastated due to the invasion of the Huns and their associates.

Finally after the death of Buddha Gupta, the vast and integrated Gupta Empire was crumbled and the local chiefs rose to power. Narasimha Gupta just had no strong influence over the Gupta Empire. As is suggested by historians, the later Guptas were ruling in diminished glory over Magadha, north Bengal and parts of Kalinga. In this process the Gupta supremacy was diminished and the Maukharis finally ousted them from Magadha and Ishanavarmana Maukhari ascended the throne assuming the title of 'Maharajadhiraja' in 554 A.D.

ECONOMIC LIFE DURING GUPTA RULE

The Guptas had ruled north India for about 200 years. Political unity, economic prosperity and extraordinary progress in every aspect of life under the Guptas were prevalent. The Gupta period had witnessed great prosperity, owing to the flourishing trade, agriculture and industry. Prosperity due to Roman trade, which began in the Kushana period, continued upto the early reign of the Guptas. The Saka Satraps of western India continued trade with the west after the fall of the Kushanas. Chandragupta II's conquest of Malwa and Saurashtra, by overthrowing the Saka rulers had established direct link of the Guptas in India with Roman trade. Brigukachchha port bore the bulk of trade with the west. Ujjaini itself had served as a major centre of trade. From Ujjaini goods were directly transformed to Bhrauch, wherefrom it was shipped off to the west. There were supplementary ports like Kalyana and ports of Sind, wherefrom the trade was carried out. Ujjaini was linked with south India and Deccan through roads. It was also linked with a road to Pataliputra and Eastern India. The inland market of Govardhana, Nasik, Paithan, Pataliputra, Beneras etc. provided the materials, which were exported through ports of Bhrauch.

Trade with Rome continued in a flourishing manner till the early Gupta period. Then it suffered disruption and from the time of the Hun invasion, it had greatly declined. Even then trade with Byzantine Empire continued. The discovery of Byzantine coins in different parts of India testifies the continuation of Byzantine trade. As a result there was considerable decline of Indian silk trade with Rome. Silk merchants of western India were thrown out of employment suddenly. The Mandasor inscription depicts the story of a guild of silk workers who had migrated from Gujrat to Dasapura, where they had taken up a different occupation.

Apart from silk, the Guptas had traded many other materials with the Romans. Historians have opined that slaves were exported to Roman countries. India exported leather goods, fur, iron products, ivory, pearl, pepper, spices and indigo to the west. India produced sugar in galore. From "Raghuvansam" it is known how sugarcane and Sali paddy was cultivated in India. Bengal was famous for the cultivation of a special type of sugarcane called Pundri-Akh. Gauda in Bengal was important for the production of molasses. Besides Indian cotton goods, both the fine and coarse quality also had a great external market.

Decline of trade with Rome did not affect India's foreign trade though. The diminution of Roman trade was compensated by flourishing trade of the Guptas with the countries of East Asia and Southeast Asia, through the port of Tamralipta. According to Cosmas, in 6th century, Sindhu, Kalyan and Chaul in the Western Coast and Kaveri Pattanam in the Coromondal coast were the important centres of maritime trade in ancient India during the Guptas. Tamralipta was the most significant one.

Apart from external trade, the Guptas in India had a flourishing inland trade, which was augmented by political peace, established by the Guptas and the vast network of roads linking different parts of the country. The towns of Beneras, Mathura, Sarnath, Pataliputra, Ujjaini, Nasik, Paithan, Kanchi, and Tamralipta were famous trading centres.

The Gupta government had laid down various laws and regulations for smooth flow of trade, which also had influenced the economic life of the Guptas. The Smritis, or law books had laid down the principle that it was royal duty to encourage trade and arts. Like the Mauryan government, the Guptas had also laid down various regulations on trade. It was said that imported commodities should be taxed at the rate of 1/5th of the value as a toll.

"Kamasutra" had stated that the Ayuktas use to look after the storehouses in villages.

Guild system was a part of life of the traders and manufacturers. The guilds had their autonomous organisation and had their own rules of organisations. There was a specific president to supervise the guild. However according to Kausambhi, after the decline of Roman trade and the emergence of rural economy, the guild system had lost its shine. Dr. Majumdar also supports this view and opines that the guild system was completely diminished in the 4th and 5th centuries.

Agriculture was not at all neglected during the Gupta period in spite of the spread of trade. Agriculture held a significant place in the economic life of the people during the Gupta period. Agriculture was the main occupation of common folk and a stable source of state revenue. Land revenue was collected from various categories of land. Land was divided into 3 categories- fallow or wasteland owned by the state, cultivated land owned by the state from which the main portions of the state income was derived, and private land. The king used to grant land to Brahmins free of tax, which was called 'Agrahaara' grant. Theoretically the king could revoke the land after the death of the grantee but actually the land remained as a hereditary to the family of the grantee, though the king had direct control over that land. Where the tenant farmers use to cultivate their land, the owner achieved Â½ or 1/3 of the produce, the remaining of which went to the tenant. Paddy, wheat, fruits, sugarcane, bamboo etc. were cultivated in the cultivable lands. From the accounts of Fa-hien it is known that paddy was cultivated in the regions of Magadha and eastern India and wheat was cultivated in northern and western India. The Gupta kings also took special care of irrigation purposes for the promotion of agricultural economy in the Gupta kingdom.

Textile industry greatly flourished during the Gupta period. Beneras was famous for silk manufacturing and Mathura was famous for cotton fabrics. Textile had a vast domestic or inland market and "Indian Muslin" was very popular abroad. Though Indian silk trade with Rome had declined after the Hun invasion, yet brisk trade of Chinese silk through land and sea routes had flourished. Apart from textile production, ivory cutting, stone cutting, metal casting, making of gold and silver ornaments, pottery etc. were prominent industries in Gupta phase. Weaponry was rigidly controlled by the state. These industrial products had overseas market also. Goods were transported through sea routes in the overseas market.

Thus during the Gupta period, trade and agriculture both had achieved a thriving prosperity, which promoted economic life of the people, thereby attaining material prosperity.

SOCIAL LIFE DURING THE GUPTA AGE

The Gupta Empire was founded in north India, in the beginning of fourth century A.D., after a long period of chaos, which ensued when the Kushana Empire ended in the middle of the third century. In the interim period, a number of new people and states had emerged, about whom there exists scanty historical records. It was only after the foundation of the Gupta Empire that there was once again unity and peace over almost the whole of North India. Known as the 'Golden Age' and 'Classical Period', there was a degree of balance and harmony in all the arts and an efficient system of administration during the Gupta period. Peaceful and balanced social life was one of the chief features of the Gupta period.

The Smritis and accounts of Fa-Hien are the chief sources of knowledge about the social life of the Guptas. Fa-Hien had stayed in India for a long period of 9 years, from 401 to 410 A.D. and visited various periods of north India, including Punjab, Uttar Pradesh, Bihar and Bengal. He had spent several years in Pataliputra and Tamralipta. Therefore he could have had a first hand knowledge of the social life of the Guptas. According to his accounts, people were very happy and content during the period of the Guptas and were free to move anywhere. Since public morality was very high during that time, therefore criminal law was lenient. People were mainly vegetarian and did not even eat onion or garlic. The habit of drinking wine among people was rare. Only the Chandalas and the sweepers drank wine and ate meat. However, they lived outside the towns and villages.

The representation of society as described by Fa-Hien depicts that town-dwellers lived a comfortable life and enjoyed a good standard of living. People living in the outskirts, like the Chandalas, were not so well of. Villagers lived on the production of their own cultivations and products manufactured by their artisans. "Kamasutra" indicates the comfortable life of the well-to-do citizens of towns. "Kamasutra" depicts the refinement and leisure of city life. It is presumed by historians that the city people beguiled themselves with poetry, writing and painting. Gatherings were held where poetry was recited and dancing performances were held. Youth of upper classes played the lute and practiced singing and even received training in the art of love, as Kamasutra testifies. Joint-family system was actually the general rule of family life. The head of the family governed the family unit. But Smritis also dictates the partition of family and familial properties. The male members dominated the family and society.

Though women were subordinate to men in society, yet their position was no less significant. Women in Gupta society were idealised in literature. Basham has pointed out that ancient literature presented contradictory attitude towards women. While women were respected as anchors of the family, at the same time were mother of children and the friend of husband, a living goddess. Dandin in "Dashakumara-charita" had proposed disparaging remarks about women in a class. He had described them as quarrelsome and disgusting. Education was permitted in a limited way to the upper class women in Gupta civilization. They not only participated in public life, but there is also reference to women teachers. There are instances also that women used to take part in governmental and administrative functions.

Agramahisini, or the chief queen had a special place in the royal palace of the Guptas. Every minister was bound to act according to the will of this chief queen or Agramahisini. Prabhabati Gupta, daughter of Chandragupta II had administered the Vakataka government after the death of her husband. Vatsayana had recommended Sastric education for women in order to sharpen the intellect of women. There is reference to women teachers in "Amarakosha", who were well versed in Vedic hymns. The practice of Swyamvara was in vogue during the Guptas. But in general women were kept in subordination. The Smritis lowered the age of girls. Hence child marriage and polygamy were widely prevalent during that time. A married woman had to live with many wives of her husband. This custom was in vogue even in the royal family. Celibacy of widows became a general rule in the Gupta society. Sometimes the custom of Sati was also recommended. It is known from the Gupta inscription that Goparaja, a feudal chief of Bhanugupta, had died while fighting with the Huns. His wife had performed self-immolation. According to historians, Sati was prevalent largely among the Kshatriyas and other martial races.

Social morality rate during the Gupta era was not very high. The Smritis treated debauchery as a small crime, which could be wiped out by 'prayschitta' (observing confession). But debauchery by the Sudras was regarded a serious crime because it affected the Varna or caste system, which was a significant feature of the Gupta society. The entire society was subdivided into several castes- the Brahmanas, the Kshatriyas, the Vaishyas and the Sudras. The Brahmanas belonged to the upper stratum of the society and enjoyed all the socio-economic privileges, while the Sudras or the lower castes were deprived of those privileges. Existence of a large number of courtesans was a momentous feature of urban life during the Gupta period. It has been suggested by historians that there was a vogue to maintain courtesans in royal families. Kamasutra also had prescribed conversational and behavioral training to the courtesans. Vatsayana had prescribed the learning of 64 katas by a courtesan, including dancing, singing, cooking and the art of dressing and art of repartee. Courtesans also could return to an honest life if they wished to. The 'Devdasi' system was widely practiced during the Gupta period. Kalidasa had referred to devdasis in Mahakala Temple of Ujjaini. However "Manu Smriti" referred them as the outcasts and social maladies.

Amusements consisted of theatrical entertainments, dances, performances and musical concerts. Though gambling was a popular pastime, animal fighting, wrestling and athletics was no less popular in the Gupta society and was in vogue both in towns and villages. Various festivals- religious and secular also provided amusement to the people. Festivals were celebrated by wearing new dresses and eating meat and drinking wine or 'sura' and chewing betel leaf or 'pan'.

Education and learning constituted a significant status in Gupta society. Education during the Gupta period was provided by the Brahmanical agraharas and in Buddhist monasteries. No distinction was however made between

Buddhist and Hindu teachings. Primary education was provided by members of the family. Formal and higher education was given in the agraharas or monasteries. Baranasi, Nasik, Kanchi were great centres of Brahmanical learning. Several universities had sprang up under the patronage of the Gupta kings. University of Nalanda was the legendary Buddhist University, which provided outstanding education regarding various branches of art, philosophy, grammar, humanities, astrology etc. University of Taxila, though had lost its former glory due to Hun invasion, yet had maintained its standard. Technical and industrial education was imparted by the guilds. According to Manu there were two types of teachers- 'acharya' and 'upadhya'. The acharyas were entrusted with fundamental teachings of Vedas, Upanishads and Kalpasutra. The acharyas took their work as 'work of charity' and refrained from taking fees from pupils. The Upadhyas took teaching as a profession and charged the pupils. Memorisation of subjects was regarded the best way to learn a thing. For scholarly education, study of Dharmashastras, Smriti, itihasa-puranas, heterodox scriptures, Naya Shastras etc. were included in the syllabus. For non-scholarly education, mathematics, science of warfare, astronomy, astrology and medicine were included. Education was generally permitted to the people belonging to the upper stratum of society. Brahmanas were eligible for all types of education, while the Kshatriyas and Sudras were eligible only for some items of learning. But the Sudras were deprived completely from any light of education. State grants were made to various institutions for the development of learning procedures.

Technical training like metallurgy, ivory and diamond cutting, goldsmithery, woodwork etc. were instructed by the guilds. The educational institutions imparting literary education had no contacts with them. Mathematics and astronomy was widely cultivated. The tremendous achievements of Varahamihir and Aryabhatta testify it. Excellence in metallurgy is proved by the Delhi Iron Pillar of King Chandra.

It has been suggested by historians that caste system and slavery was one of the chief features of the Gupta period. The law books distinguished between the Sudras and slaves and gave a higher place to the former. Rulebooks ascribed higher status to the Brahmins of the society. They were called twice born or 'Dvija'. The Smritis had underlined the need of keeping purity of blood of the Brahmanas and treated the other Varnas as impure. The 'panchaneas' or the fifth caste, which was outside the Varna system, was considered untouchable.

However in the Gupta period the rigidity of caste system was declined in comparison to the Maurya Age. Due to decentralisation of Gupta administration, the state did not enforce caste regulations rigidly. Inter-caste marriage and marriage with foreigners were permitted and widely in practice too. There was no objection in group eating of a higher caste man with a farmer, barber, milkman and Sudra family friends. Change of profession was in vogue. Therefore a guild of silk weavers if discovered that they were not being paid, could easily change their profession. Since the caste system was not rigid, people of one caste could easily adopt the profession of another caste. Farming became mostly the profession of the Sudras. Thus it is clear that though Varna system was a rigid form of caste system, yet it was not rigid during the Gupta period. According to historians the Varna system was rigid because there was influx of foreign races in the country. There was a separate residential area for separate castes prescribed in the social code. But in reality the caste system was not so rigid and change of profession had reduced the rigidity of caste distinction. The Guptas were mostly Vaishyas and they had appointed many Sudras in the infantry as soldiers, an occupation that was reserved for the Kshatriyas before. Generally the Brahmins and Kshatriyas enjoyed high esteem in the Gupta society. Slavery was highly in vogue during the Gupta era. According to Manu, there were different categories of slaves and were regarded properties of their masters. The masters enjoyed ownership over them by hereditary right. Dr. R.S. Sramana suggested the Gupta period as the "Vaishya-Sudra society", since these two castes had played the most important parts in the role of production. Hinduism, Buddhism and Jainism were the prevailing forms of religion. Jainism and Saivism were popular in south India. Idol worship was extremely popular in Gupta society. Historians have opined that in spite of caste or Varna difference, Gupta civilization was peaceful and India had witnessed a thriving prosperity under them.

●●

3

History of the Gupta Dynasty

The history of **Gupta Empire** begins with its founding by Sri-Gupta around 320 A.D., although dates are not well established. The empire covered most of Northern India and Eastern Pakistan, parts of Gujarat and Rajasthan and what is now western India and Bangladesh. The capital of the Guptas was Pataliputra, present day Patna, in the north Indian state of Bihar. The origin of the Gupta Empire is still somewhat obscure due to omissions in the historical record on the ancestry of the Guptas and their original homeland.

When the Gupta dynasty ascended the throne around 320 A.D., continuing until 550 A.D., they consolidated northern India by subjugating the local and provincial powers that had become independent after the downfall of the Kushans. The period during the Gupta Empire is referred to as the Golden Age of India, embracing art, architecture, literature, sculpture and education.

The Name Gupta

The earlier Shunga of eastern central Indian and Satavahana of southern and central India have references to many officials bearing the surname Gupta. But relationships of these persons in earlier empires from the east with the Imperial Guptas is not yet determined. Furthermore it is not yet discovered whether the term Gupta indicated a surname of a specific family or referred to a clan. However Gupta Empire records and Chinese records provided by the later I-Tsing, furnished the names of the first three rulers of the

Gupta Dynasty, Maharaja Sri Gupta, Maharaja Sri Ghatotkacha and Ghatotokacha's son, Maharajadhiraja Sri Chandragupta, considered the first Gupta emperor. Historian K. P. Jaiswal suggested that the Guptas belonged to the Jat tribe of Punjab. But his theory lacked conclusive proofs, and it was discarded. The historian H.C. Roychowdhury, however holds that the Guptas belonged to the Dharana Gotra. According to Roychowdhury, the Guptas were related to queen Dharini of Agnimitra, wife of the son of king Pushyamitra Shunga. Roychowdhury drew this theory about the pedigree of the Guptas based on the records of Prabhabati Gupta, daughter of Chandragupta II. In her records she claimed herself to be a descendant of the Dharana Gotra. Another historian of this time, S. Chattopadhya, has put forth a different theory about the ancestry of the Guptas. According to him, in the Panchobh Copper Plate, some kings bearing the title Guptas and related to the imperial Gupta Dynasty, claimed themselves as Kshatriyas. The theory of S. Chattopadhya has been generally accepted by modern scholars.

Although the identification of the Guptas as Kshatriyas is supported by the historical records such as copper plate inscriptions, the controversy about whether the term "Gupta" was originally a family surname or a full or clan name is still unresolved. This is so because the name of the first king was Sri Gupta, where the term "Gupta" seemed to be a title, but the second Gupta did not use it in the same manner. However the expression "Gupta" had been systematically used by all the Gupta rulers from Chandragupta I onwards, which had led to the acceptance of the term "Imperial Gupta dynasty," with Chandragupta I considered the first emperor of the dynasty.

Gupta Homeland

There is controversy among scholars about the original homeland of the Guptas. Jaiswal has pointed out that the

Guptas were originally inhabitants of Prayag (Allahabad), Uttar Pradesh, in north India, as the vassal of the Nagas or Bharsivas. Thereafter they rose in prominence. Another scholar, Gayal supported the theory of Jaiswal, suggesting that the original home of the Guptas was Antarvedi , embracing the regions of Oudh and Prayag. These historians have derived their theory from several Gupta Dynasty coins found in those regions, and this study of numismatic evidences led to the theory that the Guptas were the original inhabitants of that region of northeastern India. However another historian of this time in Indian history, Ganguli, has offered a different view about the original Gupta homeland. According to him the Guptas homeland is further south, the Murshidabad region of Bengal, and not Magadha in Bihar. He based his theory on the statement of I-Tsing, who had visited India during 675 and 695 A.D. Fleet and other historians however criticize Ganguli's theory because Sri Gupta ruled during the end of the third century, but I-Tsing placed him at the end of the second century. Hence the theory of historians, who have provided their views based on the accounts of I-Tsing, are considered less valid than theories based on other sources such as coinage.

The extent of the Gupta Empire and when they ascended the throne after the lapse of the prolonged Dark Age, is also subject of intense controversy among the scholars. Dr. R.C. Majumdar has pointed out that the picture of a stupa has been found in Nepal with the label "Mrigasthapana" Stupa of Varendri. This "Mrigasthapana" is the same as "Mrigashivana" of I-Tsing. As Sri Gupta built a temple in Mrigashivana and as the place was in Varendri, so historians have pointed out that Varendri might have been under the sway of the Guptas, when they ascended the throne. According to Dr. Ganguli, Bengal and parts of Bihar was also included in the Gupta Empire, when they were ruling from the seat of power.

Another theory about the origins of the Guptas is that the Guptas originated from Bengal. The mention of "Varendra

Mrigashihavan Stupa" on a mound in Nepal is a strong evidence that the Guptas originated from Bengal. Maharaja Sri-Gupta probably ruled a portion of Northern/Southern Bengal. Later Chandragupta I established his dominion over Magadha through marital policy with the Licchavis..

From these theories, several conflicting opinions about the original homeland and the Empire of the Guptas are available. According to Allan and some other scholars, the Guptas were originally concentrated in the region of Magadha and from there they extended their sway to Bengal. According to other groups, the original homeland of the Guptas was Varendri or the Varendra Bhumi in Bengal, wherefrom they extended their Empire to Magadha.

Whatever the theory is, the Imperial fabric of the Guptas initiated the Golden Age in history of ancient India and with passage of time they became the sole authority of entire Northern India.

CHANDRAGUPTA I

The Gupta dynasty first rises in eminence with the accession of **Chandra Gupta I**, son of *Ghatotkacha* to the throne of the ancestral Gupta kingdom. While his two ancestors were given the title of *Maharaja*(king), **Chandra Gupta I** is described in his inscriptions as *Maharajadhiraj*(king of kings) signifying a rise in the family fortunes. A series of gold coins issued by the king also testifies to his rising influence. The well known Gupta era which commenced on February 26, 320 AD is generally attributed to Chandra Gupta I. Hence it is surmised that the Gupta era began on the occasion of the coronation of Chandra Gupta I. According to the Puranas the Guptas ruled over territories (referred to as *Janapadas*) such as Prayag (Allahabad), Saket(Oudh) and Magadh(south Bihar). This description of the Gupta dominion precedes the reign of Samudragupta and hence must refer to the territories ruled over by Chandragupta I.

Alliance with the Lichchhavis

The coins issued by Chandra Gupta commemorate his marital union with the Lichchhavi princess Kumaradevi. The political importance of this marital union is further underlined by the fact that their son Samudra Gupta is always referred to in the genealogical accounts of the imperial Guptas as 'daughter's son of the Lichchhavis'. The maternal genealogy is never mentioned in the records of other kings. V.A. Smith places the Lichchhavi kingdom as the contemporary rulers of Magadh, while R.C. Majumdar believes that the Lichchhavi dynasty was ruling somewhere in North Bihar, between Nepal and Vaisali. A Lichchavi dynasty was also the rulers of Nepal which points to the prominent role the Lichchhavi dynasties were playing in the politics of the age in eastern India. It is probable that the Lichchhavis and the Guptas ruled over adjoining principalities and that the two kingdoms were united under Chandra Gupta by his marriage with Kumaradevi. This considerably strengthened the position of the Guptas and may have allowed its subsequent rapid expansion under Samudra Gupta.

Most records indicate that Chandragupta reigned in the period c. 319-335 A.D. The Allahabad inscription on Samudra Gupta by Harishen seems to suggest that he publicly announced Samudra Gupta as the heir apparent and may have abdicated the throne in his son's favour.

Chandragupta Maurya, sometimes known simply as Chandragupta (born c. 340 BCE, ruled c. 320 – 298 BCE, died about 290 BCE), was the founder of the Maurya Empire. Chandragupta succeeded in bringing together most of the Indian subcontinent. As a result, Chandragupta is considered the first unifier of India and its first genuine emperor. In foreign Greek and Latin accounts, Chandragupta is known as Sandrokyptos, Sandrokottos or Androcottus.

Prior to Chandragupta's consolidation of power, small regional kingdoms dominated the northwestern subcontinent, while the Nanda Dynasty dominated the Indo-Gangetic Plain. After Chandragupta's conquests, the Maurya Empire extended from Bengal and Assam in the east, to Afghanistan and Balochistan in the west, to Kashmir and Nepal in the north, and to the Deccan Plateau in the south.

His achievements, which ranged from conquering Alexander the Great's Macedonian satrapies and conquering the Nanda Empire by the time he was only about 20 years old, to defeating Seleucus I Nicator and establishing centralized rule throughout South Asia, remain some of the most celebrated in the history of India. Over two thousand years later, the accomplishments of Chandragupta and his successors, including Ashoka the Great, are objects of great study in the annals of South Asian and world history. Contents [hide]

ISHWAR CHANDRA GUPTA

Ishwar Chandra Gupta (March 1812 - January 23, 1859) was a Bengali poet and writer. Gupta was born in the village *Kanchanpolli* or *Kanchrapara* Chabbis Pargana (currently in the state of West Bengal, India).

Ishwar Chandra Gupta was brought up in his uncle's house after the death of his mother. Gupta spent most of his childhood in Kolkata. At that time, poets were named *Kobiwala* and the *kobiwalas* were not so civilized in language. Sexual words and clashes were common. But Ishwar Chandra Gupta created a different style of poetry.

He started the newspaper *Sambad Prabhakar* with Jogendra Mohan Tagore on on January 28, 1831. which finally became a daily on June 4, 1839. Many Bengali writers of the 19th century started their career with that magazine.

He revolutionized Bengali poetry by introducing a new style with double meaning:

Ke bole Ishwar Gupta, byapta charachar,

Jaar prabhate prabha paye Prabhakar.

'Ishwar' means God, 'Gupta' means hidden and 'Prabhakar' is the sun.So a translation runs:

Who says God is hidden? He is omnipresent

From Him the Sun gets its luminescence.

Also, Ishwar (Chandra) Gupta ran the journal 'Prabhakar'. So a second meaning of the poem, making a tongue-in-cheek reference to the author, runs:

Who says Ishwar Gupta is hidden? His reach touches the world

For his brilliance makes the *Prabhakar* luminiscent.

Literary Style

He brought modern era of poetry in Bangla. He did not describe the life of Gods and Goddesses, but the daily life of human beings. He also wrote biographies of many Bengali poets and musicians.

Ishwarchandra Gupta always satires the so called modern class who blindly followed the colonial British power.

Tumi ma kalpataru

Amra shob posha goru

Shikhi ni shing bankano

Khai kebol khol-bichuli-ghash

Jano ranga amla

Tule mamla

Na bhange gamla

Ma!

Pele bhushi

Tatei kushi

Ghushi khele bachbo na!

His literary works were included in the curriculum of school level, secondary and higher secondary Bengali Literature in Bangladesh.

Political Views

In the early days he was a conservative, opposing the Young Bengal movement as well as frowning on widow remarriage. His views on widow remarriage put him at odds with Ishwar Chandra Vidyasagar. He was one of the earliest advocates of a Hindu view of Indian society. Later in his life, his views began to change and he championed the cause for the remarriage of virgin widows and women's education.

Important Works

- Life of Bharat Chandra Roy
- Probodh Pravakara
- Kobitabolir Saar Sangraha

Faxian

Fa Xian (ca. 337 – ca. 422) was a Chinese Buddhist monk who traveled to Nepal, India, and Sri Lanka to acquire Buddhist scriptures between 399 and 412 . His journey is described in his work *A Record of Buddhistic Kingdoms, Being an Account by the Chinese Monk Fa-Hien of his Travels in India and Ceylon in Search of the Buddhist Books of Discipline*. He is most known for his pilgrimage to Lumbini, the birthplace of Lord Buddha.

On Fa Xian's return to China, after a two-year stay in Ceylon, a violent storm drove his ship onto an island that was probably Java. Faxian landed at Laoshan in what is now

Shandong province, 30 km east of the city of Qingdao and went to Shandong's then-capital, Qingzhou, where he remained for a year translating and editing the scriptures he had collected.

His work is a travel book, filled with accounts of early Buddhism, and the geography and history of numerous countries along the Silk Roads at the turn of the 5th century CE.

The following is from the introduction to a translation of Fa Xian's work by James Legge:

> Nothing of great importance is known about Fa-hien in addition to what may be gathered from his own record of his travels. I have read the accounts of him in the *Memoirs of Eminent Monks*, compiled in A.D. 519, and a later work, the *Memoirs of Marvellous Monks*, by the third emperor of the Ming dynasty (A.D. 1403-1424), which, however, is nearly all borrowed from the other; and all in them that has an appearance of verisimilitude can be brought within brief compass.
>
> His surname, they tell us, was Kung, and he was a native of Wu-yang in P'ing-Yang, which is still the name of a large department in Shan-hsi. He had three brothers older than himself; but when they all died before shedding their first teeth, his father devoted him to the service of the Buddhist society, and had him entered as a Sramanera, still keeping him at home in the family. The little fellow fell dangerously ill, and the father sent him to the monastery, where he soon got well and refused to return to his parents.
>
> When he was ten years old, his father died; and an uncle, considering the widowed solitariness and helplessness of the mother, urged him to renounce the monastic life, and return to her, but the boy replied, "I

did not quit the family in compliance with my father's wishes, but because I wished to be far from the dust and vulgar ways of life. This is why I chose monkhood." The uncle approved of his words and gave over urging him. When his mother also died, it appeared how great had been the affection for her of his fine nature; but after her burial he returned to the monastery.

On one occasion he was cutting rice with a score or two of his fellow-disciples, when some hungry thieves came upon them to take away their grain by force. The other Sramaneras all fled, but our young hero stood his ground, and said to the thieves, "If you must have the grain, take what you please. But, Sirs, it was your former neglect of charity which brought you to your present state of destitution; and now, again, you wish to rob others. I am afraid that in the coming ages you will have still greater poverty and distress;—I am sorry for you beforehand." With these words he followed his companions into the monastery, while the thieves left the grain and went away, all the monks, of whom there were several hundred, doing homage to his conduct and courage.

When he had finished his noviciate and taken on him the obligations of the full Buddhist orders, his earnest courage, clear intelligence, and strict regulation of his demeanour were conspicuous; and soon after, he undertook his journey to India in search of complete copies of the Vinaya-pitaka. What follows this is merely an account of his travels in India and return to China by sea, condensed from his own narrative, with the addition of some marvelous incidents that happened to him, on his visit to the Vulture Peak near Rajagriha.

It is said in the end that after his return to China, he went to the capital (evidently Nanking), and there, along with the Indian Sramana Buddha-bhadra, executed translations of some of the works which he had obtained in India; and that before he had done all that he wished to do in this way, he removed to King-chow (in the present Hoo-pih), and died in the monastery of Sin, at the age of eighty-eight, to the great sorrow of all who knew him. It is added that there is another larger work giving an account of his travels in various countries.

Such is all the information given about our author, beyond what he himself has told us. Fa-hien was his clerical name, and means "Illustrious in the Law," or "Illustrious master of the Law." The Shih which often precedes it is an abbreviation of the name of Buddha as Sakyamuni, "the Sakya, mighty in Love, dwelling in Seclusion and Silence," and may be taken as equivalent to Buddhist. It is sometimes said to have belonged to "the eastern Tsin dynasty" (A.D. 317-419), and sometimes to "the Sung," that is, the Sung dynasty of the House of Liu (A.D. 420-478). If he became a full monk at the age of twenty, and went to India when he was twenty-five, his long life may have been divided pretty equally between the two dynasties.

CHANDRAGUPTA MAURYA

Chandragupta Maurya, sometimes known simply as **Chandragupta** (born c. 340 BCE, ruled c. 320 – 298 BCE, died about 290 BCE), was the founder of the Maurya Empire. Chandragupta succeeded in bringing together most of the Indian subcontinent. As a result, Chandragupta is considered the first unifier of India and its first genuine emperor. In foreign Greek and Latin accounts, Chandragupta is known as **Sandrokyptos**, **Sandrokottos** or **Androcottus**.

Prior to Chandragupta's consolidation of power, small regional kingdoms dominated the northwestern sub-continent, while the Nanda Dynasty dominated the Indo-Gangetic Plain.

After Chandragupta's conquests, the Maurya Empire extended from Bengal and Assam in the east, to Afghanistan and Balochistan in the west, to Kashmir and Nepal in the north, and to the Deccan Plateau in the south.

His achievements, which ranged from conquering Alexander the Great's Macedonian satrapies and conquering the Nanda Empire by the time he was only about 20 years old, to defeating Seleucus I Nicator and establishing centralized rule throughout South Asia, remain some of the most celebrated in the history of India. Over two thousand years later, the accomplishments of Chandragupta and his successors, including Ashoka the Great, are objects of great study in the annals of South Asian and world history.

While many Indian historians hold the view that Chandragupta was an illegitimate child of the Nanda Dynasty of Magadha in eastern India, born to a Nanda prince and a maid named "Mura", later literary traditions imply that Chandragupta may have been raised by peacock-tamers (Sanskrit: Mayura-Poshaka), which earned him the Maurya epithet. Both the Buddhist as well as Jain traditions testify to the supposed connection between the Moriya (Maurya) and Mora or Mayura (Peacock). Yet there are other literary traditions according to which Chandragupta belonged to Moriyas, a Kshatriya clan of a little ancient republic of Pippalivana located between Rummindei in the Nepali Terai and Kasia in the Gorakhpur district of Uttar Pradesh.

There are differing theories regarding Chandragupta Maurya's origins. A common view is that Chandragupta originated from Magadha, possibly as the son of a Nanda prince and a maid named "Mura". A kshatriya people known as the "Mauryas" who had received the relics of the Gautama Buddha are also mentioned in the Mahaparinibbana Sutta of the Digha Nikaya: "Then the Moriyas of Pipphalivana came to know that at Kusinara the Blessed One had died. And they sent a message to the Mallas of Kusinara, saying: "The Blessed One was of the warrior caste, and we are too. We are worthy to receive a portion of the relics of the Blessed One. We will erect a stupa over the relics of the Blessed One and hold a festival in their honor.

Others claim that the Mauryas were the *Muras* or rather *Mors*, and another view of a Jat origin of Indo-Scythian lineage has been proposed. Another school of thought, including scholars such as B. M. Barua, J. W. McCrindle, D. B. Spooner, H. C. Seth, Hari Ram Gupta, Ranajit Pal, Gur Rattan Pal Singh and Kirpal Singh have connected Chandragupta to Gandhara (or Kamboja) in modern day Pakistan. Based on interpretations of Plutarch and Appian's writings, these scholars assert that Chandragupta Maurya may have belonged to the north-west frontier region, possibly to the Assakenoi or Ashvaka (q.v.) Kshatriya clan of Swat/ Kunar valley (modern *Koh-I-Mor* or *Mer-coh* — the *Meros* of the classical writings; probably *Meru* of Sanskrit texts and *Mor* and *Mer* in Prakritic) . It has been claimed by several scholars that Chandragupta belonged to the Ashvaka tribe of this region (*known as Mor*), and thus, the dynasty founded by him was called Moriya or Maurya. . The Ashvakas were a section of the Kambojas, who were exclusively engaged in horse-culture and were noted for providing mercenary cavalry. H.C. Raychaudhuri noted that the name Priyadarshi was adopted also by Chandragupta as also noted by W. W. Tarn.

Early Life

Very little is known about Chandragupta's youth. Much of what is known about his youth is gathered from later classical Sanskrit literature, as well as classical Greek and Latin sources which refer to Chandragupta by the names "Sandracottos" or "Andracottus". He was paragon for next rulers.

According to traditional accounts, Chanakya, a teacher at Takshasila University at the time of Alexander's invasion, found the boy Chandragupta from the Magadha kingdom in eastern India. As the story goes, Chandragupta was playing as a king with his friends and was giving justice to another boy playing criminal. He also saw the kindness inside him to help others. Chanakya saw this and was impressed with Chandragupta's sense of justice. Chanakya asked his mother about him. His mother told him that his father used to work as a servant of the king Nand who ruled over the kingdom of Maghada and due to some fault he was sent into the prison. Chanakya told her to take him to the king and ask him to give some education to Chandragupta. Then she went to his court. There Chandragupta solved a problem for the king. The king was impressed and told his minister to join him in the best university at that time, The Vishvavidhyalay of Takshasila[often known as the Takshasila University]

Plutarch reports that he met with Alexander the Great, probably around Takshasila in the northwest, and that he viewed the ruling Nanda Empire in a negative light:

> "Androcottus, when he was a stripling, saw Alexander himself, and we are told that he often said in later times that Alexander narrowly missed making himself master of the country, since its king was hated and despised on account of his baseness and low birth."
>
> —Plutarch, *Parallel Lives: Life of Alexander* 62.9

According to this tradition, the encounter would have happened around 326 BCE, suggesting a birth date for Chandragupta around 340 BC.

Junianus Justinus (Justin) describes the humble origins of Chandragupta, and explains how he later led a popular uprising against the Nanda king:

> "He was of humble origin, but was pushing to acquiring the throne by the superior power of the mind. When after having offended the king of Nanda by his insolence,

he was condemned to death by the king, he was saved by the speed of his own feet... He gathered bandits and invited Indians to a change of rule."

—Junianus Justinus, *Historiarum Philippicarum libri XLIV*, XV.4.15

Foundation of the Maurya Empire

Chandragupta Maurya with the help of Chankya defeated the Magadha kings and the bulk army of Chandravanshi clan and defeated generals of Alexander settled in Gandhara (Kamboja kingdom of Aryan Mahajanpad) which is called as Afghanistan now. At the time of Alexander's invasion, Chanakya was a teacher at Takshasila University. The king of Takshasila and Gandhara, Ambhi (also known as Taxiles), made a treaty with Alexander and did not fight against him. Chanakya saw the foreign invasion against the Indian culture and sought help from other kings to unite and fight Alexander. Porus (Parvateshwar), a king of Punjab, was the only local yadav king who was able to challenge Alexander at the Battle of the Hydaspes River, but was defeated.

Chanakya then went to Magadha further east to seek the help of Dhana Nanda, who ruled a vast Nanda Empire which extended from Bihar and Bengal in the east to eastern Punjab in the west, but he denied any such help. After this incident, Chanakya began sowing the seeds of building an empire that could protect Indian territories from foreign invasion into his disciple Chandragupta.

Chandragupta later adopted Jainism. It is said he died fasting which was according to Jainism a holy way of sacrificing mortal life.

Chanakya

Chandragupta's adviser or prime minister Chanakya, who is also known as Kautilya and was the author of the

Arthashastra, is regarded as the architect of Chandragupta's early rise to power. Chandragupta Maurya, with the help of Chanakya, began laying the foundation of the Maurya Empire. In all forms of the Chanakya legend, he is thrown out of the Nanda court by the king, whereupon he swears revenge. While in Magadha, Chanakya by chance met Chandragupta in whom he spotted great military and executive abilities. Chanakya was impressed by the prince's personality and intelligence, and immediately took the young boy under his wing to fulfill his silent vow.

Depending upon the interpretation of Justin's accounts, the second version of the above story is that Chandragupta had also accompanied Chanakya to Pataliputra and himself was insulted by Dhana Nanda (Nandrum of Justin). If this version of Justin's accounts is accepted, then the view that Chanakya had purchased Chandragupta from Bihar, on his way back to Taxila, becomes irrelevant. The shrewd Chanakya had trained Chandragupta under his expert guidance and together they planned the conquest of the Nanda Empire.

Nanda Army

According to Plutarch, at the time of Alexander's Battle of the Hydaspes River, the size of the Nanda Empire's army further east numbered 200,000 infantry, 80,000 cavalry, 8,000 chariots, and 6,000 war elephants, which was discouraging for Alexander's men and stayed their further progress into India:

> "As for the Macedonians, however, their struggle with Porus blunted their courage and stayed their further advance into India. For having had all they could do to repulse an enemy who mustered only twenty thousand infantry and two thousand horse, they violently opposed Alexander when he insisted on crossing the river Ganges also, the width of which, as they learned, was thirty-two furlongs, its depth a hundred fathoms, while its

> banks on the further side were covered with multitudes of men-at arms and horsemen and elephants. For they were told that the kings of the Ganderites and Praesii were awaiting them with eighty thousand horsemen, two hundred thousand footmen, eight thousand chariots, and six thousand fighting elephants. And there was no boasting in these reports. For Androcottus, who reigned there not long afterwards, made a present to Seleucus of five hundred elephants, and with an army of six hundred thousand men overran and subdued all India."
>
> —Plutarch, *Parallel Lives,* "Life of Alexander" 62.1-4

In order to defeat the powerful Nanda army, Chandragupta needed to raise a formidable army of his own.

Conquest of Macedonian Territories in India

After Alexander's death in 323 BC, Chandragupta, turned his attention to Northwestern India (modern Pakistan), where he defeated the satrapies (described as "prefects" in classical Western sources) left in place by Alexander (according to Justin), and may have assassinated two of his governors, Nicanor and Philip. The satrapies he fought may have included Eudemus, ruler in western Punjab until his departure in 317 BC; and Peithon, son of Agenor, ruler of the Greek colonies along the Indus until his departure for Babylon in 316 BC. The Roman historian Justin described how Sandrocottus (Greek version of Chandragupta's name) conquered the northwest:

> "Some time after, as he was going to war with the generals of Alexander, a wild elephant of great bulk presented itself before him of its own accord, and, as if tamed down to gentleness,,11 took him on its back, and became his guide in the war, and conspicuous in fields of battle. Sandrocottus, having thus acquired a throne, was in possession of India, when Seleucus was laying

the foundations of his future greatness; who, after making a league with him, and settling his affairs in the east, proceeded to join in the war against Antigonus. As soon as the forces, therefore, of all the confederates were united, a battle was fought,12 in which Antigonus was slain, and his son Demetrius put to flight. "

—Junianus Justinus, *Historiarum Philippicarum libri XLIV*, XV.4.19

Having consolidated power in the northwest, Chandragupta pushed east towards the Nanda Empire.

Conquest of the Nanda Empire

Chanakya had trained Chandragupta under his guidance and together they planned the destruction of Dhana Nanda. The *Mudrarakshasa* of Visakhadutta as well as the Jaina work *Parisishtaparvan* talk of Chandragupta's alliance with the Himalayan king Parvatka, sometimes identified with Porus.

It is noted in the *Chandraguptakatha* that the protagonist and Chanakya were initially rebuffed by the Nanda forces. Regardless, in the ensuing war, Chandragupta faced off against Bhadrasala – commander of Dhana Nanda's armies. He was eventually able to defeat Bhadrasala and Dhana Nanda in a series of battles, ending with the siege of the capital city Kusumapura and the conquest of the Nanda Empire around 321 BC, thus founding the powerful Maurya Empire in Northern India by the time he was about 20 years old.

Expansion

By the time he was only about 20 years old, Chandragupta, who had succeeded in defeating the Macedonian satrapies in India and conquering the Nanda Empire, had founded a vast empire that extended from the Bay of Bengal in the east, to the Indus River in the west, which he would further expand in later years.

Conquest of Seleucus' Eastern Territories

Seleucus I Nicator, a Macedonian satrap of Alexander, reconquered most of Alexander's former empire and put under his own authority eastern territories as far as Bactria and the Indus (Appian, History of Rome, The Syrian Wars 55), until in 305 BC he entered in a confrontation with Chandragupta:

> "Always lying in wait for the neighboring nations, strong in arms and persuasive in council, he acquired Mesopotamia, Armenia, 'Seleucid' Cappadocia, Persis, Parthia, Bactria, Arabia, Tapouria, Sogdia, Arachosia, Hyrcania, and other adjacent peoples that had been subdued by Alexander, as far as the river Indus, so that the boundaries of his empire were the most extensive in Asia after that of Alexander. The whole region from Phrygia to the Indus was subject to Seleucus. He crossed the Indus and waged war with Sandrocottus [Maurya], king of the Indians, who dwelt on the banks of that stream, until they came to an understanding with each other and contracted a marriage relationship. Some of these exploits were performed before the death of Antigonus and some afterward."
>
> —Appian, *History of Rome,* The Syrian Wars 55

The exact details of engagement are not known. As noted by scholars such as R. C. Majumdar and D. D. Kosambi, Seleucus appears to have fared poorly, having ceded large territories west of the Indus to Chandragupta. Due to his defeat, Seleucus surrendered Arachosia, Gedrosia, Paropamisadae, and Aria.

Mainstream scholarship asserts that Chandragupta received vast territory west of the Indus, including the Hindu Kush, modern day Afghanistan, and the Balochistan province of Pakistan. Archaeologically, concrete indications of Mauryan rule, such as the inscriptions of the Edicts of Ashoka, are known as far as Kandhahar in southern Afghanistan.

> "He (Seleucus) crossed the Indus and waged war with Sandrocottus [Maurya], king of the Indians, who dwelt on the banks of that stream, until they came to an understanding with each other and contracted a marriage relationship."
>
> "After having made a treaty with him (Sandrakotos) and put in order the Orient situation, Seleucos went to war against Antigonus."
>
> —Junianus Justinus, *Historiarum Philippicarum libri XLIV*, XV.4.15

It is generally thought that Chandragupta married Seleucus's daughter, or a Greek Macedonian princess, a gift from Seleucus to formalize an alliance. In a return gesture, Chandragupta sent 500 war-elephants, a military asset which would play a decisive role at the Battle of Ipsus in 302 BC. In addition to this treaty, Seleucus dispatched an ambassador, Megasthenes, to Chandragupta, and later Deimakos to his son Bindusara, at the Mauryan court at Pataliputra (modern Patna in Bihar state). Later Ptolemy II Philadelphus, the ruler of Ptolemaic Egypt and contemporary of Ashoka the Great, is also recorded by Pliny the Elder as having sent an ambassador named Dionysius to the Mauryan court..

Classical sources have also recorded that following their treaty, Chandragupta and Seleucus exchanged presents, such as when Chandragupta sent various aphrodisiacs to Seleucus:

> "And Theophrastus says that some contrivances are of wondrous efficacy in such matters [as to make people more amorous]. And Phylarchus confirms him, by reference to some of the presents which Sandrakottus, the king of the Indians, sent to Seleucus; which were to act like charms in producing a wonderful degree of

affection, while some, on the contrary, were to banish love."

—Athenaeus of Naucratis

Southern Conquests

After annexing Seleucus' eastern Persian provinces, Chandragupta had a vast empire extending across the northern parts of Southern Asia, from the Bay of Bengal to the Arabian Sea. Chandragupta then began expanding his empire further south beyond the barrier of the Vindhya Range and into the Deccan Plateau. By the time his conquests were complete, Chandragupta succeeded in unifying most of Southern Asia. Megasthenes later recorded the size of Chandragupta's acquired army as 400,000 soldiers, according to Strabo:

"Megasthenes was in the camp of Sandrocottus, which consisted of 400,000 men"

—Strabo, *Geographica,* 15.1.53

On the other hand, Pliny, who also drew from Megasthenes' work, gives even larger numbers of 600,000 infantry, 30,000 cavalry, and 9,000 war elephants:

"But the Prasii surpass in power and glory every other people, not only in this quarter, but one may say in all India, their capital Palibothra, a very large and wealthy city, after which some call the people itself the Palibothri,—nay even the whole tract along the Ganges. Their king has in his pay a standing army of 600,000-foot-soldiers, 30,000 cavalry, and 9,000 elephants: whence may be formed some conjecture as to the vastness of his resources."

—Pliny, *Natural History* VI, 22.4

Jainism

Chandragupta gave up his throne towards the end of his life and became an ascetic under the caca saint Bhadrabahu, migrating south with them and ending his days in sallekhana at Shravanabelagola, in present day Karnataka; though fifth-century inscriptions in the area support the concept of a larger southern migration around that time. A small temple marks the cave (Bhadrabahu Cave) where he is said to have died by fasting.

Successors

Chandragupta Maurya renounced his throne to his son, Bindusara, who became the new Mauryan Emperor. Bindusara would later become the father of Ashoka the Great, who was one of the most influential kings in history due to his important role in the history of Buddhism.

●●

4

Middle kingdoms of India

Middle kingdoms of India refers to the political entities in India from the 2nd century BC since the decline of the Maurya Empire, and the corresponding rise of the Satavahana dynasty, beginning with Simuka, from 230 BC. The "Middle" period lasts for some 1,500 years, and ends in the 13th century, with the rise of the Islamic Sultanates (the Delhi Sultanate was established in 1206) and the end of the Chalukya Cholas (Rajendra Chola III died 1279).

The North West

In the wake of the disintegration of the Mauryan Empire during the 2nd century BC, South Asia became a collage of regional powers with overlapping boundaries. The Indus Valley and Gangetic plains of the northwest attracted a series of invaders between 200 BC and 300 AD. The Puranas speak of many of these tribes as foreigners and impure barbarians (Mlechhas) First the Satavahanas and later the Gupta Empire, both successor states to the Mauryan Empire, attempt to contain the expansions of the successive before eventually crumbling internally due pressure exerted by these wars.

The invading tribes are influenced by and adopt Buddhism which continues to flourish under the patronage of both the invaders and the Satavahanas and Guptas and provides a cultural bridge between the two cultures. Over time, the invaders became "Indianized" as they influence society and philosophy across the gangetic plains and are conversely influenced by it. This period is marked by both intellectual and artistic achievements inspired by cultural diffusion and syncretism as the new kingdoms straddle the Silk route.

The Indo-Scythian Sakas

The **Indo-Scythians** are a branch of Sakas (Scythians), who migrated from southern Siberia into Bactria, Sogdiana, Arachosia, Gandhara, Kashmir, Punjab, and into parts of Western and Central India, Gujarat, Maharashtra and Rajasthan, from the middle of the 2nd century BCE to the 4th century CE. The first Saka king in India was Maues or Moga who established Saka power in Gandhara and gradually extended supremacy over north-western India. Indo-Scythian rule in India ended with the last Western Satrap Rudrasimha III in 395 CE.

The invasion of India by Scythian tribes from Central Asia, often referred to as the Indo-Scythian invasion, played a significant part in the history of India as well as nearby countries. In fact, the Indo-Scythian war is just one chapter in the events triggered by the nomadic flight of Central Asians from conflict with Chinese tribes which had lasting effects on Bactria, Kabol, Parthia and India as well as far off Rome in the west. The Scythian groups that invaded India and set up various kingdoms, included besides the Sakas other allied tribes, such as the Medii, Xanthii, Massagetae, Getae, Parama Kambojas, Avars, Bahlikas, Rishikas and Paradas.

The Indo-Greeks

The **Indo-Greek Kingdom** (or sometimes **Graeco-Indian Kingdom**) covered various parts of the northwest and northern Indian subcontinent during the last two centuries BC, and was ruled by more than 30 Hellenistic kings, often in conflict with each other. The kingdom was founded when the Greco-Bactrian king Demetrius invaded India early in the second century BC; in this context the boundary of "India" is the Hindu Kush. The Greeks in India were eventually divided from the Greco-Bactrian Kingdom centered in Bactria (now the border between Afghanistan and Uzbekistan). The expression "Indo-Greek Kingdom" loosely describes a number of various dynastic polities. There were numerous cities, such as Taxila Pakistan's Punjab, or Pushkalavati and Sagala. These cities would house a number of dynasties in their times, and based on Ptolemy's *Geographia* and the nomenclature of later kings, a certain Theophila in the south was also probably a satrapal or royal seat at some point.

During the two centuries of their rule, the Indo-Greek kings combined the Greek and Indian languages and symbols, as seen on their coins, and blended ancient Greek, Hindu and Buddhist religious practices, as seen in the archaeological remains of their cities and in the indications of their support of Buddhism, pointing to a rich fusion of Indian and Hellenistic influences. The diffusion of Indo-Greek culture had consequences which are still felt today, particularly through the influence of Greco-Buddhist art. The Indo-Greeks ultimately disappeared as a political entity around 10 AD following the invasions of the Indo-Scythians, although pockets of Greek populations probabiy remained for several centuries longer under the subsequent rule of the Indo-Parthians and Kushans.

The Yavanas

The **Yavanas** were described as living beyond Gandhara. There was another country mentioned in the epic as **Parama Yona**, in the far west of Yavana. This could be the Ionia of Greece, somehow related to Indian Ionians or Yavanas. The name Yavana could be the Sanskritized form of the name Ionia. Some believes that the name Ionia originated from the Sanskrit word *Ayonija* meaning *one who born not from a (human) womb* or *people with extra ordinary origins.* Yavanas, Sakas, Pahlavas and Hunas were sometimes described as Mlechhas.

Sometimes along with them, the Madras, Kambojas, Kekeyas, Sindhus and Gandharas were included. This name was used to indicate their cultrural differences with the Vedic culture, prevailed in the Kuru-Panchala Kingdoms.

The Indo-Parthians

With the rise of the Parthians, the Indus Valley was once again brought under the influence of Persia as they conquered the Indo-Scythians.They had Gandhara as their Capital city. The Indo-Parthian Kingdom was founded by Gondophernes around 20 AD when he declared his Independence from the Parthians. This Kingdom last only briefly until its conquest by the Kushans in 75 AD.

The Pahlavas

The **Pahlavas** are a people mentioned in ancient Indian texts like the Manu Smriti, various Puranas, the Ramayana, the Mahabharata, and the Brhatsamhita. In some texts the Pahlavas are synonymous with the Pallavas, a dynasty of Southern India: While the Vayu Purana distinguishes between *Pahlava* and *Pahnava*, the Vamana Purana and Matsya Purana refer to both as *Pallava*. The Brahmanda Purana and Markendeya Purana refer to both as *Pahlava* or *Pallava*. *Bhishama Parava* Mahabharata 6.11.66 . of the Mahabharata also does not distinguish between the Pahlavas and Pallavas. The Pahlavas are said to be same as the Parasikas. According to P. Carnegy , the Pahlava are probably those people who spoke Paluvi or Pehlvi, that is the Parthian language. Buhler similarly suggests Pahlava is an Indic form of *Parthava* meaning 'Parthian' . In a 4th century BCE, Vartika of Katyayana mentions the *Sakah-Parthavah* demonstrating an awareness of these Saka-Parthians, probably by way of commerce .

The Western Satraps

The **Western Satraps**, or **Western Kshatrapas** (35-405) were Saka rulers of the western and central part of India

(Saurashtra and Malwa: modern Gujarat, Southern Sindh, Maharashtra, Rajasthan and Madhya Pradesh states). Their state, or at least part of it, was called "Ariaca" according to the Periplus of the Erythraean Sea. They were successors to the Indo-Scythians, and were contemporaneous with the Kushans who ruled the northern part of the Indian subcontinent and were possibly their overlords, and the Satavahana (Andhra) who ruled in Central India. They are called "Western" in contrast to the "Northern" Indo-Scythian satraps who ruled in the area of Mathura, such as Rajuvula, and his successors under the Kushans, the "Great Satrap" Kharapallana and the "Satrap" Vanaspara. Although they called themselves "Satraps" on their coins, leading to their modern designation of "Western Satraps", Ptolemy in his 2nd century "Geographia" still called them "Indo-Scythians". Altogether, there were 27 independent Western Satrap rulers during a period of about 350 years. The word *Kshatrapa* stands for *satrap*, and its equivalent in Persian *Ksatrapavan*, which means viceroy or governor of a province.

The Kushans

The **Kushan Empire** (c. 1st–3rd centuries) originally formed in Bactria on either side of the middle course of the Oxus River or Syr Darya in what is now northern Afghanistan, Tajikistan and Uzbekistan, and, during the first century CE, they expanded their territory to include the Punjab and much of the Ganges basin, conquering a number of kingdoms across the northern part of the Indian subcontinent in the process. The Kushans conquered the central section of the main Silk Routes and, therefore, had control of the overland trade between India, Parthia, China, and the Roman Empire.

The Indo-Sassanid Kushanshahs

The rise of a new Persian dynasty, the Sassanids saw them re-exert their influence into the Indus region and conquer lands from the Kushans setting up the Kushanshahs around

240 AD. They were to maintain their influence in the region until they were overthrown by the rising Caliphate. Afterwards they were displaced in 410 CE by the invasions of the Indo-Hephthalites.

The Hephthalite Hunas

The Hephthalite were another Central Asian nomadic tribe to invade. They are also linked to the Yuezhi who founded the Kushan Empire. From their capital in Bamiyan, Afghanistan they extended their rule across the Indus and Northern India thereby pressuring the collapse of the Gupta Empire. They were eventually defeated by the Sassanid Empire in alliance with other Turkic tribes.

The Rais

The **Rai Dynasty** of Sindh were patrons of Buddhism even though they also established a huge temple of Shiva in present-day Sukkur, derived from original Shankar, close to their capital in Al-ror. This is consistent with the historical accounts from the times of Emperor Ashoka and Harsha because Indian monarchs never sponsored a state religion and usually patronized more than one faith. The influence of the **Rai** state exdended from Kashmir and Kannauj in the east, Makran and Debal (Karachi) port in the west, Surat port in south, Kandahar, Sistan, Suleyman, Ferdan and Kikanan hills in the north.

The Gandharan Kambojas

After the collapse of the Sassanid Empire to the Caliphate the Gandharan Satrapy became an independent Kingdom based from Afghanistan and vied with the Tang dynasty, Tibet, the Caliphate and other Turkic tribes for domination in the region.

The Shahis

The **Shahi, Sahi,** also called **Shahiya** dynasties ruled portions of the Kabul Valley (in eastern Afghanistan) and the old province of Gandhara (northern Pakistan from the decline of the Kushan Empire in third century to the early ninth century . The kingdom was known as Kabul-shahan or Ratbel-shahan from (565 - 670 CE) when the capitals were located in Kapisa and Kabul, and later Udabhandapura (also known as *Hund*) for its new capital. In ancient time, the title Shahi appears to be a quite popular royal title in Afghanistan and the north-western areas of the Indian sub-continent. It was used by Achaemenids , Sakas , Kushanas , Hunas , Bactrians , by the rulers of Kapisa/Kabul and Gilgit. In Persian form, the title appears as *Kshathiya, Kshathiya Kshathiyanam,* Shao of the Kushanas and the *Ssaha* of Mihirakula (Huna chief) . The Kushanas are stated to have adopted the title *Shah-in-shahi* (*"Shaonano shao"*) in imitation of Achaemenid practice .

Ancient Jaina work *Kalakacarya-kathanaka* says that the rulers of the Sakas who had invaded Ujjaini/Malwa in 62 BCE also wore the titles of *Sahi* and *Sahnusahi* . Since the title *Shahi* was used by the rulers of *Kapisa/Kabul or Gandhara* also in imitation of Kushana "Shao", it has been speculated by some writers that the Shahi dynasty of Kapisa/Kabul or Gandhara was a *foreign dynasty* and had descended from the Kushans or Turks (*Turushkas*). However, the title has been used by several rulers irrespective of any racial connotations and this may refute the above speculation. The Shahis of Kabul/Gandhara are generally split up into two eras — the Buddhist-Shahis and the Hindu-Shahis, with the change-over thought to have occurred sometime around 870 AD.

The Gangetic Plains and Deccan

Following the demise of the Mauryan Empires the Satavahanas rose as the successor state to check and contend with the influx of the Central Asian tribes from the Northwest. The Satavahanas straddling the Deccan plateau also provided a link for transmission of Buddhism and contact between the

Northern Gangetic plains and the Southern regions even as the Upanishads were gaining ground.

Eventually weakened both by contention with the northwestern invaders and internal strife they broke up and gave rise to many smalled nations around Deccan and central India regions even as the Gupta Empire arose in the gangetic plains and ushered in a **"Golden Age"** and rebirth of Empire as decentralized local administrative model and the spread of Indian culture until collapse under the Huna invasions. After the fall of Gupta Empire the gangetic region broke up into smaller states temporarily reunited under Harsha then giving rise to the Rajput dynasties. In the Deccan, the Chalukyas arose forming a formidable nation marking the migration of the centers of cultural and military power long held in the gangetic plains to the new nations forming in the southern regions of India.

The Satavahanas

The **Sâtavâhana Empire** started out as feudatories to the Mauryan Empire but declared independence soon after the death of Ashoka (232 BC). They were the first Indic rulers to issue coins struck with their rulers embossed and are known for their patronage of Buddhism resulting in buddhist monuments from Ellora to Amaravati. They formed a cultural bridge and played a vital role in trade and the transfer of ideas and culture to and from the gangetic plains to the southern tip of India.

The Satavahanas had to compete with the Sunga and the Kanva dynasty of the Mauryan Empire to establish first their independence then to expand their rule. Later they had to contend in protecting their domain from the incursions of Sakas, Yavanas and Pahlavas. In particular their struggles with the Western Kshatrapas weakened them and the kingdom split into smaller states.

The Guptas

The **Classical Age** refers to the period when most of North India was reunited after the Mauryans under the Gupta Empire (ca. 320 AD–550 AD). This period is called the Golden Age of India and was marked by extensive achievements in science, technology, engineering, art, dialectic, literature, logic, mathematics, astronomy, religion and philosophy that crystallized the elements of what is generally known as Hindu culture. These classical patterns began to spread south only much later after the end of the empire. The high points of this cultural creativity are magnificent and creative architecture, sculpture, and painting. The poet Kalidasa was the greatest writer of the time. Strong trade ties also made the region an important cultural center and set the region up as a base that would influence nearby kingdoms and regions in Burma, Sri Lanka, Malay Archipelago and Indochina.

The Gupta period marked a watershed of Indian culture: the Guptas performed Vedic sacrifices to legitimize their rule, but they also patronized Buddhism, which continued to provide an alternative to Brahmanical orthodoxy. The military exploits of the first three rulers—Chandragupta I (ca. 319–335), Samudragupta (ca. 335–376), and Chandragupta II (ca. 376–415) —brought all of North India under their leadership from capital at Pataliputra. They successfully resisted the North-Western Kingdoms until the arrival of the Hunas.

The Vakatakas

The **Vakataka Empire** was the contemporaries of the Gupta Empire and the successor state of the Satavahanas they formed the southern boundaries of the north and ruled over today's modern day states of Madhya Pradesh and Maharashtra during the 3rd and 5th centuries. The rock-cut Buddhist viharas and chaityas of Ajanta Caves (a UNESCO

World Heritage Site), built under the patronage of the Vakataka rulers. They were eventually overrun by the Chalukyas.

The Harsha Vardhana

After the collapse of the Gupta Empire, the gangetic plains fractured into numerous small nations. Harsha of Kannauj was able to briefly bind them together under his rulership. Only a defeat at the hands of the Chalukyas prevented him from expanding his reign south of the Narmada river. This unity did not last long beyond his reign and his empire fractured soon after his death in 647 AD.

The Vishnukundinas

The **Vishnukundina Empire** was an Indian dynasty that ruled over the Deccan, Orissa and parts of South India during the 5th and 6th centuries carving land out from the Vakataka Empire. The Vishnukundin reign came to an end with the conquest of the eastern Deccan by the Chalukya, Pulakesi II. Pulakesi appointed his brother Kubja Vishnuvardhana as Viceroy to rule over the conquered lands. Eventually Vishnuvardhana declared his independence and started the Eastern Chalukya dynasty.

The Rajputs

The Rajput were a Hindu clan who rose to power across a region stretching from the gangaetic plains to the Afghan mountains, and refer to the various dynasties of the many kingdoms in the region in the wake of the collapse of the Sassanid Empire and Gupta Empire and marks the transition of Buddhist ruling dynasties to Hindu ruling dynasties.

The Pratiharas

The **Pratihara Empire** (Pratihâra), also known as *Parihars,* formed an Indian dynasty that ruled much of Northern India from the 6th to the 11th centuries. They are called **Gurjara-Pratiharas** in one late inscription. At its peak of prosperity resulted in the subjugation of the Sikh kingdom, and the annexation of the Punjab and what subsequently became the North-West Frontier Province by the East India Company.

The Sikh kingdom of the Punjab was consolidated and expanded by Maharaja Ranjit Singh during the early years of the nineteenth century. During the same period, the British East India Company's territories had been expanded until they were adjacent to the Punjab.

Ranjit Singh maintained an uneasy alliance with the East India Company, while increasing the military strength of the Khalsa (the Sikh Army, which also saw itself as the embodiment of the state and religion), to deter British or Afghan aggression against his state.

When Ranjit Singh died in 1839, the Punjab began to fall into disorder. There was a succession of short-lived rulers at the central Durbar (court), and increasing tension between the Khalsa and the Durbar. The East India Company began to build up its military strength on the borders of the Punjab. Eventually, the increasing tension goaded the Khalsa to invade British territory, under weak and very possibly treacherous leaders. After the hard-fought First Anglo-Sikh War ended in defeat for the Sikh army, Punjab was partially governed by the East India Company.

Aftermath of the First Anglo-Sikh War

The Sikhs were made to cede some valuable territory (the Jullundur Doab) to the East India Company, and Maharaja Gulab Singh, the ruler of Jammu, was allowed to acquire Kashmir from the Sikh kingdom by a large cash payment to the East India Company. These conditions naturally humiliated and angered the Sikhs. Some of the Khalsa were forced to make an expedition to oust the ruling Maharajah of Kashmir in favour of Gulab Singh.

that era, the others being Pratiharas, Paramaras and Chalukyas. Chauhan dynasties established themselves in several places in North India and in the state of Gujarat in Western India. They were also prominent at Sirohi in the southwest of Rajputana, and at Bundi and Kota in the east. Inscriptions also associate them with Sambhar, the salt lake area in the Amber (later Jaipur) district (the Sakhambari branch remained near lake Sambhar and married into the ruling Gurjara-Pratihara, who then ruled an empire in Northern India). Chauhans adopted a political policy that saw them indulge largely in campaigns against the Chalukyas and the invading Muslim hordes. In the 11th century they founded the city of Ajayameru (Ajmer) in the southern part of their kingdom, and in the 12th century captured Dhilika (the ancient name of Delhi) from the Tomaras and annexed some of their territory along the Yamuna River.

The **Chauhan Kingdom** became the leading state in Northern India under King Prithviraj III (1165-1192), also known as **Prithvi Raj Chauhan** or Rai Pithora. Prithviraj III has become famous in folk tales and historical literature as the Chauhan king of Delhi who resisted and repelled the invasion by Mohammed of Ghor at the first Battle of Tarain in 1191. Armies from other Rajput kingdoms, including Mewar, assisted him. The Chauhan kingdom collapsed after Prithviraj and his armies fled the battle ground against Mohammed of Ghor in 1192 at the Second Battle of Tarain.

The Palas

Pala Empire was a Buddhist dynasty that ruled from the north-eastern region of the Indian subcontinent. The name *Pala* means *protector* and was used as an ending to the names of all Pala monarchs. The Palas were followers of the Mahayana and Tantric schools of Buddhism. Gopala was the first ruler from the dynasty. He came to power in 750 in Gaur by a democratic election. This event is recognized as one of the first democratic elections in South Asia since the time of the Mahâ Janapadas. He reigned from 750-770 and consolidated his position by extending his control over all of Bengal. The Buddhist dynasty lasted for four centuries (750-1120 AD) and ushered in a period of stability and prosperity in Bengal. They created many temples and works of art as well as supported the Universities of Nalanda and Vikramashila. Somapura Mahavihara built by Dharmapala is the greatest Buddhist Vihara in the Indian Subcontinent.

The empire reached its peak under Dharmapala and Devapala. Dharmapala extended the empire into the northern parts of the Indian Subcontinent. This triggered once again the power struggle for the control of the subcontinent. Devapala, successor of Dharmapala, expanded the empire to cover much of South Asia and beyond. His empire stretched from Assam and Utkala in the east, Kamboja (modern day Afghanistan) in the north-west and Deccan in the south. According to Pala copperplate inscription Devapala exterminated the Utkalas, conquered the Pragjyotisha (Assam), shattered the pride of the Huna, and humbled the lords of Pratiharas, Gurjara and the Dravidas.

The death of Devapala ended the period of ascendancy of the Pala Empire and several independent dynasties and kingdoms emerged during this time. However, Mahipala I rejuvenated the reign of the Palas. He recovered control over all of Bengal and expanded the empire. He survived the invasions of Rajendra Chola and the Chalukyas. After Mahipala I the Pala dynasty again saw its decline until Ramapala, the last great ruler of the dynasty, managed to retrieve the position of the dynasty to some extent. He crushed the Varendra rebellion and extended his empire farther to Kamarupa, Orissa and Northern India.

The Pala Empire can be considered as the golden era of Bengal. Never had the Bengali people reached such height of power and glory to that extent. Palas were responsible for the introduction of Mahayana Buddhism in Tibet, Bhutan and Myanmar. The Palas had extensive trade as well as influence in south-east Asia. This can be seen in the sculptures and architectural style of the Sailendra Empire (present-day Malaya, Java, Sumatra).

The Eastern Gangas

The **Eastern Ganga dynasty** rulers reigned over Kalinga which consisted of the parts of the modern day Indian states of Orissa, West Bengal, Jharkhand, Chattisgarh, and Andhra Pradesh from the 11th century to the early 15th century. Their capital was known by the name Kalinganagar, which is the modern Srimukhalingam in Srikakulam District of Andhra Pradesh bordering Orissa. Today they are most remembered as the builders of the Konark Sun Temple a World Heritage site at Konark, Orissa. It was built by King Narasimhadeva I (1238-1264). During their reign (1078-1434) a new style of temple architecture came into being, commonly called as Indo-Aryan architecture. This dynasty was founded by King Anantavarma Chodaganga Deva (1078–1147). He was a religious person and a patron of art and literature. He is credited for having built the famous Jagannath Temple of Puri in Orissa.

King Anantavarman Chodagangadeva was succeeded by a long line of illustrious rulers such as Narasimhadeva I (1238-1264). The rulers of Eastern Ganga dynasty defended their kingdom from the constant attacks of the Muslim rulers. This kingdom prospered through trade and commerce and the wealth was mostly used in the construction of temples. The rule of the dynasty came to end under the reign of King Bhanudeva IV (1414-34), in the early 15th century.

The Senas

The Palas were followed by the Sena dynasty who brought Bengal under one ruler during the twelfth century.

Vijay Sen the second ruler of this dynasty defeated the last Pala emperor Madanapala and established his reign. Ballal Sena introduced caste system in Bengal and made Nabadwip the capital. The fourth king of this dynasty Lakshman Sen expanded the empire beyond Bengal to Bihar, Assam, Orissa and probably to Varanasi. Lakshman was later defeated by the Muslims and fled to eastern Bengal were he ruled few more years. The Sena dynasty brought a revival of Hinduism and cultivated Sanskrit literature in India. It is believed by some Bengali authors that Jayadeva, the famous Sanskrit poet and author of Gita Govinda, was one of the *Pancharatnas* (meaning 5 gems) in the court of Lakshman Sen.

The South

In the first half of the millennium the South saw various smalled kingdoms rise and fall mostly independent to the turmoil in the gangetic plains and the spread of the Buddhism and Jainism to the southern tip of India. During the second half of the millennium after the fall of the Gupta Empire we see a gradual shift of the balance of power both military and cultural from the northern states to the rise of large southern kingdoms.

In fact, from the mid-seventh to the mid-thirteenth centuries, regionalism was the dominant theme of political or dynastic history of South Asia. Three features commonly characterize the sociopolitical realities of this period.

- First, the spread of Brahmanical religions was a two-way process of Sanskritization of local cults and localization of Brahmanical social order.
- Second was the ascendancy of the Brahman priestly and landowning groups that later dominated regional institutions and political developments.
- Third, because of the seesawing of numerous dynasties that had a remarkable ability to survive perennial

military attacks, regional kingdoms faced frequent defeats but seldom total annihilation.

Peninsular India was involved in an eighth-century tripartite power struggle among the Chalukyas (556–757), the Pallavas (300–888) of Kanchipuram, and the Pandyas. The Chalukya rulers were overthrown by their subordinates, the Rashtrakutas (753-973). Although both the Pallava and Pandya kingdoms were enemies, the real struggle for political domination was between the Pallava and Chalukya realms.

The emergence of the Rashtrakutas heralded a new era in the history of South India. The idiom of a Pan-Indian empire had moved to south. South Indian kingdoms had hitherto ruled areas only up to and south of the Narmada River. It was the Rashtrakutas who first forged north to the Gangetic plains and successfully contested their might against the Palas of Bengal and the Rajput Prathiharas of Gujarat.

Despite interregional conflicts, local autonomy was preserved to a far greater degree in the south where it had prevailed for centuries. The absence of a highly centralized government was associated with a corresponding local autonomy in the administration of villages and districts. Extensive and well-documented overland and maritime trade flourished with the Arabs on the west coast and with Southeast Asia. Trade facilitated cultural diffusion in Southeast Asia, where local elites selectively but willingly adopted Indian art, architecture, literature, and social customs.

The interdynastic rivalry and seasonal raids into each other's territory notwithstanding, the rulers in the Deccan and South India patronized all three religions—Buddhism, Hinduism, and Jainism. The religions vied with each other for royal favor, expressed in land grants but more importantly in the creation of monumental temples, which remain architectural wonders. The cave temples of Elephanta Island (near Mumbai or Bombay, as it was known formerly), Ajanta, and Ellora (in Maharashtra), and structural temples of Pattadakal, Aihole, Badami in Karnataka and Mahaballipuram and Kanchipuram in Tamil Nadu are enduring legacies of otherwise warring regional rulers.

By the mid-seventh century, Buddhism and Jainism began to decline as sectarian Hindu devotional cults of Shiva and Vishnu vigorously competed for popular support.

Although Sanskrit was the language of learning and theology in South India, as it was in the north, the growth of the bhakti (devotional) movements enhanced the crystallization of vernacular literature in all four major Dravidian languages: Tamil, Telugu, Malayalam, and Kannada; they often borrowed themes and vocabulary from Sanskrit but preserved much local cultural lore. Examples of Tamil literature include two major poems, Cilappatikaram (The Jewelled Anklet) and Manimekalai (The Jewelled Belt); the body of devotional literature of Shaivism and Vaishnavism—Hindu devotional movements; and the reworking of the Ramayana by Kamban in the twelfth century. A nationwide cultural synthesis had taken place with a minimum of common characteristics in the various regions of South Asia, but the process of cultural infusion and assimilation would continue to shape and influence India's history through the centuries.

The Sangam Era Kingdoms

Farther south were three ancient Tamil kingdoms—Chera (on the west), Chola (on the east), and Pandya (in the south) —. They were involved in internecine warfare seeking regional supremacy. They are mentioned in Greek and Ashokan sources as important Indian kingdoms beyond the Mauryan Empire. A corpus of ancient Tamil literature, known as Sangam (academy) works, provides much useful information about life in these kingdoms in the era 300 BC to 200 AD.

There is clear evidence of encroachment by Aryan traditions from the north into a predominantly indigenous Dravidian culture in transition.

Dravidian social order was based on different ecoregions rather than on the Aryan varna paradigm, although the Brahmans had a high status at a very early stage. Segments of society were characterized by matriarchy and matrilineal succession—which survived well into the nineteenth century—cross-cousin marriage, and strong regional identity. Tribal chieftains emerged as "kings" just as people moved from pastoralism toward agriculture sustained by irrigation based on rivers by small-scale tanks (as man-made ponds are called in India) and wells, as well as maritime trade with Rome and Southeast Asia.

Discoveries of Roman gold coins in various sites attest to extensive South Indian links with the outside world. As with Patliputra in the northeast and Taxila in the northwest (in modern Pakistan), the city of Madurai, the capital of the Pandyan Kingdom (in modern Tamil Nadu), was the center of intellectual and literary activity. Poets and bards assembled there under royal patronage at successive concourses to composed anthologies of poems and expositions on Tamil grammar. By the end of the first century BC, South Asia was crisscrossed by overland trade routes, which facilitated the movements of Buddhist and Jain missionaries and other travelers and opened the area to a synthesis of many cultures.

The Cheras

From early pre-historic times, Tamil Nadu was the home of the four Tamil kingdoms of the Chera, Chola, Pandya and Pallavas. The oldest extant literature, dated between 300 BC and 600 AD mentions the exploits of the kings and the princes, and of the poets who extolled them. Cherans, who spoke Tamil language ruled from the capital of Karur in the west and traded extensively with West Asian kingdoms. An unknown dynasty called Kalabhras invaded and displaced the three Tamil kingdoms between the fourth and the seventh centuries CE. This is referred to as the Dark Age in Tamil history. They were eventually expelled by the Pallavas and the Pandyas.

The Kalabhras

Little of their origins or the time during which they ruled is known beyond that they ruled over the entirety of the southern tip of India during the 3rd to the 6th century, overcoming the Sangam era kingdoms. The appear to be patrons of Jainism and Buddhism as the only source of information on them is the scattered mentions in the many Buddhist and Jain literature of the time. They were contemporaries of the Kadambas and the Western Ganga Dynasty. They were overcome by the rise of the Pallavas and the resurgence of the Pandyan Kingdom.

The Kadambas

The **Kadamba Dynasty** (345 - 525 CE) was an ancient royal family of Karnataka that ruled from Banavasi in present day Uttara Kannada district. The dynasty later continued to rule as a feudatory of larger Kannada empires, the Chalukya and the Rashtrakuta empires for over five hundred years during which time they branched into Goa and Hanagal. At the peak of their power under King Kakushtavarma, they ruled large parts of Karnataka. During the pre-Kadamba era the ruling families that controlled Karnataka, the Mauryas, Satavahanas and Chutus were not natives of the region and the nucleus of power resided outside present day Karnataka. The Kadambas were the first indigenous dynasty to use Kannada, the language of the soil at an administrative level. In the history of Karnataka, this era serves as a broad based historical starting point in the study of the development of region as an enduring geo-political entity and Kannada as an important regional language.

The dynasty was founded by Mayurasharma in 345 which at times showed the potential of developing into imperial proportions, an indication to which is provided by the titles and epithets assumed by its rulers. One of his successors, Kakusthavarma was a powerful ruler and even the kings of imperial Gupta Dynasty of northern India cultivated marital relationships with his family, giving a fair indication of the sovereign nature of their kingdom. Tiring of the endless battles and bloodshed, one of the later descendants, King Shivakoti adopted Jainism. The Kadambas were contemporaries of the Western Ganga Dynasty of Talakad and together they formed the earliest native kingdoms to rule the land with absolute autonomy.

The Western Gangas

The **Western Ganga Dynasty** (350–1000 CE) was an important ruling dynasty of ancient Karnataka in India. They are known as **Western Gangas** to distinguish them from the **Eastern Gangas** who in later centuries ruled over modern Orissa. The general belief is the Western Gangas began their rule during a time when multiple native clans asserted their freedom due to the weakening of the Pallava empire in South India, a geo-political event sometimes attributed to the southern conquests of Samudra Gupta. The Western Ganga sovereignty lasted from about 350 to 550 CE, initially ruling from Kolar and later moving their capital to Talakad on the banks of the Kaveri River in modern Mysore district.

After the rise of the imperial Chalukyas of Badami, the Gangas accepted Chalukya overlordship and fought for the cause of their overlords against the Pallavas of Kanchi. The Chalukyas were replaced by the Rashtrakutas of Manyakheta in 753 CE as the dominant power in the Deccan. After a century of struggle for autonomy, the Western Gangas finally accepted Rashtrakuta overlordship and successfully fought alongside them against their foes, the Chola Dynasty of Tanjavur. In the late 10th century, north of Tungabhadra river, the Rashtrakutas were replaced by the emerging Western Chalukya Empire and the Chola Dynasty saw renewed power south of the Kaveri river. The defeat of the Western Gangas by Cholas around 1000 resulted in the end of the Ganga influence over the region.

Though territorially a small kingdom, the Western Ganga contribution to polity, culture and literature of the modern south Karnataka region is considered important. The Western Ganga kings showed benevolent tolerance to all faiths but are most famous for their patronage towards Jainism resulting in the construction of monuments in places such as Shravanabelagola and Kambadahalli. The kings of this dynasty encouraged the fine arts due to which literature in Kannada and Sanskrit flourished. Chavundaraya's writing, *Chavundaraya Purana* of 978 CE, is an important work in Kannada prose. Many classics were written on various subjects ranging from religion to elephant management.

The Badami Chalukyas

The **Chalukya Empire**, natives of the Aihole and Badami region in Karnataka, were at first a feudatory of the Kadambas. They encouraged the use of Kannada in addition to the Sanskrit language in their administration. In the middle of the 6th century the Chalukyas came into their own when Pulakesi I made the hill fortress in Badami his center of power. During the rule of Pulakesi II a south Indian empire sent expeditions to the north past the Tapti River and Narmada River for the first time and successfully defied Harshavardhana, the King of Northern India (*Uttarapatheswara*). The Aihole inscription of Pulakesi II, written in classical Sanskrit language and old Kannada script dated 634, proclaims his victories against the Kingdoms of Kadambas, Western Gangas, Alupas of South Canara, Mauryas of Puri, Kingdom of Kosala, Malwa,

Lata and Gurjaras of southern Rajasthan. The inscription describes how King Harsha of Kannauj lost his *Harsha* (joyful disposition) on seeing a large number of his war elephants die in battle against Pulakesi II.

These victories earned him the title *Dakshinapatha Prithviswamy* (lord of the south). Pulakesi II continued his conquests in the east where he conquered all kingdoms in his way and reached the Bay of Bengal in present day Orissa. A Chalukya viceroyalty was set up in Gujarat and Vengi (coastal Andhra) and princes from the Badami family were dispatched to rule them. Having subdued the Pallavas of Kanchipuram, he accepted tributes from the Pandyas of Madurai, Chola dynasty and Cheras of the Kerala region. Pulakesi II thus became the master of India, south of the Narmada River. Pulakesi II is widely regarded as one of the great kings in Indian history. Hiuen-Tsiang, a Chinese traveller visited the court of Pulakesi II at this time and Persian emperor Khosrau II exchanged ambassadors. However, the continuous wars with Pallavas took a turn for the worse in 642 when the Pallava king Narasimhavarman I avenged his father's defeat, conquered and plundered the capital of Pulakesi II who may have died in battle. A century later, Chalukya Vikramaditya II marched victoriously into Kanchipuram, the Pallava capital and occupied it on three occasions, the third time under the leadership of his son and crown prince Kirtivarman II. He thus avenged the earlier humiliation of the Chalukyas by the Pallavas and engraved a Kannada inscription on the victory pillar at the Kailasanatha Temple. He later overran the other traditional kingdoms of Tamil country, the Pandyas, Cholas and Keralas in addition to subduing a Kalabhra ruler.

The Kappe Arabhatta record from this period (700) in *tripadi* (three line) metre is considered the earliest available record in Kannada poetics. The most enduring legacy of the Chalukya dynasty is the architecture and art that they left behind. More than one hundred and fifty monuments attributed to the them, built between 450 and 700, have survived in the Malaprabha basin in Karnataka. The constructions are centred in a relatively small area within the Chalukyan heartland. The structural temples at Pattadakal, a UNESCO World Heritage Site, the cave temples of Badami, the temples at Mahakuta and early experiments in temple building at Aihole are their most celebrated monuments. Two of the famous paintings at Ajanta cave no. 1, "The Temptation of the Buddha" and "The Persian Embassy" are also credited to them. Further, they influenced the architecture in far off places like Gujarat and Vengi as evidenced in the Nava Brahma temples at Alampur.

The Pallavas

The seventh century Tamil Nadu saw the rise of the Pallavas under Mahendravarman I and his son *Mamalla* Narasimhavarman I. The Pallavas were not a recognised political power before the second century. It has been widely accepted by scholars that they were originally executive officers under the Satavahana Empire. After the fall of the Satavahanas, they began to get control over parts of Andhra and the Tamil country. Later they had marital ties with the Vishnukundina who ruled over the Deccan. It was around 550 AD under King Simhavishnu that the Pallavas emerged into prominence. They subjugated the Cholas and reigned as far south as the Kaveri River. Pallavas ruled a large portion of South India with Kanchipuram as their capital. Dravidian architecture reached its peak during the Pallava rule. Narasimhavarman II built the Shore Temple which is a UNESCO World Heritage Site. Many sources describe Bodhidharma, the founder of the Zen school of Buddhism in China, as a prince of the Pallava dynasty.

The Eastern Chalukyas

Eastern Chalukyas were a South Indian dynasty whose kingdom was located in the present day Andhra Pradesh.

Their capital was Vengi and their dynasty lasted for around 500 years from the 7th century until c. 1130 C.E. when the Vengi kingdom merged with the Chola empire. The Vengi kingdom was continued to be ruled by Eastern Chalukyan kings under the protection of the Chola empire until 1189 C.E., when the kingdom succumbed to the Hoysalas and the Yadavas. They had their capital originally at Vengi now (Pedavegi, Chinavegi and Denduluru) near Eluru of the West Godavari district end later changed to Rajamahendravaram (Rajamundry).

Eastern Chalukyas were closely related to the Chalukyas of Vatapi (Badami). Throughout their history they were the cause of many wars between the more powerful Cholas and Western Chalukyas over the control of the strategic Vengi country. The five centuries of the Eastern Chalukya rule of Vengi saw not only the consolidation of this region into a unified whole, but also saw the efflorescence of Telugu culture, literature, poetry and art during the later half of their rule. It can be said to be the golden period of Andhra history.

The Pandyas

Pallavas were replaced by the Pandyas in the 8th century. Their capital Madurai was in the deep south away from the coast. They had extensive trade links with the Southeast Asian maritime empires of Srivijaya and their successors. As well as contacts, even diplomatic, reaching as far as the Roman Empire. During the 13th century of the Christian era Marco Polo mentioned it as the richest kingdom in existence. Temples like Meenakshi Amman Temple at Madurai and Nellaiappar Temple at Tirunelveli are the best examples of Pandyan Temple architecture. The Pandyas excelled in both trade as well as literature and they controlled the pearl fisheries along the South Indian coast, between Sri Lanka and India, which produced some of the finest pearls in the known ancient world.

The Rashtrakutas

In the middle of 8th century the Chalukya rule was ended by their feudatory, the Rashtrakuta family rulers of Berar (in present day Amravati district of Maharashtra). Sensing an opportunity during a weak period in the Chalukya rule, Dantidurga trounced the great Chalukyan "Karnatabala" (power of Karnata). Having overthrown the Chalukyas, the Rashtrakutas made Manyakheta their capital (modern Malkhed in Gulbarga district). Although the origins of the early Rashtrakuta ruling families in central India and the Deccan in the 6th and 7th centuries is controversial, during the eighth through the tenth centuries they emphasised the importance of the Kannada language in conjunction with Sanskrit in their administration. Rashtrakuta inscriptions are in Kannada and Sanskrit only. They encouraged literature in both languages and thus literature flowered under their rule.

The Rashtrakutas quickly became the most powerful Deccan empire, making their initial successful forays into the doab region of Ganga River and Jamuna River during the rule of Dhruva Dharavarsha. The rule of his son Govinda III signaled a new era with Rashtrakuta victories against the Pala Dynasty of Bengal and Gurjara Pratihara of north western India resulting in the capture of Kannauj. The Rashtrakutas held Kannauj intermittently during a period of a tripartite struggle for the resources of the rich Gangetic plains. Because of Govinda III's victories, historians have compared him to Alexander the Great and Pandava Arjuna of the Hindu epic Mahabharata. The Sanjan inscription states the horses of Govinda III drank the icy water of the Himalayan stream and his war elephants tasted the sacred waters of the Ganges River. Amoghavarsha I, eulogised by contemporary Arab traveller Sulaiman as one among the four great emperors of the world, succeeded Govinda III to the throne and ruled during an important cultural period that produced landmark writings in Kannada and Sanskrit. The benevolent development of Jain religion was a hallmark of his rule. Because of his religious temperament, his interest in the arts and literature and his peace loving nature, he has been compared to emperor Ashoka. The rule of Indra III in the tenth century enhanced the Rashtrakuta position as an imperial power as they conquered and held Kannauj again. Krishna III followed Indra III to the throne in 939. A patron of Kannada literature and a powerful warrior, his reign marked the submission of the Paramara of Ujjain in the north and Cholas in the south.

An Arabic writing *Silsilatuttavarikh* (851) called the Rashtrakutas one among the four principle empires of the world. *Kitab-ul-Masalik-ul-Mumalik* (912) called them the "greatest kings of India" and there were many other contemporaneous books written in their praise. The Rashtrakuta empire at its peak spread from Cape Comorin in the south to Kannauj in the north and from Banaras in the east to Broach (Bharuch) in the west. While the Rashtrakutas built many fine monuments in the Deccan, the most extensive and sumptuous of their work is the monolithic Kailasanatha temple at Ellora, the temple being a splendid achievement. In Karnataka their most famous temples are the Kashivishvanatha temple and the Jain Narayana temple at Pattadakal. All of the monuments are designated UNESCO World Heritage Sites.

The Western Chalukyas

In the late 10th century, the Western Chalukyas, also known as the Kalyani Chalukyas or 'Later' Chalukyas rose to power by overthrowing the Rashtrakutas under whom they had been serving as feudatories. Manyakheta was their capital early on before they moved it to Kalyani (modern Basavakalyan). Whether the kings of this empire belonged to the same family line as their namesakes, the Badami Chalukyas is still debated. Whatever the Western Chalukya origins, Kannada remained their language of administration and the

Kannada and Sanskrit literature of their time was prolific. Tailapa II, a feudatory ruler from Tardavadi (modern Bijapur district), re-established the Chalukya rule by defeating the Rashtrakutas during the reign of Karka II. He timed his rebellion to coincide with the confusion caused by the invading Paramara of Central India to the Rashtrakutas capital in 973. This era produced prolonged warfare with the Chola dynasty of Tamilakam for control of the resources of the Godavari River-Krishna River doab region in Vengi. Somesvara I, a brave Chalukyan king, successfully curtailed the growth of the Chola Empire to the south of the Tungabhadra River region despite suffering some defeats while maintaining control over his feudatories in the Konkan, Gujarat, Malwa and Kalinga regions. For approximately 100 years, beginning in the early 11th century, the Cholas occupied large areas of South Karnataka region (Gangavadi).

In 1076, the ascent of the most famous king of this Chalukya family, Vikramaditya VI, changed the balance of power in favour of the Chalukyas. His fifty year reign was an important period in Karnataka's history and is referred to as the "Chalukya Vikrama era". His victories over the Cholas in the late 11th and early 12th centuries put an end to the Chola influence in the Vengi region permanently. Some of the well known contemporaneous feudatory families of the Deccan under Chalukya control were the Hoysalas, the Seuna Yadavas of Devagiri, the Kakatiya dynasty and the Southern Kalachuri. At their peak, the Western Chalukyas ruled a vast empire stretching from the Narmada River in the north to the Kaveri River in the south. Vikramaditya VI is considered one of the most influential kings of Indian history. Important architectural works were created by these Chalukyas, especially in the Tungabhadra river valley, that served as a conceptual link between the building idioms of the early Badami Chalukyas and the later Hoysalas. With the weakening of the Chalukyas in the decades following the death of Vikramaditya

VI in 1126, the feudatories of the Chalukyas gained their independence.

The Kalachuris of Karnataka, whose ancestors were immigrants into the southern deccan from central India, had ruled as a feudatory from Mangalavada (modern Mangalavedhe in Maharashtra). Bijjala II, the most powerful ruler of this dynasty, was a commander (*mahamandaleswar*) during the reign of Chalukya Vikramaditya VI. Seizing an opportune moment in the waning power of the Chalukyas, Bijjala II declared independence in 1157 and annexed their capital Kalyani. His rule was cut short by his assassination in 1167 and the ensuing civil war caused by his sons fighting over the throne ended the dynasty as the last Chalukya scion regained control of Kalyani. This victory however, was short-lived as the Chalukyas were eventually driven out by the Seuna Yadavas.

The Yadavas

The **Seuna**, *Sevuna* or **Yadava dynasty** (850 - 1334) was an Indian dynasty, which at its peak ruled a kingdom stretching from the Tungabhadra to the Narmada rivers, including present-day Maharashtra, north Karnataka and parts of Madhya Pradesh, from its capital at Devagiri (present-day Daulatabad in Maharashtra). The Yadavas initially ruled as feudatories of the Western Chalukyas. Around the middle of the 12th century, they declared independence and established rule that reached its peak under Singhana II. The foundations of Marathi culture was laid by the Yadavas and the peculiarities of Maharashtra's social life developed during their rule.

The Kakatiyas

The Kakatiya dynasty was a South Indian dynasty that ruled parts of what is now Andhra Pradesh, India from 1083 to 1323. They were one of the great Telugu kingdoms that lasted for centuries.

The Kalachuris

Kalachuri Empire is this the name used by two kingdoms who had a succession of dynasties from the 10th-12th centuries, one ruling over areas in Central India (west Madhya Pradesh, Rajasthan) and were called Chedi or *Haihaya* (*Heyheya*) (northern branch) and the other southern Kalachuri who ruled over parts of Karnataka. They are disparately placed in time and space. Apart from the dynastic name and perhaps a belief in common ancestry, there is little in known sources to connect them.

The earliest known Kalachuri family (550–620 A.D) ruled over northern Maharashtra, Malwa and western Deccan. Their capital was Mahismati situated in the Narmada river valley. There were three prominent members; Krishnaraja, Shankaragana and Buddharaja. They distributed coins and epigraphs around this area.

Southern Kalachuris (1130 - 1184) at their peak ruled parts of the Deccan extending over regions of present day North Karnataka and parts of Maharashtra. This dynasty rose to power in the Deccan between 1156 and 1181 A.D. They traced their origins to *Krishna* who was the conqueror of *Kalinjar* and Dahala in Madhya Pradesh. It is said that *Bijjala* a viceroy of this dynasty established the authority over Karnataka. He wrested power from the Chalukya king Taila III. Bijjala was succeeded by his sons Someshwara and Sangama but after 1181 A.D, the Chalukyas gradually retrieved the territory. Their rule was a short and turbulent and yet very important from a the socio - religious movement point of view; a new sect called the Lingayat or Virashaiva sect was founded during these times. A unique and purely native form of Kannada literature-poetry called the *Vachanas* was also born during this time. The writers of *Vachanas* were called *Vachanakaras* (poets). Many other important works like Virupaksha Pandita's *Chennabasavapurana*, Dharani Pandita's

Bijjalarayacharite and Chandrasagara Varni's *Bijjalarayapurana* were also written.

Northern Kalachuris ruled in central India with its base at the ancient city of Tripuri (Tewar); it originated in the 8th century, expanded significantly in the 11th century, and declined in the 12th–13th centuries.

The Hoysalas

The Hoysalas had become a powerful force even during their rule from Belur in the 11th century as a feudatory of the Chalukyas (in the south Karnataka region). In the early 12th century they successfully fought the Cholas in the south, convincingly defeating them in the battle of Talakad and moved their capital to nearby Halebidu. Historians refer to the founders of the dynasty as natives of Malnad Karnataka, based on the numerous inscriptions calling them *Maleparolganda* or "Lord of the Male (hills) chiefs" (*Malepas*). With the waning of the Western Chalukya power, the Hoysalas declared their independence in the late twelfth century.

During this period of Hoysala control, distinctive Kannada literary metres such as *Ragale* (blank verse), *Sangatya* (meant to be sung to the accompaniment of a musical instrument), *Shatpadi* (seven line) etc. became widely accepted. The Hoysalas expanded the Vesara architecture stemming from the Chalukyas, culminating in the Hoysala architectural articulation and style as exemplified in the construction of the Chennakesava Temple at Belur and the Hoysaleswara temple at Halebidu. Both these temples were built in commemoration of the victories of the Hoysala Vishnuvardhana against the Cholas in 1116. Veera Ballala II, the most effective of the Hoysala rulers, defeated the aggressive Pandya when they invaded the Chola kingdom and assumed the titles "Establisher of the Chola Kingdom" (*Cholarajyapratishtacharya*), "Emperor of the south" (*Dakshina Chakravarthi*) and "Hoysala emperor" (*Hoysala Chakravarthi*). The Hoysalas extended their foothold in areas known today as Tamil Nadu around 1225, making the city of Kannanur Kuppam near Srirangam a provincial capital. This gave them control over South Indian politics that began a period of Hoysala hegemony in the southern Deccan.

In the early 13th century, with the Hoysala power remaining unchallenged, the first of the Muslim incursions into South India began. After over two decades of waging war against a foreign power, the Hoysala ruler at the time, Veera Ballala III, died in the battle of Madurai in 1343. This resulted in the merger of the sovereign territories of the Hoysala empire with the areas administered by Harihara I, founder of the Vijayanagara Empire, located in the Tungabhadra region in present day Karnataka. The new kingdom thrived for another two centuries with Vijayanagara as its capital.

The Cholas

By the 9th century, under Rajaraja Chola and his son Rajendra Chola, the Cholas rose as a notable power in south Asia. The Chola Empire stretched as far as Bengal. At its peak, the empire spanned almost 250 million acres (1,000,000 km^2). Rajaraja Chola conquered all of peninsular South India and parts of the Sri Lanka. Rajendra Chola's navies went even further, occupying coasts from Burma (now Myanmar) to Vietnam, the Andaman and Nicobar Islands, Lakshadweep, Sumatra, Java, Malaya in South East Asia and Pegu islands. He defeated Mahipala, the king of the Bengal, and to commemorate his victory he built a new capital and named it Gangaikonda Cholapuram.

The Cholas excelled in building magnificent temples. Brihadeshwara Temple in Thanjavur is a classical example of the magnificent architecture of the Chola kingdom. Brihadshwara temple is an UNESCO Heritage Site under "Great Living Chola Temples." Another example is the

Chidambaram Temple in the heart of the temple town of Chidambaram.

PATALIPUTRA

Pataliputra, modern-day Patna, was a city in ancient India, originally built by Ajatashatru in 490 BC as a small fort (Pâmaligrama) near the River Ganges, and later the capital of the ancient Mahâjanapadas kingdom of Magadha. Its key central location in north central India led rulers of successive dynasties to base their administrative capital here, from the Nandas, Mauryans, Sungas and the Guptas down to the Palas. In the Lord Buddha's day it was a village known as Pataligrama. He visited it shortly before his death and prophesied it would be great but would face destruction either by fire, water, or civil war.Two important councils were held here, the first at the death of the Buddha and the second in the reign of Asoka . During the reign of Emperor Asoka in the 3rd century BCE, it was the world's largest city, with a population of 150,000-300,000. Pataliputra reached the pinnacle of prosperity when it was the capital of the great Mauryan Emperors, Chandragupta Maurya and Ashoka the Great. The city prospered under the Mauryas and a Greek ambassador Megasthenes resided there and left a detailed account of its splendour. The city also became a flourishing Buddhist centre boasting a number of important monasteries. It remained the capital of the Gupta dynasty (III–VI centuries CE) and the Pala Dynasty (VIII-XII centuries CE). The city was largely in ruins when visited by Hsüan-tsang, and suffered further damage at the hands of Muslim raiders in the XII century. Afterwards Sher Shah Suri made Pataliputra his capital and changed the name to modern Patna.

Though parts of the city have been excavated, much of it still lies buried beneath modern Patna. During the Mauryan period, the city was described as being shaped as parallelogram, approximately 1.5 miles wide and 9 miles long. Its wooden walls were pierced by 64 gates. These were thought to have been converted to strong stone walls during the time of Ashoka. Situated at the confluence of the Ganges and Gandhaka rivers, Pataliputra soon came to dominate the riverine trade of the Indo-Gangetic plains during Magadha's early imperial period. It was a great center of trade and commerce and attracted merchants and intellectuals, such as the famed Chanakya, from all over India.

There is an on-going campaign of the people of Bihar to rename Patna with its original name, Pataliputra.

Etymology

The etymology of Pâtaliputra is unclear. "Putra" means son, and "pâþali" is a species of rice or the plant *Bignonia suaveolens*. One traditional etymology holds that the city was named after the plant. Another tradition says that Pâtaliputra means the son of Pâtali, who was the daughter of Raja Sudarshan. As it was known as Pâtali-grama originally, some scholars believe that Pâtaliputra is a transformation of Pâtalipura, "Pâtali town".

PATNA

Patna is the capital of the Indian state of Bihar. The modern city of Patna is situated on the southern bank of the Ganges. The city also straddles the rivers Kosi, Sone and Gandak. Patna is approximately 25 km long and 9 km to 10 km wide. Patna is 14th most populous cities in India with approximately 1.8 million and 168th most populous agglomerations in world . It's the largest city in Eastern India after Kolkata. Today, all major companies have their base in Patna reflecting the growing importance of the city. The city is growing at an unprecendented rate with an almost boom like situation in all sectors from retail to real estate. It is also fast emerging as hub of higher education with institutes of national repute being started in Patna.

Apart from being the administrative centre of the state and its historic importance, the city is also a major educational and medical centre. The Economy of patna is based on local service industry. Patna is recording the highest per capita gross district domestic product of Rs 31,441 in Bihar which better than the most of the metropolitan in India Patna is 21st fastest growing city and urban areas in world and 5th fastest growing city in India In June 2009, The World Bank ranked Patna as the second best city in India to start a business, after Delhi.

Patna is one of oldest continuously inhabited places in the world.. Ancient Patna, known as Pataliputra, was the capital of the Magadha Empire under the Haryanka, Nanda, Mauryan, Sunga, Gupta, Pala and Suri dynasties. Pataliputra was also a famous seat of learning and fine arts. Its population during Maurya period (around 300 BCE), was about 400,000. The walled old area, called Patna City by the locals, is a major trading centre.

The Buddhist, Hindu, and Jain pilgrim centres of Vaishali, Rajgir , Nalanda, Bodhgaya, and Pawapuri are nearby and Patna is also a sacred city for Sikhs. The Sikh Guru, Founder and first Commander-in-Chief of Sikh Khalsa Army, Guru Gobind Singh, was born Here.

Origin of Name

There are several theories regarding the source of the appellation Patna:

- It is etymologically derived from *Patan*, the name of the Hindu goddess, Patan Devi.
- It comes from *Pattan* (meaning "port" in Sanskrit), since the city, located near the confluence of four rivers, has been a thriving river port.
- It may be a short form of *Patliputra*, one of the most ancient names of this city. This name was mentioned

by Megasthenes (350-290 BCE), the Greek historian, (calling it *Palibothra* or *Palimbotra* in Greek), in his writings during the 4th century, and also appears in the records of the Chinese traveller, Fa Hien as Pa-lin-fou.

- The Greeks called it Palibothra. The Chinese called the place as Pa-lin-fou.
- The city has been known by various names during its more than two millennia long existence — Pataligram, Patliputra, Kusumpur, Pushpapura, Azimabad, and the present-day Patna.
- Patna received its current name during the reign of Sher Shah Suri, whose tomb is at Sasaram, a place near Patna.

Legend ascribes the origin of Patna to a mythological King Putraka who created Patna by magic for his queen Patali, literally Trumpet flower, which gives it its ancient name Pataligrama. It is said that in honour of the first born to the queen, the city was named Pataliputra. *Gram* is the Sanskrit for village and *Putra* means son.

Legend also says that the Emerald Buddha was created in Patna (then Pataliputra) by Nagasena in 43 BC.

From a scientific history perspective, it would be appropriate to surmise that the history of Patna started around the year 490 BCE when Ajatashatru, the king of Magadha, wanted to shift his capital from the hilly Rajagaha to a more strategically located place to combat the Licchavis of Vaishali. He chose the site on the bank of Ganges and fortified the area. From that time, the city has had a continuous history, a record claimed by few cities in the world. Gautama Buddha passed through this place in the last year of his life, and he had prophesized a great future for this place, but at the same time, he predicted its ruin from flood, fire, and feud.

With the rise of the Mauryan empire, the place became the seat of power and nerve centre of the sub-continent. From Pataliputra, the famed emperor Chandragupta Maurya (a contemporary of Alexander) ruled a vast empire, stretching from the Bay of Bengal to Afghanistan.

Early Mauryan Patliputra was mostly built with wooden structures. Emperor Ashoka, the grandson of Chandragupta Maurya, transformed the wooden capital into a stone construction around 273 BCE. Chinese scholar Fa Hein, who visited India sometime around 399-414 CE, has given a vivid description of the stone structures in his travelogue

Megasthenes (350-290 BCE), Greek historian and ambassador to the court of Chandragupta Maurya, gives the first written account of Patliputra. In his book Indika, he mentions that the city of *Palibothra* (Pataliputra, modern day Patna) was situated on the confluence of the rivers *Ganges* and *Arennovoas* (Sonabhadra - Hiranyawah) and was 9 miles (14 km) long and 1.75 miles (2.82 km) wide..*Michael Wood (historian)* in *The Story of India* (2007) Describes this city to be the greatest city on earth during its hayday.

Much later, a number of Chinese travellers came to India in pursuit of knowledge and recorded their observation about Pataliputra in their travelogues, including those of a Chinese Buddhist Fa Hien, who visited India, between 399 and 414 CE, and stayed here for many months translating Buddhist texts.

In the years that followed, the city saw many dynasties ruling the Indian subcontinent from here. It saw the rules of the Gupta empire and the Pala kings. However, it never reached the glory that it had under the Mauryas.

With the disintegration of the Gupta empire, Patna passed through uncertain times. Bakhtiar Khilji captured Bihar in the 12th century AD and destroyed many ancient seats of learning, Patna lost its prestige as the political and cultural center of India.

Guru Gobind Singh (December 22, 1666 – October 7, 1708), the tenth Guru of the Sikhs was born as Gobind Rai in Patna to Teg Bahadur, the ninth Guru of the Sikhs, and his wife Gujri. His birth place Harmandir saheb is a one of most sacred pilgrimage for Sikhs.

The Mughal period was a period of unremarkable provincial administration from Delhi. The most remarkable period during these times was under Sher Shah Suri who revived Patna in the middle of the 16th century. He built a fort and found a town on the banks of Ganga. Sher Shah's fort in Patna does not survive, but the mosque, Sher Shah Suri Masjid, built in Afghan architectural style survives.

Mughal emperor Akbar came to Patna in 1574 to crush the Afghan Chief Daud Khan. Akbar's navratna and state's official historian and author of "Ain-i-Akbari" Abul Fazl refers to Patna as a flourishing centre for paper, stone and glass industries. He also refers to the high quality of numerous strains of rice grown in Patna famous as Patna rice in Europe.

By 1620 the city of Patna, which was revived by Sher Shah Suri in year 1541, was the great entrepot of Northern India - "the largest town in Bengal and the most famous for trade". This was before the founding of the city of Calcutta.

Mughal Emperor Aurangzeb acceded to the request of his favourite grandson Prince Muhammad Azim to rename Patna as Azimabad, in 1704 while Azim was in Patna as the subedar. However, very little changed during this period other than the name.

With the decline of the Mughal empire, Patna moved into the hands of the Nawabs of Bengal, who levied a heavy tax on the populace but allowed it to flourish as a commercial centre.

The mansions of the Maharaja of Tekari Raj dominated the Patna riverfront in 1811-12.

During the 17th century, Patna became a centre of international trade. The British started with a factory in Patna in 1620 for trading in calico and silk. Soon it became a trading centre for saltpetre, urging other Europeans—French, Danes, Dutch and Portuguese—to compete in the lucrative business. Peter Mundy, writing in 1632, described Patna as "the greatest mart of the eastern region".

After the decisive Battle of Buxar (1765), Patna fell in the hands of the East India Company which installed a puppet government. Ruled during the raj by a series of ineffectual Viceroys, the most well known was Rahul Gunderjaharagand. During this period it continued as a trading centre. In 1912, Patna became the capital of Orissa Province and Bihâr when Bengal Presidency was partitioned. It soon emerged as an important and strategic centre. A number of imposing structures were constructed by the British. Credit for designing the massive and majestic buildings of colonial Patna goes to the architect, I. F. Munnings. Most of these buildings reflect either Indo-Saracenic influence (like Patna Museum and the state Assembly), or overt Renaissance influence like the Raj Bhawan and the High Court. Some buildings, like the General Post Office (GPO) and the Old Secretariat bear pseudo-Renaissance influence. Some say, the experience gained in building the new capital area of Patna proved very useful in building the imperial capital of New Delhi. Orissa was created as a separate province in 1935. Patna continued as the capital of Bihar province under the British Raj.

Patna played a major role in the Indian independence struggle. Most notable are the Champaran movement against the Indigo plantation and the 1942 Quit India Movement. Patna's contribution in the freedom struggle has been immense with outstanding national leaders like Swami Sahajanand

Saraswati, the first President of the Constituent Assembly of India Dr. Sachidanand Sinha,Dr. Rajendra Prasad,*Bihar Vibhuti* Anugrah Narayan Sinha,Basawon Singh (Sinha) , *Loknayak* Jayaprakash Narayan, Sri Krishna Sinha, Sheel Bhadra Yajee, Sarangdhar Sinha(Singh), Yogendra Shukla, and many others who worked for India's freedom relentlessly. Shrii Anandamurti formed the Ananda Marga movement in Patna in 1962 to worked for world unity and justice. He moderized the ancient practices of yoga and made the most advanced practices of meditation abvailabe to the general public. He spoke about the inequality of women (both in India and worldwide). As an example, he questioned the morality of the dowry system of marriage and the Indian caste system. His Ananda Marga organization spread worldwide and teaches both neo-humanism (oneness of family of life) and PROUT (Progressive Utilization Theory) for overall economic development. He is considered a leader in the field of philosophy and morality.

Patna continued to be the capital of the state of Bihar after independence in 1947, though Bihar itself was partitioned again in 2000 when Jharkhand was carved out as a separate state of the Indian union.

Geography

Patna is located on the south bank of the Ganges River, called Ganga locally. An impressing characteristic about the geography of Patna is its meshing of rivers of which the Ganges River is most ascendant and then conjoined by the Four mighty rivers; Ghagra, Gandak, Punpun and Sone. The Ganga is a respectable river in its passing along the district of the city of Patna where it seems to be to the full as large as in any part of its course for the huge flow of the Kosi. Just to the north of Patna across the [Ganges River/river Ganga] flows the river Gandak making it a unique place having four large rivers in its vicinity. It is the largest riverine city in the world.

The bridge over the river Ganga named Mahatma Gandhi Setu, is 5575m long and is one of the longest (single river) bridge in the world.

Climate

Patna, as most of Bihar, has a subtropical climate with hot summers from late March to early June, the monsoon season from late June to late September and a mild winter from November to February. The table below details historical monthly averages for climate variables. Highest ever recorded is 55 °C, lowest ever is -6 °C and annual rainfall is 1000 mm.

Economy

From the very ancient time Patna has rich socioeconomic background. Patna has long been a major agricultural center of trade, its most active exports being grain, sugarcane, sesame, and medium-grained Patna rice. It is also an important business center of eastern India.

In the last few years, the growth in Patna has been quite phenomenonal. With the improvement in the law and order after the regime change, all the major companies have setup shop in Patna. The companies have started to recognize Patna's growing upper and middle class's purchasing power. This has led to a boom in the real estate sector and prices for commercial as well as residential complexes have hit the roof despite the global economic meltdown. The modern Patna, though still not comparable to the developed state capitals, is changing for the better. By the end of next year, the city will boast of 4 new malls that are coming up in different parts of the capital. This includes the P&M Mall & Multiplex that is being promoted by Prakash Jha's company. A slew of residential properties are also being developed in response to the huge demand for these in Patna. Large format retailers such as Big Bazaar and the Future Group are planning to setup their stores by next year. A number of restaurant joints such as Yo China, Moti Mahal, Smoking Joes and Dosa Plaza have established their presence in Patna.

Being the state capital, with a growing middle income group households, Patna has also emerged as a big and rapidly expanding consumer market, both for Fast Moving Consumer Goods (FMCG), as also for other consumer durable items. A large and growing population, and expanding boundaries of the city, is also spurring growth of service sector.Several Multi National companies have also come up at Patna, One example can be Tata Consultancy Services

The hinterland of Patna is endowed with excellent agro-climatic resources and the gains of the green revolution have enabled the older eastern part of Patna (locally called as Patna City) to develop as a leading grain market of the state of Bihar, and one of the biggest in eastern India.

Financial Express reported on April 7, 2008 that even as Bihar has the lowest per capita income in the country at Rs 5,772 against the national average of Rs 22,946, some of its southern districts are much better off compared with those in the north. This disparity within the state is clearly reflected in Bihar's latest economic survey for 2007-08. The survey shows that Patna, Munger, and Begusarai in south Bihar were the three best-off districts out of a total of 38 districts, recording the highest per capita gross district domestic product (GDP) of Rs 31,441, Rs 10,087, and Rs 9,312, respectively in 2004-05. In contrast, right at the bottom of the rank, with the lowest per capita GDP, were the northern districts of Araria at Rs 4,578, Sitamarhi at Rs 4,352, and Sheohar at Rs 3,636.

Demographics

The population of Patna is over 1,885,470. The population density is 1132 persons per square kilometre. There are 839 females to every 1,000 males. The overall literacy rate is 62.9%, and the female literacy rate is 50.8%.

Many languages are spoken in Patna. Hindi and Urdu is the official language. The native dialect is Magadhi or Magahi, named after Magadha, the ancient name of Bihar. Dialects from other regions of Bihar spoken widely in Patna are Angika, Bhojpuri, and Maithili. Other languages widely spoken in Patna include Bengali, Oriya, and English.

Culture

Though geographically located in the Magadh region of Bihar, many residents of Patna are natives of one of the four other regions of Bihar - Bhojpur, Mithila, Vajj, or Ang, which differ only slightly from each other. Intermarriages and cultural intermixing among the people of the five regions has been so common that it may be difficult for an outsider to discern the differences. Intermixing of people is also common at the village level (e.g. resident of Gulni include people from Gaya, Ganga-par and other villages).

People are religious and family-oriented, and their lives are deeply rooted in tradition. The interests of the family take precedence over that of an individual. Families are generally large, though the government is actively encouraging family planning to curb rapid population growth. Extended families often live together in one home because of economic necessity. Although the culture is same among the regions, the dialects spoken are quite different. Many talented people of Bihar have emigrated for better opportunities.

Transportation and Connectivity

Patna was among pioneer selected towns of India having horse-drawn trams as urban transport. Now days, Public transport in Patna is provided by buses, auto rickshaws and a Local trains.Auto rickshaws are the most popular means of public transportation in Patna, as they charge lower . Most run on diesel and are yellow and black in colour. Buses are also one of the popular means of public transportation in Patna.

Public transport is one area where Patna lacks quite a lot. As of now, only private buses ply on city roads and often very crowded and uncomfortable. So if you are looking at comfort, there are many car rentals in Patna that provide A/C & Non-A/C cars on hire at reasonable rates. Recently, the government has appointment a private consultant to overhaul the public transport system. The government has also placed orders for over 50 low floor A/C and Non-A/C buses to ease congestion on city roads under JNNURM. This move will improve public transport facilities in and around Patna.

Patna is also an important transit point of Bihar for the tourists dropping in from the other states of India. Patna is well-connected by air, rail and road transport. Patna has its own airport known as Lok Nayak Jayaprakash Airport or Airport Patna. It is an national airport and it is connected to all major city of India via daily flights.

Patna is well served by a network of well maintained roads. Patna] is also connected through National Highway NH 19, NH 30-NH 31 & NH 83. Road distance from other major City. from Delhi - 1,015 km North-East (by road), from Mumbai - 1,802 km North-East (by road) and From Kolkata - 556 km North-West (by road).

Railways also served as means of public transportation in Patna. However Patna is a major junction in the rail map of India. The five main railway stations are Patna Junction, Rajendranagar Terminal, Gulzarbag Station, Danapur Junction and Patna Shahib Station.Among them Patna Shahib Station is oldest one. The main line of the Eastern Railway passes through the entire length of the district running parallel to the Ganga. There are three railway lines running across the district from north to south viz., the Patna - Gaya Branch line the Fatuha - Islampur Light Railway and the Bakhtiarpur-Rajgir Branch line. Except the Light Railway, the other two are branches of the Eastern Railway. With the opening of the famous Patna-Hajipur Bridge (Mahatma Gandhi Setu), the ferry service connencting the capital with the North-Eastern Railway System has Ceased to function.

Bihar is connected by National Waterways No. 1 which established in October 1986. This National Waterways has fixed terminals at Haldia, BISN (Kolkata), Pakur, Farrakka and **Patna**. This National Waterways has also floating terminals facilities at Haldia, Kolkata, Diamond Harbour, Katwa, Tribeni,Baharampur, Jangipur, Bhagalpur, Semaria, Doriganj, Ballia, Ghazipur, Varanasi, Chunar and Allahabad.

Places of Interest

Patna has a 3,000-year history. The rich culture and heritage of Bihar is evident from the innumerable ancient monuments that dot the region. Patna is home to many tourist attractions. About 2,500,000 (2.5 million) tourists visit Patna every year.

Kumhrar, Agam Kuan is the site of the ruins of the Ashokan Patliputra. Didarganj Yakshi is a fine example of Mauryan art and may be India's most famous piece of art. The famous Hanuman Mandir has the second highest budget in North India after the famous Vaishno Devi shrine. Patan Devi is the oldest temple and Patna's name is derived from Patan, the name of the Hindu goddess of this temple. Birla Mandir and Kali Mandir are other famous Hindu temples.

Takht Shri Harmandir Saheb is one of the Five Takhts of Sikhism and consecrates the birthplace of the tenth Guru of the Sikhs, Gobind Singh. There are five other Gurdwaras in Patna which are related to different Sikh gurus; these are Gurdwara Pahila Bara, Gurdwara Gobind Ghat, Gurdwara Guru ka Bagh, Gurdwara Bal Leela and Gurdwara Handi Sahib.

Phulwari Sharif, Maner Sharif, Sher Shah Suri Masjid, Pathar ki Masjid, Nagholkothi and Begu Hajjam's mosque are of great religious importance to Muslims and examples of unique Mughal architecture of the Middle Ages.

Padri Ki Haveli, High Court, Golghar and State Secretariat Building are examples of unique British architecture.

Darbhanga House, Sadaqat Ashram, Kargil Chowk and Saheed Smarak are monuments and Gandhi Maidan is located in the center of Patna. Mahatma Gandhi Setu is one of the longest single river bridges in the world. Patna Museum, Patna Planetarium, Sri Krishna Science Centre, Sanjay Gandhi Jaivik Udyan, Patna and Qila House (Jalan House) are the different types of infotainment complexes.

Patna is also a gateway to famous locations like Bodh Gaya, Gaya, Vaishali, Pawapuri, Nalanda, Rajgir, Maner, Vikramshila and Muzaffarpur.

Education

Patna has gradually emerged as one of the major center of learning in East India. Schools in Patna are either run by the state government or run by private trusts, organisations, missionaries. Government schools are affiliated with the Bihar School Examination Board and most private schools are affiliated with the ICSE and CBSE boards. Some of the prominent old schools Patna like *St Joseph's Convent High School, St Michael's Higher Secondary School, St. Xavier's High School*, were established by missionaries during the British Raj.

In the recent years, Patna has become a hub for imparting quality education in fields like Technology, Medicine, Management, Law and Fashion. In the past few years, many institutions of national repute have opened up in Patna tremendously increasing the opportunities in higher education in the state capital. Colleges such as *Indian Institute of Technology*

Patna, Birla Institute of Technology, Patna and National Institute of Technology, Patna are the prominent engineering college in Patna. Other colleges include the newly opened National Institute of Fashion Technology Patna and medical schools such as *Indira Gandhi Institute of Medical Sciences, Patna Medical College and Hospital and Nalanda Medical College and Hospital.*Anugrah Narayan College & B N College are among the best known colleges for commerce & humanities besides for a range of PG courses.

After coming to power, the Nitish Kumar led government opened the Chanakya National Law University, a national law university and a B-school that goes by the name of Chandragupt Institute of Management. Both these institutes have done tremendously well given that they are still in their infancy. They have been successful in attracting students from not just within Bihar but also students from far flung states. *A N Sinha Institute of Social Sciences, Rajendra Memorial Research Institute, Bihar Research Institute* are the research institutes in Patna. The Patna University, the first university in Bihar, was established in 1917, and was the 7th oldest University of the Indian subcontinent. . Patna also houses one of India's world-renowned libraries, the Khuda Baksh Oriental Library and the Sinha Library, which is one of the largest in the region.

Lately, Patna has also emerged as a major center for engineering and civil services coaching. All the major private IIT-JEE coaching institutes have opened up their branches here and this has helped in reducing the number of students who used to got to places like Kota & Delhi for engineering/ medical coaching.

Sports

As in the rest of India, cricket is the most popular sport in Patna. There are several cricket grounds (or maidans) located across the city, including the Moin-ul-Haq Stadium, which is second largest in eastern India, next only to "Eden Gardens" of Kolkata.. The stadium features a swimming pool and a cricket academy. This statdium has served as venue for two One day international matches and several national sport event. Patna Golf Club situated west of the Government House to the South Bihar Gymkhana Club. It is 165 acres Golf Field . and includes some very tough holes, this well-maintained course will prove interesting to amateur and pros alike. . Patna Indoor Stadium also known as Rainbow Field is indoor - outdoor sporting complex and will be renamed after Abhinav Bindra. Patna will be a team in Indian Premier League according to IPL expension plan 2012-13

●●

5

Maurya Empire

The **Maurya Empire** was a geographically extensive and powerful empire in **ancient India**, ruled by the **Mauryan dynasty** from 321 to 185 B.C.E.

Originating from the kingdom of Magadha in the Indo-Gangetic plains (modern Bihar, eastern Uttar Pradesh and Bengal) in the eastern side of the Indian subcontinent, the empire had its capital city at Pataliputra (modern Patna). The Empire was founded in 322 BC by Chandragupta Maurya, who had overthrown the Nanda Dynasty and rapidly expanded his power westwards across central and western India taking advantage of the disruptions of local powers in the wake of the withdrawal westward by Alexander the Great's Greek and Persian armies. By 320 BC the empire had fully occupied Northwestern India, defeating and conquering the satraps left by Alexander.

At its greatest extent, the Empire stretched to the north along the natural boundaries of the Himalayas, and to the east stretching into what is now Assam. To the west, it reached beyond modern Pakistan, annexing Balochistan and much of what is now Afghanistan, including the modern Herat and Kandahar provinces. The Empire was expanded into India's central and southern regions by the emperors Chandragupta and Bindusara, but it excluded a small portion of unexplored tribal and forested regions near Kalinga (modern Orissa).

The Mauryan Empire was one of the largest empires to rule the Indian subcontinent. Its decline began 60 years after

Ashoka's rule ended, and it dissolved in 185 BC with the foundation of the Sunga Dynasty in Magadha.

Under Chandragupta, the Mauryan Empire conquered the trans-Indus region, which was under Macedonian rule. Chandragupta then defeated the invasion led by Seleucus I, a Greek general from Alexander's army. Under Chandragupta and his successors, both internal and external trade, and agriculture and economic activities, all thrived and expanded across India thanks to the creation of a single and efficient system of finance, administration and security. After the Kalinga War, the Empire experienced half a century of peace and security under Ashoka: India was a prosperous and stable empire of great economic and military power whose political influence and trade extended across Western and Central Asia and Europe. Mauryan India also enjoyed an era of social harmony, religious transformation, and expansion of the sciences and of knowledge. Chandragupta Maurya's embrace of Jainism increased social and religious renewal and reform across his society, while Ashoka's embrace of Buddhism was the foundation of the reign of social and political peace and non-violence across all of India. Ashoka sponsored the spreading of Buddhist ideals into Sri Lanka, Southeast Asia, West Asia and Mediterranean Europe.

Chandragupta's minister Kautilya Chanakya wrote the *Arthashastra*, one of the greatest treatises on economics, politics, foreign affairs, administration, military arts, war, and religion ever produced in the India. Archaeologically, the period of Mauryan rule in South Asia falls into the era of Northern Black Polished Ware (NBPW). The *Arthashastra* and the Edicts of Ashoka are primary sources of written records of the Mauryan times. The Mauryan empire is considered one of the most significant periods in Indian history. The *Lion Capital of Asoka* at Sarnath, is the emblem of India.

Alexander set up a Greek-Macedonian garrison and satrapies (vassal states) in the trans-Indus region of modern day Pakistan, ruled previously by kings Ambhi of Taxila and Porus of Pauravas (modern day Jhelum).

Chanakya and Chandragupta Maurya

Following Alexander's advance into the Punjab, a brahmin named Chanakya (real name Vishnugupta, also known as Kautilya) traveled to Magadha, a kingdom that was large and militarily-powerful and feared by its neighbors, but was dismissed by its king Dhana, of the Nanda Dynasty. However, the prospect of battling Magadha deterred Alexander's troops from going further east: he returned to Babylon, and re-deployed most of his troops west of the Indus river. When Alexander died in Babylon, soon after in 323 BCE, his empire fragmented, and local kings declared their independence, leaving several smaller satraps in a disunited state. Chandragupta Maurya deposed Dhana. The Greek generals Eudemus, and Peithon, ruled until around 316 BCE, when Chandragupta Maurya (with the help of Chanakya, who was now his advisor) surprised and defeated the Macedonians and consolidated the region under the control of his new seat of power in Magadha.

Chandragupta Maurya's rise to power is shrouded in mystery and controversy. On the one hand, a number of ancient Indian accounts, such as the drama *Mudrarakshasa* (*Poem of Rakshasa - Rakshasa* was the prime minister of Magadha) by Visakhadatta, describe his royal ancestry and even link him with the Nanda family. A kshatriya tribe known as the Maurya's are referred to in the earliest Buddhist texts, Mahaparinibbana Sutta. However, any conclusions are hard to make without further historical evidence. Chandragupta first emerges in Greek accounts as "Sandrokottos". As a young man he is said to have met Alexander. He is also said to have met the Nanda king, angered him, and made a narrow escape. Chanakya's original intentions were to train a guerilla army under Chandragupta's command. The Mudrarakshasa of Visakhadutta as well as the Jaina work Parisishtaparvan talk of Chandragupta's alliance with the Himalayan king Parvatka, sometimes identified with Porus (Sir John Marshall "Taxila", p18, and al.) This Himalayan alliance gave Chandragupta a composite and powerful army made up of Yavanas (Greeks), Kambojas, Shakas (Scythians), Kiratas (Nepalese), Parasikas (Persians) and Bahlikas (Bactrians).

With the help of these frontier martial tribes from Central Asia, Chandragupta was able to defeat the Nanda/Nandin rulers of Magadha and found the powerful Maurya empire in northern India.

Conquest of Magadha

Chanakya encouraged Chandragupta Maurya and his army to take over the throne of Magadha. Using his intelligence network, Chandragupta gathered many young men from across Magadha and other provinces, men upset over the corrupt and oppressive rule of king Dhana, plus resources necessary for his army to fight a long series of battles. These men included the former general of Taxila, other accomplished students of Chanakya, the representative of King Porus of Kakayee, his son Malayketu, and the rulers of small states.

Preparing to invade Pataliputra, Maurya hatched a plan. A battle was announced and the Magadhan army was drawn from the city to a distant battlefield to engage Maurya's forces. Maurya's general and spies meanwhile bribed the corrupt general of Nanda. He also managed to create an atmosphere of civil war in the kingdom, which culminated in the death of the heir to the throne. Chanakya managed to win over popular sentiment. Ultimately Nanda resigned, handing power to Chandragupta, and went into exile and was never heard of again. Chanakya contacted the prime minister, Rakshasas, and made him understand that his loyalty was to Magadha, not to the Magadha dynasty, insisting that he continue in office. Chanakya also reiterated that choosing to resist would start a war that would severely affect Magadha and destroy the city. Rakshasa accepted Chanakya's reasoning, and Chandragupta Maurya was legitimately installed as the new King of Magadha. Rakshasa became Chandragupta's chief advisor, and Chanakya assumed the position of an elder statesman.

Chandragupta Maurya

Approximate Dates of Mauryan Dynasty

Emperor	*Reign start*	*Reign end*
Chandragupta Maurya	322 BCE	298 BCE
Bindusara	297 BCE	272 BCE
Asoka The Great	273 BCE	232 BCE
Dasaratha	232 BCE	224 BCE
Samprati	224 BCE	215 BCE
Salisuka	215 BCE	202 BCE
Devavarman	202 BCE	195 BCE
Satadhanvan	195 BCE	187 BCE
Brihadratha	187 BCE	185 BCE

Chandragupta was again in conflict with the Greeks when Seleucus I, ruler of the Seleucid Empire, tried to reconquer the northwestern parts of India, during a campaign in 305 BCE, but failed. The two rulers finally concluded a peace treaty: a marital treaty (Epigamia) was concluded, implying either a marital alliance between the two dynastic lines or a recognition of marriage between Greeks and Indians, Chandragupta received the satrapies of Paropamisade (Kamboja and Gandhara), Arachosia (Kandhahar) and Gedrosia (Balochistan), and Seleucus I received 500 war elephants that were to have a decisive role in his victory against western Hellenistic kings at the Battle of Ipsus in 301 BCE. Diplomatic relations were established and several Greeks, such as the historian Megasthenes, Deimakos and Dionysius resided at the Mauryan court.

Chandragupta established a strong centralized state with a complex administration at Pataliputra, which, according to Megasthenes, was *"surrounded by a wooden wall pierced by 64 gates and 570 towers— (and) rivaled the splendors of contemporaneous Persian sites such as Susa and Ecbatana."* Chandragupta's son Bindusara extended the rule of the Mauryan empire towards southern India. He also had a Greek ambassador at his court, named Deimachus (Strabo 1–70).

Megasthenes describes a disciplined multitude under Chandragupta, who live simply, honestly, and do not know writing:

> " The Indians all live frugally, especially when in camp. They dislike a great undisciplined multitude, and consequently they observe good order. Theft is of very rare occurrence. Megasthenes says that those who were in the camp of Sandrakottos, wherein lay 400,000 men, found that the thefts reported on any one day did not exceed the value of two hundred drachmae, and this among a people who have no written laws, but are ignorant of writing, and must therefore in all the business of life trust to memory. They live, nevertheless, happily enough, being simple in their manners and frugal. They never drink wine except at sacrifices. Their beverage is a liquor composed from rice instead of barley, and their food is principally a rice-pottage." Strabo XV. i. 53-56, quoting Megasthenes

Bindusara

Ashoka the Great

Chandragupta's grandson was Ashokavardhan Maurya, better known as Ashoka the Great (ruled 273- 232 BCE).

As a young prince, Ashoka was a brilliant commander who crushed revolts in Ujjain and Taxila. As monarch he was ambitious and aggressive, re-asserting the Empire's superiority in southern and western India. But it was his conquest of Kalinga which proved to be the pivotal event of his life. Although Ashoka's army succeeded in overwhelming Kalinga forces of royal soldiers and civilian units, an estimated 100,000 soldiers and civilians were killed in the furious warfare, including over 10,000 of Ashoka's own men. Hundreds of thousands of people were adversely affected by the destruction and fallout of war. When he personally witnessed the devastation, Ashoka began feeling remorse, and he cried 'what have I done?'. Although the annexation of Kalinga was completed, Ashoka embraced the teachings of Gautama Buddha, and renounced war and violence. For a monarch in ancient times, this was an historic feat.

Ashoka implemented principles of *ahimsa* by banning hunting and violent sports activity and ending indentured and forced labor (many thousands of people in war-ravaged Kalinga had been forced into hard labor and servitude). While he maintained a large and powerful army, to keep the peace and maintain authority, Ashoka expanded friendly relations with states across Asia and Europe, and he sponsored Buddhist missions. He undertook a massive public works building campaign across the country. Over 40 years of peace, harmony and prosperity made Ashoka one of the most successful and famous monarchs in Indian history. He remains an idealized figure of inspiration in modern India.

The Edicts of Ashoka, set in stone, are found throughout the Subcontinent. Ranging from as far west as Afghanistan and as far south as Andhra (Nellore District), Ashoka's edicts state his policies and accomplishments. Although predominantly written in Prakrit, two of them were written in Greek, and one in both Greek and Aramaic. Ashoka's edicts refer to the Greeks, Kambojas, and Gandharas as peoples forming a frontier region of his empire. They also attest to Ashoka's having sent envoys to the Greek rulers in the West as far as the Mediterranean. The edicts precisely name each of the rulers of the Hellenic world at the time such as *Amtiyoko* (Antiochus), *Tulamaya* (Ptolemy), *Amtikini* (Antigonos), *Maka* (Magas) and *Alikasudaro* (Alexander) as recipients of Ashoka's proselytism. The Edicts also accurately locate their territory "600 yojanas away" (a yojanas being about 7 miles), corresponding to the distance between the center of India and Greece (roughly 4,000 miles).

Administration

The Empire was divided into four provinces, which one of the four, look like a giant crescents. with the imperial capital at Pataliputra. From Ashokan edicts, the names of the four provincial capitals are Tosali (in the east), Ujjain in the west, Suvarnagiri (in the south), and Taxila (in the north). The head of the provincial administration was the *Kumara* (royal prince), who governed the provinces as king's representative. The *kumara* was assisted by Mahamatyas and council of ministers. This organizational structure was reflected at the imperial level with the Emperor and his *Mantriparishad* (Council of Ministers).

Historians theorize that the organization of the Empire was in line with the extensive bureaucracy described by Kautilya in the Arthashastra: a sophisticated civil service governed everything from municipal hygiene to international trade. The expansion and defense of the empire was made possible by what appears to have been the largest standing army of its time. According to Megasthenes, the empire wielded a military of 600,000 infantry, 30,000 cavalry, and 9,000 war elephants. A vast espionage system collected intelligence for both internal and external security purposes. Having renounced offensive warfare and expansionism, Ashoka nevertheless continued to maintain this large army, to protect the Empire and instill stability and peace across West and South Asia.

Economy

For the first time in South Asia, political unity and military security allowed for a common economic system and enhanced trade and commerce, with increased agricultural productivity. The previous situation involving hundreds of kingdoms, many small armies, powerful regional chieftains, and internecine warfare, gave way to a disciplined central authority. Farmers were freed of tax and crop collection burdens from regional kings, paying instead to a nationally-administered and strict-but-fair system of taxation as advised by the principles in the *Arthashastra*. Chandragupta Maurya established a single currency across India, and a network of regional governors and administrators and a civil service provided justice and security for merchants, farmers and traders. The Mauryan army wiped out many gangs of bandits, regional private armies, and powerful chieftains who sought to impose their own supremacy in small areas. Although regimental in revenue collection, Maurya also sponsored many public works and waterways to enhance productivity, while internal trade in India expanded greatly due to newfound political unity and internal peace.

Under the Indo-Greek friendship treaty, and during Ashoka's reign, an international network of trade expanded. The Khyber Pass, on the modern boundary of Pakistan and Afghanistan, became a strategically-important port of trade and intercourse with the outside world. Greek states and Hellenic kingdoms in West Asia became important trade partners of India. Trade also extended through the Malay peninsula into Southeast Asia. India's exports included silk goods and textiles, spices and exotic foods. The Empire was enriched further with an exchange of scientific knowledge and technology with Europe and West Asia. Ashoka also sponsored the construction of thousands of roads, waterways, canals, hospitals, rest-houses and other public works. The easing of many overly-rigorous administrative practices, including those regarding taxation and crop collection, helped increase productivity and economic activity across the Empire.

In many ways, the economic situation in the Maurya Empire is comparable to the Roman Empire several centuries later, which both had extensive trade connections and both had organizations similar to corporations. While Rome had organizational entities which were largely used for public state-driven projects, Mauryan India had numerous private commercial entities which existed purely for private commerce. This was due to the Mauryas having to contend with pre-existing private commercial entities hence they were more concerned about keeping the support of these pre-existing organizations, while the Romans did not have such pre-existing entities to contend with hence they were able to prevent such entities from developing. (See also Economic history of India.)

RELIGION

Jainism

Emperor Chandragupta Maurya became the first major Indian monarch to initiate a religious transformation at the highest level when he embraced Jainism, a religious movement resented by orthodox Hindu priests who usually attended the imperial court. At an older age, Chandragupta renounced his throne and material possessions to join a wandering group of Jain monks. Chandragupta was a disciple of Acharya Bhadrabahu. It is said that in his last days, he observed the rigorous but self purifying Jain ritual of santhara i.e. fast unto death, at Shravana Belagola in Karnataka. However, his successor, Emperor Bindusara, was an Ajivika and distanced himself from Jain and Buddhist movements. Samprati, the grandson of Ashoka also embraced Jainism. Samrat Samprati was influenced by the teachings of Jain monk Arya Suhasti Suri and he is known to have built 125,000 Jain Temples across India. Some of them are still found in towns of Ahmedabad, Viramgam, Ujjain & Palitana. It is also said that just like Ashoka, Samprati sent messengers & preachers to Greece, Persia & middle-east for the spread of Jainism. But to date no research has been done in this area. Thus, Jainism became a vital force under the Mauryan Rule. Chandragupta & Samprati are credited for the spread of Jainism in Southern India. Lakhs of Jain Temples & Jain Stupas were erected during their reign. But due to lack of royal patronage & its strict principles, along with the rise of Shankaracharya & Ramanujacharya, Jainism, once the major religion of southern India, began to decline.

Buddhism

But when Ashoka embraced Buddhism, following the Kalinga War, he renounced expansionism and aggression, and the harsher injunctions of the *Arthashastra* on the use of force, intensive policing, and ruthless measures for tax collection and against rebels. Ashoka sent a mission led by his son Mahinda and daughter Sanghamitta to Sri Lanka, whose king Tissa was so charmed with Buddhist ideals that he adopted them himself and made Buddhism the state religion. Ashoka sent many Buddhist missions to West Asia, Greece and South East Asia, and commissioned the construction of monasteries, schools and publication of Buddhist literature across the empire. He is believed to have built as many as 84,000 stupas across India i.e. Sanchi and Mahabodhi Temple, and he increased the popularity of Buddhism in Afghanistan,Thailand and north Asian countries. Ashoka helped convene the Third Buddhist Council of India and South Asia's Buddhist orders, near his capital, a council that undertook much work of reform and expansion of the Buddhist religion.

Brahmanism

While himself a Buddhist, Ashoka retained the membership of Brahmana priests and ministers in his court, and he maintained religious freedom and tolerance although the Buddhist faith grew in popularity with his patronage. Brahmanic society began embracing the philosophy of *ahimsa*, and given the increased prosperity and improved law enforcement, crime and internal conflicts reduced dramatically. Also greatly discouraged was the caste system and orthodox discrimination, as Brahmanism began to absorb the ideals and values of Jain and Buddhist teachings. Social freedom began expanding in an age of peace and prosperity.

Architectural Remains

Architectural remains of the Maurya period are rather few. Remains of a hypostyle building with about 80 columns of a height of about 10 meters have been found in Kumhrar, 5 km from Patna Railway station, and is one of the very few site that has been connected to the rule of the Mauryas in that city. The style is rather reminiscent of Persian Achaemenid architecture.

The grottoes of Barabar Caves, are another example of Mauryan architecture, especially the decorated front of the Lomas Rishi grotto. These were offered by the Mauryas to the Buddhist sect of the Ajivikas.

The most widespread example of Maurya architecture are the Pillars of Ashoka, often exquisitely decorated, with more than 40 spread throughout the sub-continent.

Natural History in the Times of the Mauryas

The protection of animals in India became serious business by the time of the Maurya dynasty; being the first empire to provide a unified political entity in India, the attitude of the Mauryas towards forests, its denizens and fauna in general is of interest.

The Mauryas firstly looked at forests as a resource. For them, the most important forest product was the elephant. Military might in those times depended not only upon horses and men but also battle-elephants; these played a role in the defeat of Seleucus, Alexander's governor of the Punjab. The Mauryas sought to preserve supplies of elephants since it was cheaper and took less time to catch, tame and train wild elephants than to raise them. Kautilya's *Arthashastra* contains not only maxims on ancient statecraft, but also unambiguously specifies the responsibilities of officials such as the *Protector of the Elephant Forests*:

> On the border of the forest, he should establish a forest for elephants guarded by foresters. The Superintendent should with the help of guards...protect the elephants whether along on the mountain, along a river, along lakes or in marshy tracts...They should kill anyone slaying an elephant.
>
> —Arthashastra

The Mauryas also designated separate forests to protect supplies of timber, as well as lions and tigers, for skins. Elsewhere the *Protector of Animals* also worked to eliminate thieves, tigers and other predators to render the woods safe for grazing cattle.

The Mauryas valued certain forest tracts in strategic or economic terms and instituted curbs and control measures over them. They regarded all forest tribes with distrust and controlled them with bribery and political subjugation. They employed some of them, the food-gatherers or *aranyaca* to guard borders and trap animals. The sometimes tense and conflict-ridden relationship nevertheless enabled the Mauryas to guard their vast empire.

When Ashoka embraced Buddhism in the latter part of his reign, he brought about significant changes in his style of governance, which included providing protection to fauna, and even relinquished the royal hunt. He was the first ruler in history to advocate conservation measures for wildlife and even had rules inscribed in stone edicts. The edicts proclaim that many followed the king's example in giving up the slaughter of animals; one of them proudly states:

Our king killed very few animals.

—Edict on Fifth Pillar

However, the edicts of Ashoka reflect more the desire of rulers than actual events; the mention of a 100 'panas' (coins) fine for poaching deer in royal hunting preserves shows that rule-breakers did exist. The legal restrictions conflicted with the practices freely exercised by the common people in hunting, felling, fishing and setting fires in forests.

CONTACTS WITH THE HELLENISTIC WORLD

Foundation of the Empire

Relations with the Hellenistic world may have started from the very beginning of the Maurya Empire. Plutarch reports that Chandragupta Maurya met with Alexander the Great, probably around Taxila in the northwest:

"Sandrocottus, when he was a stripling, saw Alexander himself, and we are told that he often said in later times that Alexander narrowly missed making himself master of the country, since its king was hated and despised on account of his baseness and low birth". Plutarch 62-3

Reconquest of the Northwest (c. 310 BCE)

Chandragupta ultimately occupied Northwestern India, in the territories formerly ruled by the Greeks, where he fought the satraps (described as "Prefects" in Western sources) left in place after Alexander (Justin), among whom may have been Eudemus, ruler in the western Punjab until his departure in 317 BCE or Peithon, son of Agenor, ruler of the Greek colonies along the Indus until his departure for Babylon in 316 BCE.

> "India, after the death of Alexander, had assassinated his prefects, as if shaking the burden of servitude. The author of this liberation was Sandracottos, but he had transformed liberation in servitude after victory, since, after taking the throne, he himself oppressed the very people he has liberated from foreign domination" Justin XV.4.12-13

> "Later, as he was preparing war against the prefects of Alexander, a huge wild elephant went to him and took him on his back as if tame, and he became a remarkable fighter and war leader. Having thus acquired royal power, Sandracottos possessed India at the time Seleucos was preparing future glory." Justin XV.4.19

Conflict and Alliance with Seleucus (305 BCE)

Seleucus I Nicator, the Macedonian satrap of the Asian portion of Alexander's former empire, conquered and put under his own authority eastern territories as far as Bactria and the Indus (Appian, History of Rome, The Syrian Wars 55), until in 305 BCE he entered in a confrontation with Chandragupta:

> "Always lying in wait for the neighboring nations, strong in arms and persuasive in council, he [Seleucus] acquired Mesopotamia, Armenia, 'Seleucid' Cappadocia, Persis, Parthia, Bactria, Arabia, Tapouria, Sogdia, Arachosia, Hyrcania, and other adjacent peoples that had been subdued by Alexander, as far as the river Indus, so that the boundaries of his empire were the most extensive in Asia after that of Alexander. The whole region from Phrygia to the Indus was subject to Seleucus". Appian, History of Rome, The Syrian Wars 55

Though no accounts of the conflict remain, it is clear that Seleucus fared poorly against the Indian Emperor as he failed in conquering any territory, and in fact, was forced to surrender much that was already his. Regardless, Seleucus and Chandragupta ultimately reached a settlement and through a treaty sealed in 305 BCE, Seleucus, according to Strabo, ceded a number of territories to Chandragupta, including southern Afghanistan and parts of Persia.

Accordingly, Seleucus obtained five hundred war elephants, a military asset which would play a decisive role at the Battle of Ipsus in 301 BCE.

Marital Alliance

It is generally thought that Chandragupta married Seleucus's daughter, or a Greek Macedonian princess, a gift from Seleucus to formalize an alliance. In a return gesture, Chandragupta sent 500 war-elephants, a military asset which would play a decisive role at the Battle of Ipsus in 302 BC. In addition to this treaty, Seleucus dispatched an ambassador, Megasthenes, to Chandragupta, and later Deimakos to his son Bindusara, at the Mauryan court at Pataliputra (modern Patna in Bihar state). Later Ptolemy II Philadelphus, the ruler of Ptolemaic Egypt and contemporary of Ashoka the Great, is also recorded by Pliny the Elder as having sent an ambassador named Dionysius to the Mauryan court..

Mainstream scholarship asserts that Chandragupta received vast territory west of the Indus, including the Hindu Kush, modern day Afghanistan, and the Balochistan province of Pakistan. Archaeologically, concrete indications of Mauryan rule, such as the inscriptions of the Edicts of Ashoka, are known as far as Kandhahar in southern Afghanistan.

> "He (Seleucus) crossed the Indus and waged war with Sandrocottus [Maurya], king of the Indians, who dwelt on the banks of that stream, until they came to an

understanding with each other and contracted a marriage relationship."

The treaty on "Epigamia" implies lawful marriage between Greeks and Indians was recognized at the State level, although it is unclear whether it occurred among dynastic rulers or common people, or both. .

Exchange of Ambassadors

Seleucus dispatched an ambassador, Megasthenes, to Chandragupta, and later Deimakos to his son Bindusara, at the Mauryan court at Pataliputra (Modern Patna in Bihar state). Later Ptolemy II Philadelphus, the ruler of Ptolemaic Egypt and contemporary of Ashoka, is also recorded by Pliny the Elder as having sent an ambassador named Dionysius to the Mauryan court.

Exchange of Presents

Classical sources have also recorded that following their treaty, Chandragupta and Seleucus exchanged presents, such as when Chandragupta sent various aphrodisiacs to Seleucus:

> "And Theophrastus says that some contrivances are of wondrous efficacy in such matters [as to make people more amorous]. And Phylarchus confirms him, by reference to some of the presents which Sandrakottus, the king of the Indians, sent to Seleucus; which were to act like charms in producing a wonderful degree of affection, while some, on the contrary, were to banish love" Athenaeus of Naucratis, "The deipnosophists" Book I, chapter 32

His son Bindusara 'Amitraghata' (Slayer of Enemies) also is recorded in Classical sources as having exchanged present with Antiochus I:

> "But dried figs were so very much sought after by all men (for really, as Aristophanes says, "There's really

nothing nicer than dried figs"), that even Amitrochates, the king of the Indians, wrote to Antiochus, entreating him (it is Hegesander who tells this story) to buy and send him some sweet wine, and some dried figs, and a sophist; and that Antiochus wrote to him in answer, "The dry figs and the sweet wine we will send you; but it is not lawful for a sophist to be sold in Greece" Athenaeus, "Deipnosophistae" XIV.67

Greek Populations in India

Greek populations apparently remained in the northwest of the Indian subcontinent under Ashoka's rule. In his Edicts of Ashoka, set in stone, some of them written in Greek, Ashoka describes that Greek populations within his realm converted to Buddhism:

"Here in the king's domain among the Greeks, the Kambojas, the Nabhakas, the Nabhapamkits, the Bhojas, the Pitinikas, the Andhras and the Palidas, everywhere people are following Beloved-of-the-Gods' instructions in Dharma". Rock Edict Nb13 (S. Dhammika).

Fragments of Edict 13 have been found in Greek, and a full Edict, written in both Greek and Aramaic has been discovered in Kandahar. It is said to be written in excellent Classical Greek, using sophisticated philosophical terms. In this Edict, Ashoka uses the word Eusebeia ("Piety") as the Greek translation for the ubiquitous "Dharma" of his other Edicts written in Prakrit:

"Ten years (of reign) having been completed, King Piodasses (Ashoka) made known (the doctrine of) Piety (*åPóÝâåéá*, Eusebeia) to men; and from this moment he has made men more pious, and everything thrives throughout the whole world. And the king abstains from (killing) living beings, and other men and those who (are) huntsmen and fishermen of the king have desisted from hunting. And if some (were) intemperate, they have ceased from their intemperance as was in their power; and obedient to their father and mother and to the elders, in opposition to the past also in the future, by so acting on every occasion, they will live better and more happily". (Trans. by G.P. Carratelli)

Buddhist Missions to the West (c.250 BCE)

Also, in the Edicts of Ashoka, Ashoka mentions the Hellenistic kings of the period as a recipient of his Buddhist proselytism, although no Western historical record of this event remain:

> "The conquest by Dharma has been won here, on the borders, and even six hundred yojanas (5,400-9,600 km) away, where the Greek king Antiochos rules, beyond there where the four kings named Ptolemy, Antigonos, Magas and Alexander rule, likewise in the south among the Cholas, the Pandyas, and as far as Tamraparni (Sri Lanka)." (Edicts of Ashoka, 13th Rock Edict, S. Dhammika).

Ashoka also claims that he encouraged the development of herbal medicine, for men and animals, in their territories:

> "Everywhere within Beloved-of-the-Gods, King Piyadasi's [Ashoka's] domain, and among the people beyond the borders, the Cholas, the Pandyas, the Satiyaputras, the Keralaputras, as far as Tamraparni and where the Greek king Antiochos rules, and among the kings who are neighbors of Antiochos, everywhere has Beloved-of-the-Gods, King Piyadasi, made provision for two types of medical treatment: medical treatment for humans and medical treatment for animals. Wherever medical herbs suitable for humans or animals are not available, I have had them imported and grown. Wherever medical roots or fruits are not available I have

had them imported and grown. Along roads I have had wells dug and trees planted for the benefit of humans and animals". 2nd Rock Edict

The Greeks in India even seem to have played an active role in the propagation of Buddhism, as some of the emissaries of Ashoka, such as Dharmaraksita, are described in Pali sources as leading Greek ("Yona") Buddhist monks, active in Buddhist proselytism (the Mahavamsa, XII).

Subhagsena and Antiochos III (206 BCE)

Sophagasenus was an Indian Mauryan ruler of the 3rd century BCE, described in ancient Greek sources, and named Subhagsena or Subhashsena in Prakrit. His name is mentioned in the list of Mauryan princes, and also in the list of the Yadava dynasty, as a descendant of Pradyumna. He may have been a grandson of Ashoka, or Kunala, the son of Ashoka. He ruled an area south of the Hindu Kush, possibly in Gandhara. Antiochos III, the Seleucid king, after having made peace with Euthydemus in Bactria, went to India in 206 BC and is said to have renewed his friendship with the Indian king there:

> "He (Antiochus) crossed the Caucasus and descended into India; renewed his friendship with Sophagasenus the king of the Indians; received more elephants, until he had a hundred and fifty altogether; and having once more provisioned his troops, set out again personally with his army: leaving Androsthenes of Cyzicus the duty of taking home the treasure which this king had agreed to hand over to him". Polybius 11.39

Decline

Ashoka was followed for 50 years by a succession of weaker kings. Brhadrata, the last ruler of the Mauryan dynasty, held territories that had shrunk considerably from the time of emperor Ashoka, although he still upheld the Buddhist faith.

Sunga Coup (185 BCE)

Brihadrata was assassinated in 185 BCE during a military parade, by the commander-in-chief of his guard, the Brahmin general Pusyamitra Sunga, who then took over the throne and established the Sunga dynasty. Buddhist records such as the Asokavadana write that the assassination of Brhadrata and the rise of the Sunga empire led to a wave of persecution for Buddhists, and a resurgence of Hinduism. According to Sir John Marshall, Pusyamitra may have been the main author of the persecutions, although later Sunga kings seem to have been more supportive of Buddhism. Other historians, such as Etienne Lamotte and Romila Thapar, among others, have argued that archaeological evidence in favor of the allegations of persecution of Buddhists are lacking, and that the extent and magnitude of the atrocities have been exaggerated.

Establishment of the Indo-Greek Kingdom (180 BCE)

The fall of the Mauryas left the Khyber Pass unguarded, and a wave of foreign invasion followed. The Greco-Bactrian king, Demetrius, capitalized on the break-up, and he conquered southern Afghanistan and Pakistan around 180 BC, forming the Indo-Greek Kingdom. The Indo-Greeks would maintain holdings on the trans-Indus region, and make forays into central India, for about a century. Under them, Buddhism flourished, and one of their kings Menander became a famous figure of Buddhism, he was to establish a new capital of Sagala, the modern city of Sialkot. However, the extent of their domains and the lengths of their rule are subject to much debate. Numismatic evidence indicates that they retained holdings in the subcontinent right up to the birth of Christ. Although the extent of their successes against indigenous powers such as the Sungas, Satavahanas, and Kalingas are unclear, what is clear is that Scythian tribes, renamed Indo-Scythians, brought about the demise of the Indo-Greeks from around 70 BCE and retained lands in the trans-Indus, the region of Mathura, and Gujarat.

SAMUDRAGUPTA

Samudragupta, ruler of the Gupta Empire (c.AD 335 – 380), and successor to Chandragupta I, is considered to be one of the greatest military geniuses in Indian history, and sometimes also called the 'Napoleon of India' . His name is taken to be a title acquired by his conquests (*Samudra* referring to the 'oceans'). Samudragupta is believed to have been his father's chosen successor even though he had several older brothers. Therefore, some believe that after the death of Chandragupta I, there was a struggle for succession in which Samudragupta prevailed.

The main source of Samudragupta's history is an inscription engraved on one of the stone pillars set up by him in Allahabad. In this inscription Samudragupta details his conquests. This inscription is also important because of the political geography of India that it indicates by naming the different kings and peoples who populated India in the first half of the fourth century AD. The inscription or more aptly the eulogy to the Great Gupta's martial exploits states that its author is Harishena, who was an important poet of Samudragupta's court.

The beginning of Samudragupta's reign was marked by the defeat of his immediate neighbours, Achyuta, ruler of Ahichchhatra, and Nagasena. Following this Samudragupta began a campaign against the kingdoms to the south. This southern campaign took him south along the Bay of Bengal. He passed through the forest tracts of Madhya Pradesh, crossed the Orissa coast, marched through Ganjam, Vishakapatnam, Godavari, Krishna and Nellore districts and may have reached as far as Kancheepuram. Here however he did not attempt to maintain direct control. After capturing his enemies he reinstated them as tributary kings. This act prevented the Gupta Empire from attaining the almost immediate demise of the Maurya Empire of Ashoka and is a testament to his abilities as a statesman. The details of Samudragupta's campaigns are too numerous to recount here. These can be found in the first reference below. However it is clear that he possessed a powerful navy in addition to his army. In addition to tributary kingdoms, many other rulers of foreign states like the Saka and Kushana kings accepted the suzerainty of Samudragupta and offered him their services.

Much is known about Samudragupta through coins issued by him. These were of eight different types and all made of pure gold. His conquests brought him the gold and also the coin-making expertise from his acquaintance with the Kushana. Samudragupta is also known to have been a man of culture. He was a patron of learning, a celebrated poet and a musician. Several coins depict him playing on the Indian lyre or Veena. He gathered a galaxy of poets and scholars and took effective actions to foster and propagate religious, artistic and literary aspects of Indian culture. Though he favoured the Hindu religion like the other Gupta kings, he was reputed to possess a tolerant spirit vis-a-vis other religions. A clear illustration of this is the permission granted by him to the king of Ceylon to build a monastery for Buddhist pilgrims in Bodh Gaya.

KUMARAGUPTA I

Kumaragupta I (Mahendraditya) was ruler of the Gupta Empire from 415-455 CE. Like his father and predecessor, Chandragupta II, Kumaragupta was an able ruler. He retained, intact, the vast empire, which extended from North Bengal to Kathiawar and from the Himalayas to the Narmada. He ruled efficiently for nearly forty years. However, the last days of his reign were not good. The Gupta empire was threatened by the invasions of Pushyamitras. The Pushyamitras were a tribe of foreigners who were settled in Central India. However,

Kumaragupta was successful in defeating the invaders and performed Ashvamedha Yajna (horse sacrifice) to celebrate his victory. He issued new coins with images of Lord Kartikeya.

Iron Pillar

Kumaragupta erected an iron pilar, today visible at the Qutb complex. The iron pillar is one of the world's foremost metallurgical curiosities. The pillar was originally located in the temple of Muttra, with the idol of Garuda at the top. It is the only piece of the Hindu temple remaining, which stood there before being destroyed by Qutb-ud-din Aybak to build the Qutub Minar and Quwwat-ul-Islam mosque. Qutub built around it when he constructed the mosque.

Made up of 98% wrought iron of impure quality, it is 23 feet, 8 inches high and has a diameter of 16 inches. The pillar is a testament to the high level of skill achieved by ancient Indian iron smiths in the extraction and processing of iron. It has attracted the attention of archaeologists and metallurgists as it has withstood corrosion for the last 1600 years, despite harsh weather.

Succession after Kumaragupta I

Rev: Garuda bird, circled by legend in Brahmi "*Parama-bhagavata rajahiraja Sri Kumaragupta Mahendraditya*" ("Most devout King of Kings Kumaragupta Mahendraditya").

The modern scholars are divided in opinion regarding the immediate successor of Kumaragupta I. While some scholars opine that he was succeeded by his son Skandagupta, other scholars contend that he was succeeded by his other son, Purugupta. Some scholars even think that both Skandagupta and Purugupta are the same person.

The Junagadh rock inscription of Skandagupta mentions:

> ...whom the goddess of fortune and splendour of her own accord selected as her husband, having in succession

(and) with judgment skillfully taken into consideration and thought over all the causes of virtues and faults, (and) having discarded all (the other) sons of kings (as not coming up to her standard).

The full significance of this passage is obscure. It is, however, certain that the superior ability and prowess of Skandagupta in a time of crisis led to his choice as ruler in preference to other possible claimants after the death of Kumara Gupta I and proud of his successes against the barbarians, Skandagupta assumed the title of Vikramaditya.

The continuous attacks of the Huns weakened the Gupta empire. Skandagupta died in 467 CE. After his death, the Gupta empire began to decline.

Dated Inscriptions

An inscription on a figure of a yaksha from Mathura in the reign of Kumaragupta has been dated to 432 CE, and a pedestal (with no king's name on it - but presumably from Kumaragupta's reign - has been dated to 442 CE. The Bilsad inscription is the oldest record of his reign and it dates to Gupta year 96, which corresponds to 415 CE.

Decline of the Gupta Empire

Inscriptions prove that the Gupta sovereignty was acknowledged in the Jabbalpur region in the Narmada valley as late as AD 528, and in North Bengal till AD 543-544. Kumaragupta II is believed to have been ruling in AD 473-474, Buddhagupta from AD 476-495, Vainyagupta in AD 508 and Bhanugupta in AD 510-511. The Gupta empire became to disintegrate and till the middle of the sixth century AD, they had merely became petty chiefs.

The last known date of his reign occurs on an inscription on one of his silver coins, corresponding to 445 CE.

SKANDAGUPTA

Skandagupta (died 467) was a ruler of northern India under the Gupta dynasty. He is generally considered the last of the great Gupta Emperors. He faced some of the greatest challenges in the annals of the empire having to contend with the Pushyamitras and the Hunas. He defeated the Pushyamitras, a tribe who were settled in central india but then rebelled. He was also faced with invading Indo-Hephthalites or "White Huns", known in India as *Hunas,* from the northwest. Skandagupta had warred against the Huns during the reign of his father, and was celebrated throughout the empire as a great warrior. He crushed the Huna invasion in 455, and managed to keep them at bay; however, the expense of the wars drained the empire's resources and contributed to its decline. Skandagupta died in 467 and was succeeded by Buddhagupta, whose kindom in the plains of Northern India was continuously attacked by the Huns. Skandagupta's name appear in Javanese text `Tantrikamandaka', and Chinese writer, Wang-hiuen-tse refers that an ambassador was sent to his court by King Meghvarma of Sri Lanka, who had asked his permission to build a Buddhist monastery at Bodh Gaya for the monks traveling from Sri Lanka. But the most detailed and authentic record of his reign is preserved in the rock pillar of the Allahabad, composed by Harisena.

RAMAGUPTA

Ramagupta was a legendary king of India, a ruler of the Gupta empire and the elder son and successor of Samudragupta. The actual existence of this king is in some dispute.

According to legend, Ramagupta decided to expand his kingdom by attacking the Sakas in Gujarat. The campaign soon took a turn for the worse and the Gupta army was trapped. The Saka king, Rudrasimha III, demanded that

Ramagupta hand over his wife Dhruvswamini in exchange for peace. The weak king was inclined to accept these terms, to the outrage of his wife and his brother Chandragupta. Using subterfuge, Chandragupta went to the Saka camp, killed the Saka king and won the victory and also the esteem of the people and the queen. A short while later, Ramagupta was deposed and killed by his brother, who became Chandragupta II. Chandragupta II also married his erstwhile sister-in-law, Dhruvswamini.

This tale has parallels to the story of Rani Padmini of Chittor and the subterfuge she used to free her husband. Dhruvadevi was the chief queen of Chandragupta II and the mother of his heir Kumara Gupta I. Chandragupta II also claimed the conquest of the Saka kingdom. What part the shadowy figure of Ramagupta played in these stories is unclear.

A few Jain tirthankara idols have been found at Durjanpur near Vidisha that mention Ramagupta as the reigning king.

Devi Chandraguptam

In the play Devi Chandraguptam by Vishakhadatta, Ramagupta is portrayed as a weak and impotent king, afraid and incapable of warfare. The play holds that Ramagupta usurped the right to the throne of his younger brother ChandraguptaII and also married his betrothed Dhruvswamini by force.

●●

6
Han Dynasty

The **Han Dynasty** was the second imperial dynasty of China, preceded by the Qin Dynasty (221–206 BCE) and succeeded by the Three Kingdoms (220–265 CE). It was founded by the peasant rebel leader Liu Bang, known posthumously as Emperor Gaozu of Han. It was briefly interrupted by the Xin Dynasty (9–23 CE) of the former regent Wang Mang. This interregnum separates the Han into two periods: the Western Han (206 BCE–9 CE) and Eastern Han (25–220 CE). Spanning over four centuries, the period of the Han Dynasty is considered a golden age in Chinese history. To this day, China's majority ethnic group refers to itself as the "Han people".

The Han Empire was divided into areas directly controlled by the central government, known as commanderies, and a number of semi-autonomous kingdoms. These kingdoms gradually lost all vestiges of their independence, particularly following the Rebellion of the Seven States. The Xiongnu, a nomadic confederation of Central Asian tribes which dominated the eastern Eurasian Steppe, defeated the Han in battle in 200 BCE. Following the defeat a political marriage alliance was negotiated in which the Han became the *de facto* inferior partner. When, despite the treaty, the Xiongnu continued to raid Han borders, Emperor Wu of Han (r. 141–87 BCE) launched several military campaigns against them, which eventually forced the Xiongnu to accept vassal status as Han tributaries. These campaigns expanded Han sovereignty into the Tarim Basin of Central Asia, and helped establish the vast trade network known as the Silk Road, which reached as far as the Mediterranean world. Han forces managed to divide the Xiongnu into two competing nations, the Southern and Northern Xiongnu, and forced the Northern Xiongnu across the Ili River. Despite this victory, the territories north of Han's borders were quickly overrun by the nomadic Xianbei Confederation.

After 92 CE, the palace eunuchs increasingly involved themselves in court politics, engaging in violent power struggles between the various consort clans of the empresses and empress dowagers, causing Han's ultimate downfall. Imperial authority was also seriously challenged by massive Daoist religious societies which instigated the Yellow Turban Rebellion and the Five Pecks of Rice Rebellion. Following the death of Emperor Ling (r. 168–189 CE), the palace eunuchs suffered wholesale massacre by military officers, allowing warlords to divide the empire. When Cao Pi, King of Wei, usurped the throne from Emperor Xian, the Han Dynasty was ended.

The Han Dynasty was an age of economic prosperity, and saw a significant growth of the money economy first established during the Zhou Dynasty (c. 1050–256 BCE). The coinage issued by the central government mint in 119 BCE remained the standard coinage of China until the Tang Dynasty (618–907 CE). To pay for its military campaigns and the settlement of newly conquered frontier territories, the government nationalized the private salt and iron industries in 117 BCE. These government monopolies were repealed during Eastern Han, and the lost revenue was recouped through heavily taxing private entrepreneurs. The emperor was at the pinnacle of Han society. He presided over the Han government, but shared power with both the nobility and appointed ministers who came largely from the scholarly gentry class. From the reign of Emperor Wu onward, the Chinese court officially sponsored Confucianism in education and court politics, synthesized with the cosmology of later scholars such as Dong Zhongshu. This policy endured until the fall of the Qing Dynasty in 1911 CE. Science and technology during Han saw significant advances, including papermaking, the nautical steering rudder, the use of negative numbers in mathematics, the raised-relief map, the hydraulic-powered armillary sphere for astronomy, and a seismometer employing an inverted pendulum.

Western Han

China's first imperial dynasty was the Qin Dynasty (221–206 BCE). The Qin had unified the Chinese Warring States by conquest, but their empire became unstable after the death of the first emperor Qin Shi Huang. Within four years the dynasty's authority had collapsed in the face of rebellion. Two former rebel leaders, Xiang Yu (d. 202 BCE) of Chu and Liu Bang (d. 195 BCE) of Han, engaged in a war to decide who would become hegemon of China, which had fissured into 18 Kingdoms, each claiming allegiance to either Xiang Yu or Liu Bang. Although Xiang Yu proved to be a capable commander, Liu Bang defeated him at the Battle of Gaixia, in modern-day Anhui. Liu Bang assumed the title 'emperor' (*huangdi*) at the urging of his followers and is known posthumously as Emperor Gaozu (r. 202–195 BCE). Chang'an was chosen as the new capital of the reunified empire under Han.

At the beginning of the Western Han Dynasty, thirteen centrally-controlled commanderies—including the capital region—existed in the western third of the empire, while the eastern two-thirds was divided into ten semi-autonomous kingdoms. To placate his prominent commanders from the war with Chu, Emperor Gaozu enfeoffed some of them as kings. By 157 BCE, the Han court had replaced all of these kings with royal Liu family members, since the loyalty of non-relatives to the throne was questioned. After several insurrections by Han kings—the largest being the Rebellion of the Seven States in 154 BCE—the imperial court enacted a series of reforms beginning in 145 BCE, limiting the size and power of these kingdoms and dividing them into smaller ones or new commanderies. Kings were no longer able to appoint their own staff; this duty was assumed by the imperial court. Kings became nominal heads of their fiefs, and collected a portion of tax revenues as their personal incomes. The kingdoms were never entirely abolished and existed throughout the remainder of Western and Eastern Han.

To the north of China proper, the nomadic Xiongnu chieftain Modu Chanyu (r. 209–174 BCE) conquered various tribes inhabiting the eastern portion of the Eurasian Steppe. By the end of his reign, he controlled Manchuria, Mongolia, and the Tarim Basin, subjugating over twenty states east of Samarkand. Emperor Gaozu was troubled about the abundant Han-manufactured iron weapons traded to the Xiongnu along the northern borders, and he established a trade embargo against the group. In retaliation, the Xiongnu invaded what is now Shanxi province, where they defeated the Han forces at Baideng in 200 BCE. After negotiations, the *heqin* agreement in 198 BCE nominally held the leaders of the Xiongnu and the Han as equal partners in a royal marriage alliance, but the Han were forced to send large amounts of tribute items like silk clothes, food, and wine to the Xiongnu.

Despite the tribute and a negotiation between Laoshang Chanyu (r. 174–160 BCE) and Emperor Wen (r. 180–157 BCE) to reopen border markets, many of the chanyu's Xiongnu subordinates chose not to obey the treaty and periodically raided Han territories south of the Great Wall for additional goods. In a court conference assembled by Emperor Wu (r. 141–87 BCE) in 135 BCE, the majority-consensus of the ministers was to retain the heqin agreement. Emperor Wu accepted this despite continuing Xiongnu raids. However, a court conference the following year convinced the majority that a limited engagement at Mayi involving the assassination of the Chanyu would throw the Xiongnu realm into chaos and benefit the Han. When this plot failed in 133 BCE, Emperor Wu launched a series of massive military invasions of Xiongnu territory. The assault culminated in 119 BCE at the Battle of Mobei, where the Han commanders Huo Qubing (d. 117 BCE) and Wei Qing (d. 106 BCE) forced the Xiongnu court to flee north of the Gobi Desert.

After Wu's reign, Han forces continued to prevail against the Xiongnu. The Xiongnu leader Huhanye Chanyu (r. 58–31 BCE) finally submitted to Han as a tributary vassal in 51 BCE. His rival claimant to the throne, Zhizhi Chanyu (r. 56–36 BCE), was killed by Chen Tang and Gan Yanshou at the Battle of Zhizhi, in modern Taraz, Kazakhstan.

In 121 BCE, Han forces expelled the Xiongnu from a vast territory spanning the Hexi Corridor to Lop Nur. They repelled a joint Xiongnu-Qiang invasion of this northwestern territory in 111 BCE. In that year, the Han court established four new frontier commanderies in this region: Jiuquan, Zhangyi, Dunhuang, and Wuwei. The majority of people on the frontier were soldiers. On occasion, the court forcibly moved peasant farmers to new frontier settlements, along with government-owned slaves and convicts who performed hard labor. The court also encouraged commoners, such as farmers, merchants, landowners, and hired laborers to voluntarily migrate to the frontier.

Even before Han's expansion into Central Asia, diplomat Zhang Qian's travels from 139–125 BCE had established Chinese contacts with many surrounding civilizations. Zhang encountered Dayuan (Fergana), Kangju (Sogdiana), and Daxia (Bactria, formerly the Greco-Bactrian Kingdom); he also gathered information on Shendu (Indus River valley of North India) and Anxi (the Arsacid Empire). All of these countries eventually received Han embassies. These connections marked the beginning of the Silk Road trade network that extended to the Roman Empire, bringing Han items like silk to Rome and Roman goods such as glasswares to China. From roughly 115–60 BCE, Han forces fought the Xiongnu over control of the oasis city-states in the Tarim Basin. Han was eventually victorious and established the Protectorate of the Western Regions in 60 BCE, which dealt with the region's defense and foreign affairs. The naval conquest of Nanyue in 111 BCE expanded the Han realm into what are now modern Guangdong, Guangxi, and northern Vietnam. Yunnan was brought into the Han realm with the conquest of the Dian Kingdom in 109 BCE and into the northern part of the Korean Peninsula with the colonial establishments of Xuantu Commandery and Lelang Commandery in 108 BCE. In China's first known nationwide census taken in 2 CE, the population was registered as having 57,671,400 individuals in 12,366,470 households.

To pay for his military campaigns and colonial expansion, Emperor Wu nationalized several private industries, creating new central government monopolies administered largely by former merchants. These monopolies included salt, iron, and liquor production, as well as bronze-coin currency. The liquor monopoly lasted only from 98–81 BCE, and the salt and iron monopolies were eventually abolished in early Eastern Han. The issuing of coinage remained a central government monopoly throughout the rest of the Han Dynasty. The government monopolies were eventually repealed when a political faction known as the Reformists gained greater influence in the court. The Reformists opposed the Modernist faction that had dominated court politics in Emperor Wu's reign and during the subsequent regency of Huo Guang (d. 68 BCE). The Modernists argued for an aggressive and expansionary foreign policy supported by revenues from heavy government intervention in the private economy. The Reformists, however, overturned these policies, favoring a cautious, non-expansionary approach to foreign policy, frugal budget reform, and lower tax rates imposed on private entrepreneurs.

Wang Mang's Reign and Civil War

Wang Zhengjun (71 BCE–13 CE) was first empress, then empress dowager, and finally grand empress dowager during the reigns of the Emperors Yuan (r. 49–33 BCE), Cheng (r. 33–7 BCE), and Ai (r. 7–1 BCE), respectively. During this time, a succession of her male relatives held the title of regent. Following the death of Ai, Wang Zhengjun's nephew Wang Mang (45–23 CE) was appointed regent for Emperor Ping (r. 1 BCE–6 CE). When Ping died in 6 CE, the Empress Dowager appointed Wang Mang to act as emperor for the child Liu Ying (d. 25 CE). Wang promised to relinquish his control to Liu Ying once he came of age. Despite this promise, and against protest and revolts from the nobility, Wang Mang claimed that the divine Mandate of Heaven called for the end of the Han Dynasty and the beginning of his own: the Xin Dynasty (9–23 CE).

Wang Mang initiated a series of major reforms that were ultimately unsuccessful. These reforms included outlawing slavery, nationalizing land to equally distribute between households, and introducing new currencies, a change which debased the value of coinage. Although these reforms provoked considerable opposition, Wang's regime met its ultimate downfall with the massive floods of c. 3 CE and 11 CE. Gradual silt buildup in the Yellow River had raised its water level and overwhelmed the flood control works. The Yellow River split into two new branches: one emptying to the north and the other to the south of the Shandong Peninsula, though Han engineers managed to dam the southern branch by 70 CE. The flood dislodged thousands of peasant farmers, many of whom joined roving bandit and rebel groups such as the Red Eyebrows to survive. Wang Mang's armies were incapable of quelling these enlarged rebel groups. Eventually, an insurgent mob forced their way into the Weiyang Palace and killed Wang Mang.

Emperor Gengshi of Han (r. 23–25 CE), a descendant of Emperor Jing (r. 157–141 BCE), attempted to restore the Han Dynasty and occupied Chang'an as his capital. However, he was overwhelmed by the "Red Eyebrow" rebels who deposed, assassinated, and replaced him with the puppet monarch Liu Penzi. Emperor Gengshi's brother Liu Xiu, known posthumously as Emperor Guangwu (r. 25–57 CE), after distinguishing himself at the Battle of Kunyang in 23 CE, was urged to succeed Gengshi as emperor. Under Guangwu's rule the Han Empire was restored. Guangwu made Luoyang his capital in 25 CE, and by 27 CE his officers Deng Yu and Feng Yi had forced the Red Eyebrows to surrender and executed their leaders for treason. From 26 until 36 CE, Emperor Guangwu had to wage war against other regional warlords who claimed the title of emperor; when these warlords were defeated, China reunified under the Han.

The period between the foundation of the Han Dynasty and Wang Mang's reign is known as the Western Han Dynasty or Former Han Dynasty (202 BCE–9 CE). During this period the capital was at Chang'an (modern Xi'an). From the reign of Guangwu the capital was moved eastward to Luoyang. The era from his reign until the fall of Han is known as the Eastern Han Dynasty or the Later Han Dynasty (25–220 CE).

Eastern Han

During the widespread rebellion against Wang Mang, the Korean state of Goguryeo was free to raid Han's Korean commanderies; Han did not reaffirm its control over the region until 30 CE. The Trýng Sisters of Vietnam rebelled against Han in 40 CE. Their rebellion was crushed by Han general Ma Yuan (d. 49 CE) in a campaign from 42–43 CE. Wang Mang renewed hostilities against the Xiongnu, who were estranged from Han until their leader Bi, a rival claimant to the throne against his cousin Punu, submitted to Han as a tributary vassal in 50 CE. This created two rival Xiongnu states: the Southern Xiongnu led by Bi, an ally of Han, and the Northern Xiongnu led by Punu, an enemy of Han.

During the turbulent reign of Wang Mang, Han lost control over the Tarim Basin, which was conquered by the Northern Xiongnu in 63 CE and used as a base to invade Han's Hexi Corridor in Gansu. Dou Gu (d. 88 CE) defeated the Northern Xiongnu at the Battle of Yiwulu in 73 CE, evicting them from Turpan and chasing them as far as Lake Barkol before establishing a garrison at Hami. After the new Protector General of the Western Regions Chen Mu (d. 75 CE) was killed by allies of the Xiongnu in Karasahr and Kucha, the garrison at Hami was withdrawn. At the Battle of Ikh Bayan in 89 CE, Dou Xian (d. 92 CE) defeated the Northern Xiongnu chanyu who then retreated into the Altai Mountains. After the Northern Xiongnu fled into the Ili River valley in 91 CE, the nomadic Xianbei occupied the area from the borders of the Buyeo Kingdom in Manchuria to the Ili River of the Wusun people. The Xianbei reached their apogee under Tanshihuai (d. 180 CE), who consistently defeated Chinese armies. However, Tanshihuai's confederation disintegrated after his death.

Ban Chao (d. 102 CE) enlisted the aid of the Kushan Empire, occupying the area of modern India, Pakistan, Afghanistan, and Tajikistan, to subdue Kashgar and its ally Sogdiana. When a request by Kushan ruler Vima Kadphises (r. c. 90–c. 100 CE) for a marriage alliance with the Han was rejected in 90 CE, he sent his forces to Wakhan (Afghanistan) to attack Ban Chao. The conflict ended with Kushan withdrawing due to lack of supplies. In 91 CE, the office of Protector General of the Western Regions was reinstated when it was bestowed on Ban Chao.

In addition to tributary relations with Kushan, the Han Empire received gifts from the Arsacids, from a king in modern

Burma, from a ruler in Japan, and initiated an unsuccessful mission to Daqin (Rome) in 97 CE with Gan Ying as emissary. A Roman embassy of Emperor Marcus Aurelius (r. 161–180 CE) is believed to have reached the court of Emperor Huan of Han (r. 146–168 CE) in 166 CE, yet Rafe de Crespigny asserts that this was most likely a group of Roman merchants. Other travelers to Eastern-Han China included Buddhist monks who translated works into Chinese, such as An Shigao of Parthia, and Lokaksema from Kushan-era Gandhara, India.

Eunuchs in State Affairs

Emperor Zhang's (r. 75–88 CE) reign came to be viewed by later Eastern Han scholars as the high point of the dynastic house. Subsequent reigns were increasingly marked by eunuch intervention in court politics and their involvement in the violent power struggles of the imperial consort clans. With the aid of the eunuch Zheng Zhong (d. 107 CE), Emperor He (r. 88–105 CE) had Empress Dowager Dou (d. 97 CE) put under house arrest and her clan stripped of power. This was in revenge for Dou's purging of the clan of his natural mother—Consort Liang—and then concealing her identity from him. After Emperor He's death, his wife Empress Deng Sui (d. 121 CE), managed state affairs as the regent empress dowager during a turbulent financial crisis and the widespread Qiang rebellion that lasted from 107 to 118 CE.

When Empress Dowager Deng died, Emperor An (r. 106–125 CE) was convinced by the accusations of the eunuchs Li Run and Jiang Jing that Deng and her family had planned to depose him. An dismissed Deng's clan members from office, exiled them and forced many to commit suicide. After An's death, his wife, Empress Dowager Yan (d. 126 CE) placed the child Marquess of Beixiang on the throne in an attempt to retain power within her family. However, palace eunuch Sun Cheng (d. 132 CE) masterminded a successful overthrow of her regime to enthrone Emperor Shun of Han (r. 125–144

CE). Yan was placed under house arrest, her relatives were either killed or exiled, and her eunuch allies were slaughtered. The regent Liang Ji (d. 159 CE), brother of Empress Liang Na (d. 150 CE), had the brother-in-law of Consort Deng Mengnü (later empress) (d. 165 CE) killed after she resisted his attempts to control her. Afterward, Emperor Huan employed eunuchs to depose Liang Ji, who was then forced to commit suicide.

Students from the Imperial University organized a widespread student protest against the eunuchs of Emperor Huan's court. Huan further alienated the bureaucracy when he initiated grandiose construction projects and hosted thousands of concubines in his harem at a time of economic crisis. Palace eunuchs imprisoned the official Li Ying (Ngº◎) and his associates from the Imperial University on a dubious charge of treason. In 167 CE, the Grand Commandant Dou Wu (d. 168 CE) convinced his son-in-law, Emperor Huan, to release them. However the emperor permanently barred Li Ying and his associates from serving in office, marking the beginning of the Partisan Prohibitions.

Following Huan's death, Dou Wu and the Grand Tutor Chen Fan (d. 168 CE) attempted a coup d'état against the eunuchs Hou Lan (d. 172 CE), Cao Jie (d. 181 CE), and Wang Fu. When the plot was uncovered, the eunuchs arrested Empress Dowager Dou (d. 172 CE) and Chen Fan. General Zhang Huan favored the eunuchs. He and his troops confronted Dou Wu and his retainers at the palace gate where each side shouted accusations of treason against the other. When the retainers gradually deserted Dou Wu, he was forced to commit suicide.

Under Emperor Ling (r. 168–189 CE) the eunuchs had the partisan prohibitions renewed and expanded, while themselves auctioning off top government offices. Many affairs of state were entrusted to the eunuchs Zhao Zhong (d. 189 CE) and Zhang Rong (d. 189 CE) while Emperor Ling spent much of his time roleplaying with concubines and participating in military parades.

End of the Han

The partisan prohibitions were repealed during the Yellow Turban Rebellion and Five Pecks of Rice Rebellion in 184 CE, largely because the court did not want to continue to alienate a significant portion of the gentry class who might otherwise join the rebellions. The Yellow Turbans and Five-Pecks-of-Rice adherents belonged to two different hierarchical Daoist religious societies led by faith healers Zhang Jiao (d. 184 CE) and Zhang Lu (d. 216 CE), respectively. Zhang Lu's rebellion, in modern northern Sichuan and southern Shanxi, was not quelled until 215 CE. Zhang Jiao's massive rebellion across eight provinces was annihilated by Han forces within a year, however the following decades saw much smaller recurrent uprisings. Although the Yellow Turbans were defeated, many generals appointed during the crisis never disbanded their assembled militia forces and used these troops to amass power outside of the collapsing imperial authority.

General-in-Chief He Jin (d. 189 CE), half-brother to Empress He (d. 189 CE), plotted with Yuan Shao (d. 202 CE) to overthrow the eunuchs by having several generals march to the outskirts of the capital. There, in a written petition to Empress He, they demanded the eunuchs' execution. After a period of hesitation, Empress He consented. When the eunuchs discovered this, however, they had her brother He Miao rescind the order. The eunuchs assassinated He Jin on September 22, 189 CE. Yuan Shao then besieged Luoyang's Northern Palace while his brother Yuan Shu (d. 199 CE) besieged the Southern Palace. On September 25 both palaces were breached and approximately two thousand eunuchs were killed. Zhang Rang had previously fled with Emperor Shao (r. 189 CE) and his brother Liu Xie—the future Emperor

Xian of Han (r. 189–220 CE). While being pursued by the Yuan brothers, Zhang committed suicide by jumping into the Yellow River.

General Dong Zhuo (d. 192 CE) found the young emperor and his brother wandering in the countryside. He escorted them safely back to the capital and was made Minister of Works, taking control of Luoyang and forcing Yuan Shao to flee. After Dong Zhuo demoted Emperor Shao and promoted his brother Liu Xie as Emperor Xian, Yuan Shao led a coalition of former officials and officers against Dong, who burned Luoyang to the ground and resettled the court at Chang'an in May 191 CE. Dong Zhuo later poisoned Emperor Shao. Dong was killed by his adopted son Lü Bu (d. 198 CE) in a plot hatched by Wang Yun (d. 192 CE). Emperor Xian fled from Chang'an in 195 CE to the ruins of Luoyang. Xian was persuaded by Cao Cao (155–220 CE), then Governor of Yan Province in modern western Shandong and eastern Henan, to move the capital to Xuchang in 196 CE.

Yuan Shao challenged Cao Cao for control over the emperor. Yuan's power was greatly diminished after Cao defeated him at the Battle of Guandu in 200 CE. After Yuan died, Cao killed Yuan Shao's son Yuan Tan (173–205 CE), who had fought with his brothers over the family inheritance. His brothers Yuan Shang and Yuan Xi were killed in 207 CE by Gongsun Kang (d. 221 CE), who sent their heads to Cao Cao.

After Cao's defeat at the naval Battle of Red Cliffs in 208 CE, China was divided into three spheres of influence, with Cao Cao dominating the north, Sun Quan (182–252 CE) dominating the south, and Liu Bei (161–223 CE) dominating the west. Cao Cao died in March 220 CE. By December his son Cao Pi (187–226 CE) had Emperor Xian relinquish the throne to him and is known posthumously as Emperor Wen of Wei. This formally ended the Han Dynasty and initiated an age of conflict between three states: Cao Wei, Eastern Wu, and Shu Han.

SOCIETY AND CULTURE

Social Class

In the hierarchical social order, the emperor was at the apex of Han society and government. However the emperor was often a minor, ruled over by a regent such as the empress dowager or one of her male relatives. Ranked immediately below the emperor were the kings who were of the same Liu family clan. The rest of society, including nobles lower than kings and all commoners excluding slaves belonged to one of twenty ranks.

Each successive rank gave its holder greater pensions and legal privileges. The highest rank, of full marquess, came with a state pension and a territorial fiefdom. Holders of the rank immediately below, that of ordinary marquess, received a pension, but had no territorial rule. Officials who served in government belonged to the wider commoner social class and were ranked just below nobles in social prestige. The highest government officials could be enfeoffed as marquesses. By the Eastern Han period, local elites of unattached scholars, teachers, students, and government officials began to identify themselves as members of a larger, nationwide gentry class with shared similar values and a commitment to mainstream scholarship. When the government became noticeably corrupt in mid-to-late Eastern Han, many gentrymen even considered the cultivation of morally-grounded personal relationships more important than serving in public office.

The farmer, or specifically the small landowner-cultivator, was ranked just below scholars and officials in the social hierarchy. Other agricultural cultivators were of a lower status, such as tenants, wage laborers, and in rare cases slaves. Artisans and craftsmen had a legal and socioeconomic status between that of owner-cultivator farmers and common merchants. State-registered merchants, who were forced by law to wear white-colored clothes and pay high commercial taxes, were considered by the gentry as social parasites with a contemptible status. These were often petty shopkeepers of urban marketplaces; merchants such as industrialists and itinerant traders working between a network of cities could avoid registering as merchants and were often wealthier and more powerful than the vast majority of government officials. Wealthy landowners, such as nobles and officials, often provided lodging for retainers who provided valuable work or duties, sometimes including fighting bandits or riding into battle. Unlike slaves, retainers could come and go from their master's home as they pleased. Medical physicians, pig breeders, and butchers had a fairly high social status, while occultist diviners, runners, and messengers had low status.

Marriage, Gender, and Kinship

The Han-era family was patrilineal and typically had four to five nuclear family members living in one household. Multiple generations of extended family members did not occupy the same house, unlike families of later dynasties. According to Confucian family norms, various family members were treated with different levels of respect and intimacy. For example, there were different accepted time frames for mourning the death of a father versus a paternal uncle. Arranged marriages were the norm, with the father's input on his offspring's spouse being considered more important than the mother's. Monogamous marriages were also the norm, although nobles and high officials were wealthy enough to afford and support concubines as additional lovers. Under certain conditions dictated by custom, not law, both men and women were able to divorce their spouses and remarry.

Apart from the passing of noble titles or ranks, inheritance practices did not involve primogeniture; each son received an equal share of the family property. Since the father usually sent his adult married sons away with a portion of the family fortune, unlike later dynasties, sons did not always receive their inheritance after the death of their father. Daughters were not formally included in a father's will, although they did receive a portion of the family fortune through their marriage dowries.

Women were expected to obey the will of their father, then their husband, and then their adult son in old age. However, it is known from contemporary sources that there were many deviations to this rule, especially in regard to mothers over their sons, and empresses who ordered around and openly humiliated their fathers and brothers. Women were exempt from the annual corvée labor duties, but often engaged in a range of income-earning occupations aside from their domestic chores of cooking and cleaning.

The most common occupation for women was weaving clothes for the family, sale at market or for large textile enterprises that employed hundreds of women. Other women helped on their brothers' farms or became singers, dancers, sorceresses, respected medical physicians, and successful merchants who could afford their own silk clothes. Some women formed spinning collectives, aggregating the resources of several different families.

Education, Literature, and Philosophy

The early Western Han court simultaneously accepted the philosophical teachings of Legalism, Huang-Lao Daoism, and Confucianism in making state decisions and shaping government policy. However, the Han court under Emperor Wu gave Confucianism exclusive patronage. He abolished all academic chairs or erudites (*boshi* ZSëX) not dealing with the Confucian Five Classics in 136 BCE and encouraged nominees for office to receive a Confucian-based education at the Imperial University that he established in 124 BCE. Unlike the original ideology espoused by Confucius, or Kongzi (551–479 BCE), Han Confucianism in Emperor Wu's reign was the creation of Dong Zhongshu (179–104 BCE). Dong Zhongshu was a scholar and minor official who aggregated the ethical Confucian ideas of ritual, filial piety, and harmonious relationships with five phases and yin-yang cosmologies. Much to the interest of the ruler, Dong's synthesis justified the imperial system of government within the natural order of the universe. The Imperial University grew in importance as the student body grew to over 30,000 by the 2nd century CE. A Confucian-based education was also made available at commandery-level schools and private schools opened in small towns, where teachers earned respectable incomes from tuition payments.

Some important texts were created and studied by scholars. Philosophical works written by Yang Xiong (53 BCE–18 CE), Huan Tan (43 BCE–28 CE), Wang Chong (27–100 CE), and Wang Fu (78–163 CE) questioned whether human nature was innately good or evil and posed challenges to Dong's universal order. The *Records of the Grand Historian* by Sima Tan (d. 110 BCE) and his son Sima Qian (145–86 BCE) established the standard model for all of imperial China's Standard Histories, such as the *Book of Han* written by Ban Biao (3–54 CE), his son Ban Gu (32–92 CE), and his daughter Ban Zhao (45–116 CE). There were dictionaries such as the *Shuowen Jiezi* by Xu Shen (c. 58–c. 147 CE) and the *Fangyan* by Yang Xiong. Biographies on important figures were written by various gentrymen. Poems and rhapsodies were popular forms of literature amongst the gentry.

Law and Order

Han scholars such as Jia Yi (201–169 BCE) portrayed the previous Qin Dynasty as a brutal regime. However, archaeological evidence from Zhangjiashan and Shuihudi reveal that many of the statutes in the Han law code compiled by Chancellor Xiao He (d. 193 BCE) were derived from Qin law.

Various cases for rape, physical abuse and murder were prosecuted in court. Women, although usually having less rights by custom, were allowed to level civil and criminal charges against men. While suspects were jailed, convicted criminals were never imprisoned. Instead, punishments were commonly monetary fines, periods of forced hard labor for convicts, and the penalty of death by beheading. Early Han punishments of torturous mutilation were borrowed from Qin law. A series of reforms abolished mutilation punishments with progressively less-severe beatings by the bastinado.

Acting as a judge in lawsuits was one of many duties of the Magistrates of counties and Administrators of commanderies. Complex, high profile or unresolved cases were often deferred to the Minister of Justice in the capital or even the emperor. In each Han county was several districts, each overseen by a chief of police. Order in the cities was maintained by government officers in the marketplaces and constables in the neighborhoods.

Cuisine

The most common staple crops consumed during Han were wheat, barley, rice, foxtail millet, proso millet and beans. Commonly-eaten fruits and vegetables included chestnuts, pears, plums, peaches, melons, apricots, strawberries, red bayberries, jujubes, calabash, bamboo shoots, mustard plant and taro. Domesticated animals that were also eaten included chickens, Mandarin ducks, geese, cows, sheep, pigs, camels and dogs. Turtles and fish were taken from streams and lakes. Commonly-hunted game, such as owl, pheasant, magpie, sika deer, and Chinese Bamboo Partridge were consumed. Seasonings included sugar, honey, salt and soy sauce. Beer and wine were regularly consumed.

Clothing

The types of clothing worn and the materials used during the Han period depended upon social class. Wealthy folk could afford silk robes, skirts, socks, and mittens, coats made of badger or fox fur, duck plumes, and slippers with inlaid leather, pearls, and silk lining. Peasants commonly wore clothes made of hemp, wool, and ferret skins.

Religion, Cosmology, and Metaphysics

Families throughout Han China made ritual sacrifices of animals and foodstuffs to deities, spirits, and ancestors at temples and shrines, in the belief that these items could be utilized by those in the spiritual realm. It was thought that each person had a two-part soul: the spirit-soul which journeyed to the afterlife paradise of immortals (*xian*), and the body-soul which remained in its grave or tomb on earth and was only reunited with the spirit-soul through a ritual ceremony. In addition to his many other roles, the emperor acted as the highest priest in the land who made sacrifices to Heaven, the main deities known as the Five Powers, and the spirits of mountains and rivers. It was believed that the three realms of Heaven, Earth, and Mankind were linked by natural cycles of yin and yang and the five phases. If the emperor did not behave according to proper ritual, ethics, and morals, he could disrupt the fine balance of these cosmological cycles and cause calamities such as earthquakes, floods, droughts, epidemics, and swarms of locusts.

It was believed that immortality could be achieved if one reached the lands of the Queen Mother of the West or Mount Penglai. Han-era Daoists assembled into small groups of hermits who attempted to achieve immortality through breathing exercises, sexual techniques and use of medical elixirs. By the 2nd century CE, Daoists formed large hierarchical religious societies such as the Way of the Five Pecks of Rice. Its followers believed that the sage-philosopher

Laozi (fl. 6th century BCE) was a holy prophet who would offer salvation and good health if his devout followers would confess their sins, ban the worship of unclean gods who accepted meat sacrifices and chant sections of the *Daodejing*.

Buddhism first entered China during the Eastern Han and was first mentioned in 65 CE. Liu Ying (d. 71 CE), a half-brother to Emperor Ming of Han (r. 57–75 CE), was one of its earliest Chinese adherents, although Chinese Buddhism at this point was heavily associated with Huang-Lao Daoism. China's first known Buddhist temple, the White Horse Temple, was erected during Ming's reign. Important Buddhist canons were translated into Chinese during the 2nd century CE, including the *Sutra of Forty-two Chapters*, *Perfection of Wisdom*, *Shurangama Sutra*, and *Pratyutpanna Sutra*.

GOVERNMENT

Central Government

In Han government, the emperor was the supreme judge and lawgiver, the commander-in-chief of the armed forces and sole designator of official nominees appointed to the top posts in central and local administrations; those who earned a 600-*shi* salary-rank or higher. Theoretically, there were no limits to his power. However, state organs with competing interests and institutions such as the court conference—where ministers were convened to reach majority consensus on an issue—pressured the emperor to accept the advice of his ministers on policy decisions. If the emperor rejected a court conference decision, he risked alienating his high ministers. Nevertheless, emperors sometimes did reject the majority opinion reached at court conferences.

Below the emperor were his cabinet members known as the Three Excellencies. These were the Chancellor/Minister over the Masses, Imperial Counselor/Excellency of Works, and Grand Commandant/Grand Marshal.

The Chancellor, whose title was changed to Minister over the Masses in 8 BCE, was chiefly responsible for drafting the government budget. The Chancellor's other duties included managing provincial registers for land and population, leading court conferences, acting as judge in lawsuits and recommending nominees for high office. He could appoint officials below the salary-rank of 600-*shi*.

The Imperial Counselor's chief duty was to conduct disciplinary procedures for officials. He shared similar duties with the Chancellor, such as receiving annual provincial reports. However, when his title was changed to Excellency of Works in 8 BCE, his chief duty became oversight of public works projects.

The Grand Commandant, whose title was changed to Grand Marshal in 119 BCE before reverting back to Grand Commandant in 51 CE, was the irregularly-posted commander of the military and then regent during Western Han. In Eastern Han he was chiefly a civil official who shared many of the same censorial powers as the other two Excellencies.

Ranked below the Three Excellencies were the Nine Ministers, who each headed a specialized ministry. The Minister of Ceremonies was the chief official in charge of religious rites, rituals, prayers and the maintenance of ancestral temples and altars. The Minister of the Household was in charge of the emperor's security within the palace grounds, external imperial parks and wherever the emperor made an outing by chariot. The Minister of the Guards was responsible for securing and patrolling the walls, towers, and gates of the imperial palaces. The Minister Coachman was responsible for the maintenance of imperial stables, horses, carriages and coach-houses for the emperor and his palace attendants, as well as the supply of horses for the armed forces. The Minister of Justice was the chief official in charge of upholding, administering, and interpreting the law. The Minister Herald was the chief official in charge of receiving honored guests at the imperial court, such as nobles and foreign ambassadors. The Minister of the Imperial Clan oversaw the imperial court's interactions with the empire's nobility and extended imperial family, such as granting fiefs and titles. The Minister of Finance was the treasurer for the official bureaucracy and the armed forces who handled tax revenues and set standards for units of measurement. The Minister Steward served the emperor exclusively, providing him with entertainment and amusements, proper food and clothing, medicine and physical care, valuables and equipment.

Local Government

In descending order of size, the Han Empire, excluding kingdoms and marquessates, was divided into political units of provinces (*zhou*), commanderies (*jun*), and counties (*xian*). A county was divided into several districts, the latter composed of a group of hamlets, each containing about a hundred families.

The heads of provinces, whose official title was changed from Inspector to Governor and vice versa several times during Han, were responsible for inspecting several commandery-level and kingdom-level administrations. Based on their reports, the officials in these local administrations would be promoted, demoted, dismissed or prosecuted by the imperial court.

A governor could take various actions without permission from the imperial court. The lower-ranked inspector had executive powers only during times of crisis, such as raising militias across the commanderies under his jurisdiction to suppress a rebellion.

A commandery consisted of a group of counties, and was headed by an Administrator. He was the top civil and military leader of the commandery and handled defense, lawsuits, seasonal instructions to farmers and recommendations of nominees for office sent annually to the capital in a quota system first established by Emperor Wu. The head of a large county of about 10,000 households was called a Prefect, while the heads of smaller counties were called Chiefs, and both could be referred to as Magistrates. A Magistrate maintained law and order in his county, registered the populace for taxation, mobilized commoners for annual corvée duties, repaired schools and supervised public works.

Kingdoms and Marquessates

Kingdoms—roughly the size of commanderies—were ruled exclusively by the emperor's male relatives as semi-autonomous fiefs. Before 157 BCE some kingdoms were ruled by non-relatives, granted to them in return for their services to Emperor Gaozu. The administration of each kingdom was very similar to that of the central government. Although the emperor appointed the Chancellor of each kingdom, kings appointed all the remaining civil officials in their fiefs.

However, in 145 BCE, after several insurrections by the kings, Emperor Jing removed the kings' rights to appoint officials with salaries higher than 400-*shi*. The Imperial Counselors and Nine Ministers (excluding the Minister Coachman) of every kingdom were abolished, although the Chancellor was still appointed by the central government.

With these reforms, kings were reduced to being nominal heads of their fiefs, gaining a personal income from only a portion of the taxes collected in their kingdom. Similarly, the officials in the administrative staff of a full marquess's fief were appointed by the central government. A marquess's Chancellor was ranked as the equivalent of a county Prefect. Like a king, the marquess collected a portion of the tax revenues in his fief as personal income.

Military

At the beginning of the Han Dynasty, every male commoner aged twenty-three was liable for conscription into the military. The minimum age for the military draft was reduced to twenty after Emperor Zhao's (r. 87–74 BCE) reign. Conscripts underwent one year of training and one year of service as non-professional soldiers. The year of training was served in one of three branches of the armed forces: infantry, cavalry or navy. The year of active service was served either on their frontier, in a king's court or under the Minister of the Guards in the capital.

During the Eastern Han, conscription could be avoided if one paid a commutable tax. The Eastern Han court favored the recruitment of a volunteer army. The latter comprised the Southern Army (*Nanjun*), while the smaller professional standing army, stationed in the capital, was the Northern Army (*Beijun*). Led by Colonels (*Xiaowei*), the Northern Army consisted of five regiments, each with approximately 750 soldiers and 150 junior officers. When central authority collapsed after 189 CE, wealthy landowners and regional warlords relied upon their retainers to act as their own personal troops (*buqu*).

During times of war, a much larger militia was raised across the country to supplement the Northern Army. In these circumstances, a General (*Jiangjun*) led a division, which was divided into regiments led by Colonels and sometimes Majors, (*Sima*). Regiments were divided into companies and led by Captains. Platoons were the smallest units of soldiers.

ECONOMICS

Variations in Currency

In the beginning of the Han, Emperor Gaozu closed the government mint in favor of private minting of coins. This decision was reversed in 186 BCE by his widow Grand Empress Dowager Lü Zhi (d. 180 BCE), who abolished private minting. In 182 BCE, Lü Zhi issued a bronze coin that was much lighter in weight than previous coins. This caused widespread inflation that was not reduced until 175 BCE when Emperor Wen allowed private minters to manufacture coins that were precisely 2.6 g (0.09 oz) in weight.

In 144 BCE Emperor Jing abolished private minting in favor of central-government and commandery-level minting; he also introduced a new coin. Emperor Wu introduced another in 120 BCE but replaced this a year later with the *wushu* coin weighing 3.2 g (0.11 oz). The *wushu* became China's standard coin until the Tang Dynasty (618–907 CE). Its use was interrupted briefly by a range of new currencies introduced during Wang Mang's regime until it was reinstated in 40 CE.

Since commandery-issued coins were often of inferior quality and lighter weight, the central government closed commandery mints and monopolized the issue of coinage in 113 BCE. This central government issuance of coinage was overseen by the Superintendent of Waterways and Parks, this duty being transferred to the Minister of Finance during Eastern Han.

Taxation and Property

Aside from the landowner's land tax paid in a portion of their crop yield, the poll tax and property taxes were paid in coin cash. The annual poll tax rate for adult men and women was 120 coins and 20 coins for minors. Merchants were required to pay a higher rate of 240 coins. The poll tax stimulated a money economy that necessitated the minting of over 28,000,000,000 coins from 118 BCE to 5 CE, an average of 220,000,000 coins a year.

The widespread circulation of coin cash allowed successful merchants to invest money in land, empowering the very social class the government attempted to suppress through heavy commercial and property taxes. Emperor Wu even enacted laws which banned registered merchants from owning land, yet powerful merchants were able to avoid registration and own large tracts of land.

The small landowner-cultivators formed the majority of the Han tax base; this revenue was threatened during the latter half of Eastern Han when many peasants fell into debt and were forced to work as farming tenants for wealthy landlords. The Han government enacted reforms in order to keep small landowner-cultivators out of debt and on their own farms. These reforms included reducing taxes, temporary remissions of taxes, granting loans and providing landless peasants temporary lodging and work in agricultural colonies until they could recover from their debts.

In 168 BCE, the land tax rate was reduced from one-fifteenth of a farming household's crop yield to one-thirtieth, and later to a one-hundredth of a crop yield for the last decades of the dynasty. The consequent loss of government revenue was compensated for by increasing property taxes.

The labor tax took the form of conscripted labor for one month per year, which was imposed upon male commoners aged fifteen to fifty-six. This could be avoided in Eastern Han with a commutable tax, since hired labor became more popular.

Private Manufacture and Government Monopolies

In the early Western Han, a wealthy salt or iron industrialist, whether a semi-autonomous king or wealthy merchant, could boast funds that rivaled the imperial treasury and amass a peasant workforce of over a thousand. This kept many peasants away from their farms and denied the government a significant portion of its land tax revenue. To eliminate the influence of such private entrepreneurs, Emperor Wu nationalized the salt and iron industries in 117 BCE and allowed many of the former industrialists to become officials administering the monopolies. By Eastern Han times, the central government monopolies were repealed in favor of production by commandery and county administrations, as well as private businessmen.

Liquor was another profitable private industry nationalized by the central government in 98 BCE. However, this was repealed in 81 BCE and a property tax rate of 2 coins for every 0.2 L (0.05 gallons) was levied for those who traded it privately. By 110 BCE Emperor Wu also interfered with the profitable trade in grain when he eliminated speculation by selling government-stored grain at a lower price than demanded by merchants. Apart from Emperor Ming's creation of a short-lived Office for Price Adjustment and Stabilization, which was abolished in 68 CE, central government price control regulations were largely absent during the Eastern Han.

Science, Technology, and Engineering

The Han Dynasty was a unique period in the development of premodern Chinese science and technology, comparable to the level of scientific and technological growth during the Song Dynasty (960–1279).

Writing Materials

Typical ancient Chinese writing materials were bronzewares and animal bones. By the beginning of the Han Dynasty, the chief writing materials were clay tablets, silk cloth, and rolled scrolls made from bamboo strips sewn together with hempen string; these were passed through drilled holes and secured with clay stamps.

The oldest known Chinese piece of hard, hempen wrapping paper dates to the 2nd century BCE. The standard papermaking process was invented by Cai Lun (50–121 CE) in 105 CE. The oldest known surviving piece of paper with writing on it was found in the ruins of a Han watchtower that had been abandoned in 110 CE, in Inner Mongolia.

Metallurgy and Agriculture

Evidence suggests that blast furnaces, that convert raw iron ore into pig iron, which can be remelted in a cupola furnace to produce cast iron by means of a cold blast and hot blast, were operational in China by the late Spring and Autumn Period (722–481 BCE). The bloomery was nonexistent in ancient China; however, the Han-era Chinese produced wrought iron by injecting excess oxygen into a furnace and causing decarburization. Cast iron and pig iron could be converted into wrought iron and steel using the finery forge and puddling process.

The Han-era Chinese used bronze and iron to make a range of weapons, culinary tools, carpenters' tools and domestic wares. A significant product of these improved iron-smelting techniques was the manufacture of new agricultural tools. The three-legged iron seed drill, invented by the 2nd century BCE, enabled farmers to carefully plant crops in rows instead of casting seeds out by hand. The heavy moldboard iron plow, also invented during the Han Dynasty, required only one man to control it, two oxen to pull it. It had three plowshares, a seed box for the drills, a tool which turned down the soil and could sow roughly 45,730 m^2 (11.3 acres) of land in a single day.

To protect crops from wind and drought, the Grain Intendant Zhao Guo created the alternating fields system (*daitianfa*) during Emperor Wu's reign. This system switched the positions of furrows and ridges between growing seasons. Once experiments with this system yielded successful results, the government officially sponsored it and encouraged peasants to use it. Han farmers also used the pit field system (*aotian* ùQ0u) for growing crops, which involved heavily-fertilized pits that did not require plows or oxen and could be placed on sloping terrain. In southern and small parts of central Han-era China, paddy fields were chiefly used to grow rice, while farmers along the Huai River used transplantation methods of rice production.

Structural Engineering

Timber was the chief building material during the Han Dynasty; it was used to build palace halls, multiple-story residential towers and halls and single-story houses. Because wood decays rapidly, the only remaining evidence of Han wooden architecture is a collection of scattered ceramic roof tiles. The oldest surviving wooden halls in China date to the Tang Dynasty (618–907).

Though Han wooden structures decayed, some Han-dynasty ruins made of brick, stone, and rammed earth remain intact. This includes stone pillar-gates, brick tomb chambers, rammed-earth city walls, rammed-earth and brick beacon towers, rammed-earth sections of the Great Wall, rammed-earth platforms where elevated halls once stood, and two rammed-earth castles in Gansu with crenellations. The ruins of rammed-earth walls that once surrounded the capitals Chang'an and Luoyang still stand, along with their drainage systems of brick arches, ditches, and ceramic water pipes. Monumental stone pillar-gates, twenty-nine of which survive from the Han period, formed entrances of walled enclosures at shrine and tomb sites. These pillars feature artistic imitations of wooden and ceramic building components such as roof tiles, eaves, and balustrades. Architectural historian Robert L. Thorp points out the scarcity of Han-era archaeological remains, and claims that often unreliable Han-era literary and artistic sources are used by historians for clues about lost Han architecture.

The courtyard house is the most common type of home portrayed in Han artwork. Ceramic architectural models of buildings, like houses and towers, were found in Han tombs, perhaps to provide lodging for the dead in the afterlife. These provide valuable clues about lost wooden architecture. The artistic designs found on ceramic roof tiles of tower models are in some cases exact matches to Han roof tiles found at archaeological sites.

Over ten thousand Han-era underground tombs have been found, many of them featuring archways, vaulted chambers, and domed roofs. Underground vaults and domes did not require buttress supports since they were held in place by earthen pits. The use of brick vaults and domes in aboveground Han structures is unknown.

From Han literary sources, it is known that wooden-trestle beam bridges, arch bridges, simple suspension bridges, and floating pontoon bridges existed in Han China. However, there are only two known references to arch bridges in Han literature, and only a single Han relief sculpture in Sichuan depicts an arch bridge.

Underground mine shafts, some reaching depths of over 100 meters, or 300 feet, were created for the extraction of metal ores. Borehole drilling and derricks were used to lift brine to iron pans where it was distilled into salt. The distillation furnaces were heated by natural gas funneled to the surface through bamboo pipelines. Dangerous amounts of additional gas were siphoned off via carburetor chambers and exhaust pipes.

Mechanical and Hydraulic Engineering

Evidence of Han-era mechanical engineering comes largely from the choice observational writings of sometimes disinterested Confucian scholars. Professional artisan-engineers (*jiang*) did not leave behind detailed records of their work. Han scholars, who often had little or no expertise in mechanical engineering, sometimes provided insufficient information on the various technologies they described. Nevertheless, some Han literary sources provide crucial information. For example, in 15 BCE the philosopher Yang Xiong described the invention of the belt drive for a quilling machine, which was of great importance to early textile manufacturing. The inventions of the artisan-engineer Ding Huan are mentioned in the *Miscellaneous Notes on the Western Capital*. Around 180 CE, Ding created a manually-operated rotary fan used for air conditioning within palace buildings. Ding also used gimbals as pivotal supports for one of his incense burners and invented the world's first known zoetrope lamp.

Modern archaeology has led to the discovery of Han artwork portraying inventions which were otherwise absent in Han literary sources. As observed in Han miniature tomb models, but not in literary sources, the crank handle was used to operate the fans of winnowing machines that separated grain from chaff. The odometer cart, invented during Han, measured journey lengths, using mechanical figures banging drums and gongs to indicate each distance traveled. This invention is depicted in Han artwork by the 2nd century CE, yet detailed written descriptions were not offered until the 3rd century CE. Modern archaeologists have also unearthed specimens of devices used during the Han Dynasty, for example a pair of sliding metal calipers used by craftsmen for making minute measurements. These calipers contain inscriptions of the exact day and year they were manufactured. These tools are not mentioned in any Han literary sources.

The waterwheel appeared in Chinese records during the Han. As mentioned by Huan Tan in about 20 CE, they were used to turn gears that lifted iron trip hammers, and were used in pounding, threshing and polishing grain. However, there is no sufficient evidence for the watermill in China until about the 5th century. The Nanyang Commandery Administrator Du Shi (d. 38 CE) created a waterwheel-powered reciprocator that worked the bellows for the smelting of iron. Waterwheels were also used to power chain pumps that lifted water to raised irrigation ditches. The chain pump was first mentioned in China by the philosopher Wang Chong in his 1st-century-CE *Balanced Discourse.*

The armillary sphere, a three-dimensional representation of the movements in the celestial sphere, was invented in Han China by the 1st century BCE. Using a water clock, waterwheel and a series of gears, the Court Astronomer Zhang Heng (78–139 CE) was able to mechanically rotate his metal-ringed armillary sphere. To address the problem of slowed timekeeping in the pressure head of the inflow water clock, Zhang was the first in China to install an additional tank between the reservoir and inflow vessel. Zhang also invented a seismometer (*Houfeng didong yi*) in 132 CE to detect the exact cardinal or ordinal direction of earthquakes from hundreds of kilometers away. This employed an inverted pendulum that, when disturbed by ground tremors, would trigger a set of gears that dropped a metal ball from one of eight dragon mouths (representing all eight directions) into a metal toad's mouth.

Mathematics

Three Han mathematical treatises still exist. These are the *Book on Numbers and Computation*, the *Arithmetical Classic of the Gnomon and the Circular Paths of Heaven* and the *Nine Chapters on the Mathematical Art*. Han-era mathematical achievements include solving problems with right-angle triangles, square roots, cube roots, and matrix methods, finding more accurate approximations for pi, providing mathematical proof of the Pythagorean theorem, use of the decimal fraction, Gaussian elimination to solve linear equations, and continued fractions to find the roots of equations.

One of the Han's greatest mathematical advancements was the world's first use of negative numbers. Negative numbers first appeared in the *Nine Chapters on the Mathematical Art* as black counting rods, where positive numbers were represented by red counting rods. Negative numbers are used in the Bakhshali manuscript of ancient India, but its exact date of compilation is unknown. Negative numbers were also used by the Greek mathematician Diophantus in about 275 CE, but were not widely accepted in Europe until the 16th century CE.

Astronomy

Mathematics were essential in drafting the astronomical calendar, a lunisolar calendar that used the Sun and Moon as time-markers throughout the year. Use of the ancient Sifen calendar, which measured the tropical year at $365^{1}/_{4}$ days, was replaced in 104 BCE with the Taichu calendar that measured the tropical year at $365^{385}/_{1539}$ days and the lunar month at $29^{43}/_{81}$ days. However, Emperor Zhang later reinstated the Sifen calendar.

Han Chinese astronomers made star catalogues and detailed records of comets that appeared in the night sky, including recording the 12 BCE appearance of the comet now known as Halley's comet.

Han-era astronomers adopted a geocentric model of the universe, theorizing that it was shaped like a sphere surrounding the earth in the center. They assumed that the Sun, Moon, and planets were spherical and not disc-shaped. They also thought that the illumination of the Moon and planets was caused by sunlight, that lunar eclipses occurred when the Earth obstructed sunlight falling onto the Moon, and that a solar eclipse occurred when the Moon obstructed sunlight from reaching the Earth. Although others disagreed with his model, Wang Chong accurately described the water cycle of the evaporation of water into clouds.

Cartography, Nautics, and Vehicles

Evidence found in Chinese literature, and archaeological evidence, show that cartography existed in China before the Han. Some of the earliest Han maps discovered were ink-penned silk maps found amongst the Mawangdui Silk Texts in a 2nd-century-BCE tomb. The general Ma Yuan created the world's first known raised-relief map from rice in the 1st century CE. This date could be revised if the tomb of Qin Shi Huang is excavated and the account in the *Records of the Grand Historian* concerning a model map of the empire is proven to be true.

Although the use of the graduated scale and grid reference for maps was not thoroughly described until the published work of Pei Xiu (224–271 CE), there is evidence that in the early 2nd century CE, cartographer Zhang Heng was the first to use scales and grids for maps.

The Han-era Chinese sailed in a variety of ships differing from those of previous eras, such as the tower ship. The *junk* design was developed and realized during Han. Junks featured a square-ended bow and stern, a flat-bottomed hull or carvel-shaped hull with no keel or sternpost, and solid transverse bulkheads in the place of structural ribs found in Western vessels. Moreover, Han ships were the first in the world to be steered using a rudder at the stern, in contrast to the simpler steering oar used for riverine transport, allowing them to sail on the high seas.

Although ox-carts and chariots were previously used in China, the wheelbarrow was first used in Han China in the 1st century BCE. Han artwork of horse-drawn chariots shows that the Warring-States-Era heavy wooden yoke placed around a horse's chest was replaced by the softer *breast strap*. Later, during the Northern Wei (386–534 CE), the fully-developed horse collar was invented.

Medicine

Han-era medical physicians believed that the human body was subject to the same forces of nature that governed the greater universe, namely the cosmological cycles of yin and yang and the five phases. Each organ of the body was associated with a particular phase. Illness was viewed as a sign that *qi* or "vital energy" channels leading to a certain organ had been disrupted. Thus, Han-era physicians prescribed medicine that was believed to counteract this imbalance. For example, since the wood phase was believed to promote the fire phase, medicinal ingredients associated with the wood phase could be used to heal an organ associated with the fire phase. To this end, the physician Zhang Zhongjing (c. 150–c. 219 CE) prescribed regulated diets rich in certain foods that were thought to curb specific illnesses. These are now known to be nutrition disorders caused by the lack of certain vitamins consumed in one's diet. Besides dieting, Han physicians also prescribed moxibustion, acupuncture, and calisthenics as methods of maintaining one's health. When surgery was performed by the physician Hua Tuo (d. 208 CE), he used anesthesia to numb his patients' pain and prescribed a rubbing ointment that allegedly sped the process of healing surgical wounds.

●●

7
Tang Dynasty

The **Tang Dynasty** (June 18, 618 – June 4, 907) was an imperial dynasty of China preceded by the Sui Dynasty and followed by the Five Dynasties and Ten Kingdoms Period. It was founded by the Li family, who seized power during the decline and collapse of the Sui Empire. The dynasty was interrupted briefly by the Second Zhou Dynasty (October 16, 690 – March 3, 705) when Empress Wu Zetian seized the throne, becoming the first and only Chinese empress regnant, ruling in her own right.

The Tang Dynasty, with its capital at Chang'an (present-day Xi'an), the most populous city in the world at the time, is regarded by historians as a high point in Chinese civilization—equal to or surpassing that of the earlier Han Dynasty—as well as a golden age of cosmopolitan culture. Its territory, acquired through the military campaigns of its early rulers, was greater than that of the Han period, and rivaled that of the later Yuan Dynasty, Ming Dynasty and Qing Dynasty. The enormous Grand Canal of China, built during the previous Sui Dynasty, facilitated the rise of new urban settlements along its route as well as increased trade between mainland Chinese markets. The canal is to this day the longest in the world. In two censuses of the 7th and 8th centuries, the Tang records stated that the population (by number of registered households) was about 50 million people.[a] However, even when the central government was breaking down and unable to compile an accurate census of the population in the 9th century, it is estimated that the population in that century had grown to the size of about 80 million people. With its large population base, the dynasty was able to raise professional and conscripted armies of hundreds of thousands of troops to contend with nomadic powers in dominating Inner Asia and the lucrative trade routes along the Silk Road. Various kingdoms and states paid tribute to the Tang court, while the Tang also conquered or subdued several regions which it indirectly controlled through a protectorate system. Besides political hegemony, the Tang also exerted a powerful cultural influence over neighboring states such as those in Korea and Japan.

In Chinese history, the Tang Dynasty was largely a period of progress and stability, except during the An Shi Rebellion and the decline of central authority in the latter half of the dynasty. Like the previous Sui Dynasty, the Tang Dynasty maintained a civil service system by drafting officials through standardized examinations and recommendations to office. This civil order was undermined by the rise of regional military governors known as jiedushi during the 9th century. Chinese culture flourished and further matured during the Tang era; it is considered the greatest age for Chinese poetry. Two of China's most famous historical poets, Du Fu and Li Bai, belonged to this age, as well as the poets Meng Haoran, Du Mu, and Bai Juyi. Many famous visual artists lived during this era, such as the renowned painters Han Gan, Zhang Xuan, and Zhou Fang. There was a rich variety of historical literature compiled by scholars, as well as encyclopedias and books on geography. There were many notable innovations during the Tang, including the development of woodblock printing, the government compilations of *materia medica*, improvements in cartography and the application of hydraulics to power air conditioning fans. The religious and philosophical ideology of Buddhism became a major aspect of Chinese culture, with native Chinese sects becoming the most prominent. However, Buddhism would eventually be persecuted by the state and would decline in influence. Although the dynasty and central government were in decline by the 9th century, art and culture continued to flourish. The weakened central government largely withdrew from managing the economy, but the country's mercantile affairs stayed intact and commercial trade continued to thrive regardless.

Establishment

The Li family belonged to the northwest military aristocracy prevalent during the reign of the Sui emperors. The mothers of both Emperor Yang of Sui (r. 604-617) and the founding emperor of Tang were sisters, making these two emperors of different dynasties first cousins. Li Yuan (later to become Emperor Gaozu of Tang, r. 618-626) was the Duke of Tang and former governor of Taiyuan when other government officials were fighting off bandit leaders in the collapse of the Sui Empire, caused in part by a failed Korean campaign. With prestige and military experience, he later rose in rebellion along with his son Li Shimin (later Emperor Taizong, r. 626-649) and his equally militant daughter Princess Pingyang (d. 623) who raised her own troops and commanded them. In 617, Li Yuan occupied Chang'an and acted as regent over a puppet child emperor of the Sui, relegating Emperor Yang to the position of *Taishang Huang*, or retired emperor/father of the present emperor. With the news of Emperor Yang's murder by his general Yuwen Huaji (d. 619), on June 18, 618, Li Yuan declared himself the emperor of a new dynasty, the Tang.

Li Yuan ruled until 626 before being forcefully deposed by his son Li Shimin, Prince of Qin. Li Shimin had commanded troops since the age of 18, had prowess with a bow, sword, lance, and was known for his effective cavalry charges. Fighting a numerically superior army, he defeated Dou Jiande (573-621) at Luoyang in the Battle of Hulao on May 28, 621. In a violent elimination of royal family due to fear of assassination,

Li Shimin ambushed and killed two of his brothers, Li Yuanji (b. 603) and Crown Prince Li Jiancheng (b. 589) in the Incident at Xuanwu Gate on July 2, 626. Shortly thereafter, his father abdicated in his favor and Li Shimin ascended the throne. He is conventionally known by his temple name Taizong. Although killing two brothers and deposing his father contradicted the Confucian value of filial piety, Taizong showed himself to be a capable leader who listened to the advice of the wisest members of his council. In 628, Emperor Taizong held a Buddhist memorial service for the casualties of war, and in 629 had Buddhist monasteries erected at the sites of major battles so that monks could pray for the fallen on both sides of the fight. This was during the campaign against Eastern Tujue, a Göktürk khanate that was destroyed after the capture of Jiali Khan Ashini Duobi by the famed Tang military officer Li Jing (571-649), who later became a Chancellor of the Tang Dynasty. With this victory, the Turks accepted Taizong as their Khagan, or Great Khan, in addition to his rule as the Son of Heaven.

ADMINISTRATION AND POLITICS

Initial Reforms

Taizong set out to solve internal problems within the government which had constantly plagued past dynasties. Building upon the Sui legal code, he issued a new legal code that subsequent Chinese dynasties would model theirs upon, as well as neighboring polities in Vietnam, Korea, and Japan. The earliest law code to survive though was the one established in the year 653, which was divided into 500 articles specifying different crimes and penalties ranging from ten blows with a light stick, one hundred blows with a heavy rod, exile, penal servitude, or execution. The legal code clearly distinguished different levels of severity in meted punishments when different members of the social and political hierarchy committed the same crime. For example, the severity of punishment was different when a servant or nephew killed a master or an uncle than when a master or uncle killed a servant or nephew. The Tang Code was largely retained by later codes such as the early Ming Dynasty (1368-1644) code of 1397, yet there were several revisions in later times, such as improved property rights for women during the Song Dynasty (960-1279).

The Tang had three departments (*shìng*), which were obliged to draft, review, and implement policies respectively. There were also six ministries (*bù*) under the administrations that implemented policy, each of which was assigned different tasks. These divisional state bureaus included the personnel administration, finance, rites, military, justice, and public works—an administrative model which would last until the fall of the Qing Dynasty (1644-1912). Although the founders of the Tang related to the glory of the earlier Han Dynasty (202 BC-220 AD), the basis for much of their administrative organization was very similar to the previous Southern and Northern Dynasties. The Northern Zhou (557-581) divisional militia (fubing) was continued by the Tang government, along with farmer-soldiers serving in rotation from the capital or frontier in order to receive appropriated farmland. The equal-field system of the Northern Wei Dynasty (386-534) was also kept, although there were a few modifications.

Although the central and local governments kept an enormous number of records about land property in order to assess taxes, it became common practice in the Tang for literate and affluent people to create their own private documents and signed contracts. These had their own signature and that of a witness and scribe in order to prove in court (if necessary) that their claim to property was legitimate. The prototype of this actually existed since the ancient Han Dynasty, while contractual language became even more common and embedded into Chinese literary culture in later dynasties.

The center of the political power of the Tang was the capital city of Chang'an (modern Xi'an), where the emperor maintained his large palace quarters, and entertained political emissaries with music, sports, acrobatic stunts, poetry, paintings, and dramatic theater performances. The capital was also filled with incredible amounts of riches and resources to spare. When the Chinese prefectural government officials traveled to the capital in the year 643 to give the annual report of the affairs in their districts, Emperor Taizong discovered that many had no proper quarters to rest in, and were renting rooms with merchants. Therefore, Emperor Taizong ordered the government agencies in charge of municipal construction to build every visiting official his own private mansion in the capital.

Imperial Examinations

Following the Sui Dynasty's example, the Tang abandoned the nine-rank system in favor of a large civil service system. Students of Confucian studies were potential candidates for the imperial examinations, the graduates of which could be appointed as state bureaucrats in the local, provincial, and central government. There were two types of exams that were given, *mingjing* ('illuminating the classics examination') and *jinshi* ('presented scholar examination'). The *mingjing* was based upon the Confucian classics, and tested the student's knowledge of a broad variety of texts. The *jinshi* tested a student's literary abilities in writing essay-style responses to questions on matters of governance and politics, as well as their skills in composing poetry. Candidates were also judged on their skills of deportment, appearance, speech, and level of skill in calligraphy, all of which were subjective criteria that allowed the already wealthy members of society to be chosen over ones of more modest means who were unable to be educated in rhetoric or fanciful writing skills. There was a disproportionate number of civil officials coming from aristocratic as opposed to non-aristocratic families. The exams were open to all male subjects whose fathers were not of the artisan or merchant classes, although having wealth or noble status was not a prerequisite in receiving a recommendation. In order to promote widespread Confucian education, the Tang government established state-run schools and issued standard versions of the Five Classics with selected commentaries.

This competitive procedure was designed to draw the best talent into government. But perhaps an even greater consideration for the Tang rulers, aware that imperial dependence on powerful aristocratic families and warlords would have destabilizing consequences, was to create a body of career officials having no autonomous territorial or functional power base. The Tang law code ensured equal division of inherited property amongst legitimate heirs, allowing a bit of social mobility and preventing the families of powerful court officials in becoming landed nobility through primogeniture. As it turned out, these scholar-officials acquired status in their local communities and in family ties, while they also shared values that connected them to the imperial court. From Tang times until the end of the Qing Dynasty in 1912, scholar-officials functioned often as intermediaries between the grassroots level and the government. Yet the potential of a widespread examination system was not fully realized until the Song Dynasty, where the merit-driven scholar official largely shed his aristocratic habits and defined his social status through the examination system. As historian Patricia Ebrey states of the Song period scholar-officials:

The examination system, used only on a small scale in Sui and Tang times, played a central role in the fashioning of this new elite. The early Song emperors, concerned above all to avoid domination of the government by military men, greatly expanded the civil service examination system and the government school system.

Nevertheless, the Sui and Tang dynasties institutionalized and set the foundations for the civil service system and this new elite class of exam-drafted scholar-officials.

Religion and Politics

From the outset, religion played a role in Tang politics. In his bid for power, Li Yuan had attracted a following by claiming descent from the Daoist sage Laozi (fl. 6th century BC). People bidding for office would have monks from Buddhist temples pray for them in public in return for cash donations or gifts if the person was to be selected. Before the persecution of Buddhism in the 9th century, Buddhism and Daoism were accepted side by side, and Emperor Xuanzong of Tang (r. 712-756) invited monks and clerics of both religions to his court. At the same time Xuanzong exalted the ancient Laozi by granting him grand titles, wrote commentary on the Daoist *Laozi*, set up a school to prepare candidates for examinations on Daoist scriptures, and called upon the Indian monk Vajrabodhi (671-741) to perform Tantric rites to avert a drought in the year 726. In 742 Emperor Xuanzong personally held the incense burner during the ceremony of the Ceylonese monk Amoghavajra (705-774) reciting "mystical incantations to secure the victory of Tang forces." While religion played a role in politics, politics also played a role in religion. In the year 714, Emperor Xuanzong forbade shops and vendors in the city of Chang'an to sell copied Buddhist sutras, instead giving the Buddhist clergy of the monasteries the sole right to distribute sutras to the laity. In the previous year of 713, Emperor Xuanzong had liquidated the highly lucrative Inexhaustible Treasury, which was run by a prominent Buddhist monastery in Chang'an. This monastery collected vast amounts of money, silk, and treasures through multitudes of anonymous people's repentances, leaving the donations on the monastery's premise. Although the monastery was generous in donations, Emperor Xuanzong issued a decree abolishing their treasury on grounds that their banking practices were fraudulent, collected their riches, and distributed the wealth to various other Buddhist monasteries, Daoist abbeys, and to repair statues, halls, and bridges in the city.

Taxes and the Census

The Tang Dynasty government attempted to create an accurate census of the size of their empire's population, mostly for effective taxation and matters of military conscription for each region. The early Tang government established both the grain tax and cloth tax at a relatively low rate for each household under the empire. This was meant to encourage households to enroll for taxation and not avoid the authorities, thus providing the government with the most accurate estimate possible. In the census of 609, the population was tallied by efforts of the government at a size of 9 million households, or about 50 million people. Again, the Tang census of the year 742 approximated the size China's population to about 50 million people. Patricia Ebrey writes that even if a rather significant number of people had avoided the registration process of the tax census, the population size during the Tang had not grown significantly since the earlier Han Dynasty (the census of the year 2 recording a population of roughly 58 million people in China). S.A.M. Adshead disagrees, estimating that there were about 75 million people by 750.

In the Tang census of the year 754, there were 1,859 cities, 321 prefectures, and 1,538 counties throughout the empire. Although there were many large and prominent cities during the Tang, the rural and agrarian areas comprised the majority of China's population at some 80 to 90 percent. There was also a dramatic migratory shift of the population from northern to southern China, as the North held 75% of the overall population at the dynasty's inception, but by its end was reduced to 50%.

Chinese population size would not dramatically increase until the Song Dynasty period, where the population doubled to 100 million people due to extensive rice cultivation in central and southern China, coupled with rural farmers holding more abundant yields of food that they could easily provide the growing market.

MILITARY AND FOREIGN POLICY

Protectorates and Tributaries

The 7th century and first half of the 8th century is generally considered the zenith era of the Tang Dynasty. Emperor Tang Xuanzong brought the Middle Kingdom to its golden age while the Silk Road thrived, with sway over Indochina in the south, and to the west Tang China was master of the Pamirs (modern-day Tajikistan) and protector of Kashmir bordering Persia.

Some of the kingdoms paying tribute to the Tang Dynasty included Kashmir, Nepal, Khotan, Kucha, Kashgar, Japan, Korea, Champa, and kingdoms located in Amu Darya and Syr Darya valley. Turkic nomads addressed the Emperor of Tang China as *Tian Kehan*. After the widespread Göktürk revolt of Shabolüe Khan (d. 658) was put down at Issyk Kul in 657 by Su Dingfang (591-667), Emperor Gaozong established several protectorates governed by a Protectorate General or Grand Protectorate General, which extended the Chinese sphere of influence as far as Herat in Western Afghanistan. Protectorate Generals were given a great deal of autonomy to handle local crises without waiting for central admission. After Xuanzong's reign, military governors (jiedushi) were given enormous power, including the ability to maintain their own armies, collect taxes, and pass their titles on hereditarily. This is commonly recognized as the beginning of the fall of Tang's central government.

Soldiers and Conscription

By the year 737, Emperor Xuanzong discarded the policy of conscripting soldiers that were replaced every three years, replacing them with long-service soldiers who were more battle-hardened and efficient. It was more economically feasible as well, since training new recruits and sending them out to the frontier every three years drained the treasury. By the late 7th century, the *fubing* troops began abandoning military service and the homes provided to them in the equal-field system. The supposed standard of 100 *mu* of land alotted to each family was in fact decreasing in size in places where population expanded and the wealthy bought up most of the land. Hard-pressed peasants and vagrants were then induced into military service with benefits of exemption from both taxation and corvée labor service, as well as provisions for farmland and dwellings for dependents who accompanied soldiers on the frontier. By the year 742 the total number of enlisted troops in the Tang armies had risen to about 500,000 men.

Turkic and Western Regions

The Sui and Tang carried out very successful military campaigns against the steppe nomads. Chinese foreign policy to the north and west now had to deal with Turkic nomads, who were becoming the most dominant ethnic group in Central Asia. To handle and avoid any threats posed by the Turks, the Sui government repaired fortifications and received their trade and tribute missions. They sent royal princesses off to marry Turkic clan leaders, a total of four of them in 597, 599, 614, and 617. The Sui stirred trouble and conflict amongst ethnic groups against the Turks. As early as the Sui Dynasty, the Turks had become a major militarized force employed by the Chinese. When the Khitans began raiding northeast China in 605, a Chinese general led 20,000 Turks against them, distributing Khitan livestock and women to the Turks as a reward. On two occasions between 635 to 636, Tang royal princesses were married to Turk mercenaries or generals in Chinese service. Throughout the Tang Dynasty until the end of 755, there were approximately ten Turkic generals serving under the Tang. While most of the Tang army was made of *fubing* Chinese conscripts, the majority of the troops led by Turkic generals were of non-Chinese origin, campaigning largely in the western frontier where the presence of *fubing* troops was low. Some "Turkic" troops were nomadisized Han Chinese, a desinicized people.

Civil war in China was almost totally diminished by 626, along with the defeat in 628 of the Ordos Chinese warlord Liang Shidu; after these internal conflicts, the Tang began an offensive against the Turks. In the year 630, Tang armies captured areas of the Ordos Desert, modern-day Inner Mongolia province, and southern Mongolia from the Turks. After this military victory, Emperor Taizong won the title of Great Khan amongst the various Turks in the region who pledged their allegiance to him and the Chinese empire (with several thousand Turks traveling into China to live at Chang'an). On June 11, 631, Emperor Taizong also sent envoys to the Xueyantuo bearing gold and silk in order to persuade the release of enslaved Chinese prisoners who were captured during the transition from Sui to Tang from the northern frontier; this embassy succeeded in freeing 80,000 Chinese men and women who were then returned to China.

While the Turks were settled in the Ordos region (former territory of the Xiongnu), the Tang government took on the military policy of dominating the central steppe. Like the earlier Han Dynasty, the Tang Dynasty (along with Turkic allies) conquered and subdued Central Asia during the 640s and 650s. During Emperor Taizong's reign alone, large campaigns were launched against not only the Göktürks, but also separate campaigns against the Tuyuhun, the Tufan, the Xiyu states, and the Xueyantuo.

The Tang Empire fought with the Tibetan Empire for control of areas in Inner and Central Asia, which was at times settled with marriage alliances such as the marrying of Princess

Wencheng (d. 680) to Songtsän Gampo (d. 649). There was a long string of conflicts with Tibet over territories in the Tarim Basin between 670-692 and in 763 the Tibetans even captured the capital of China, Chang'an, for fifteen days during the An Shi Rebellion. In fact, it was during this rebellion that the Tang withdrew its western garrisons stationed in what is now Gansu and Qinghai, which the Tibetans then occupied along with the territory of what is now Xinjiang. Hostilities between the Tang and Tibet continued until they signed a formal peace treaty in 821. The terms of this treaty, including the fixed borders between the two countries, are recorded in a bilingual inscription on a stone pillar outside the Jokhang temple in Lhasa.

During the Islamic conquest of Persia (633-656), the son of the last ruler of the Sassanid Empire, Prince Pirooz, fled to Tang China. According to the *Book of Tang*, Pirooz was made the head of a Governorate of Persia in what is now Zaranj, Afghanistan. During this conquest of Persia, the Islamic Caliph Uthman Ibn Affan (r. 644-656) sent an embassy to the Tang court at Chang'an. By the 740s, the Arabs of Khurasan had established a presence in the Ferghana basin and in Sogdiana. At the Battle of Talas in 751, Qarluq mercenaries under the Chinese defected, which forced Tang commander Go Seonji (d. 756, also known as Gao Xianzhi, a general of Goguryeo descent) to retreat. Although the battle itself was not of the greatest significance militarily, this was a pivotal moment in history; it marks the spread of Chinese papermaking into regions west of China, ultimately reaching Europe by the 12th century.

Although they had fought at Talas, on June 11, 758, an Abbasid embassy arrived at Chang'an simultaneously with the Uyghur Turks in order to pay tribute. From even further west, a tribute embassy came to the court of Taizong in 643 from the Patriarch of Antioch.

Korea and Japan

In the east, the Chinese military campaigns were less successful than elsewhere. Like the emperors of the Sui Dynasty before him, Taizong established a military campaign in 644 against the Korean kingdom of Goguryeo in the Goguryeo-Tang Wars; however, this led to its defeat in the First Goguryeo–Tang War. Since the ancient Han and Jin dynasties once had commanderies in ancient northern Korea, the Tang Chinese desired to conquer the region. Allying with the Korean Silla Kingdom, the Chinese fought against Baekje and their Yamato Japanese allies in the Battle of Baekgang in August of 663, a decisive Tang–Silla victory. The Tang Dynasty navy had several different ship types at its disposal to engage in naval warfare, these ships described by Li Quan in his *Taipai Yinjing* (Canon of the White and Gloomy Planet of War) of 759. The Battle of Baekgang was actually a restoration movement by remnant forces of Baekje, since their kingdom was toppled in 660 by a joint Tang–Silla invasion, led by notable Korean general Kim Yushin (595-673) and Chinese general Su Dingfang. In another joint invasion with Silla, the Tang army severely weakened the Goguryeo Kingdom in the north by taking out its outer forts in the year 645. With joint attacks by Silla and Tang armies under commander Li Shiji (594-669), the Kingdom of Goguryeo was destroyed by 668.

Although they were formerly enemies, the Tang accepted officials and generals of Goguryeo into their administration and military, such as the brothers Yeon Namsaeng (634-679) and Yeon Namsan (639-701). From 668 to 676, the Tang Empire would control northern Korea. However, in 671 Silla began fighting the Tang forces there. At the same time the Tang faced threats on its western border when a large Chinese army was defeated by the Tibetans on the Dafei River in 670. By 676, the Tang army was driven out of Korea by Unified Silla. Following a revolt of the Eastern Turks in 679, the Tang abandoned its Korean campaigns.

Although the Tang had fought the Japanese, they still held cordial relations with Japan. There were numerous Imperial embassies to China from Japan, diplomatic missions that were not halted until 894 by Emperor Uda (r. 887-897), upon persuasion by Sugawara no Michizane (845-903). The Japanese Emperor Temmu (r. 672-686) even established his conscripted army on that of the Chinese model, his state ceremonies on the Chinese model, and constructed his palace at Fujiwara on the Chinese model of architecture. Many Chinese Buddhist monks came to Japan to help further the spread of Buddhism as well. Two 7th century monks in particular, Zhi Yu and Zhi You, visited the court of Emperor Tenji (r. 661-672), whereupon they presented a gift of a South Pointing Chariot that they had crafted. This 3rd century mechanically-driven directional-compass vehicle (employing a differential gear) was again reproduced in several models for Tenji in 666, as recorded in the *Nihon Shoki* of 720. Japanese monks also visited China; such was the case with Ennin (794-864), who wrote of his travel experiences including travels along China's Grand Canal. The Japanese monk Enchin (814-891) stayed in China from 839 to 847 and again from 853 to 858, landing near Fuzhou, Fujian and setting sail for Japan from Taizhou, Zhejiang during his second trip to China.

Trade and Spread of Culture

Through use of the land trade along the Silk Road and maritime trade by sail at sea, the Tang were able to gain many new technologies, cultural practices, rare luxury, and contemporary items. From the Middle East, India, Persia, and Central Asia the Tang were able to acquire new ideas in fashion, new types of ceramics, and improved silver-smithing. The Chinese also gradually adopted the foreign concept of stools and chairs as seating, whereas the Chinese beforehand always sat on mats placed on the floor. To the Middle East, the Islamic world coveted and purchased in bulk Chinese goods such as silks, lacquerwares, and porcelain wares. Songs, dances, and musical instruments from foreign regions became popular in China during the Tang Dynasty. These musical instruments included oboes, flutes, and small lacquered drums from Kucha in the Tarim Basin, and percussion instruments from India such as cymbals. At the court there were nine musical ensembles (expanded from seven in the Sui Dynasty) representing music from throughout Asia.

There was great contact and interest in India as a hub for Buddhist knowledge, with famous travelers such as Xuanzang (d. 664) visiting the South Asian subcontinent. After a 17-year long trip, Xuanzang managed to bring back valuable Sanskrit texts to be translated into Chinese. There was also a Turkic–Chinese dictionary available for serious scholars and students, while Turkic folksongs gave inspiration to some Chinese poetry. In the interior of China, trade was facilitated by the Grand Canal and the Tang government's rationalization of the greater canal system that reduced costs of transporting grain and other commodities. The state also managed roughly 32,100 km (19,900 mi) of postal service routes by horse or boat.

Silk Road

The Silk Road was the most important pre-modern Eurasian trade route. During this period of the Pax Sinica, the Silk Road reached its golden age, whereby Persian and Sogdian merchants benefited from the commerce between East and West. At the same time, the Chinese empire welcomed foreign cultures, making the Tang capital arguably the most cosmopolitan area in the world.

Although the Silk Road from China to the West was initially formulated during the reign of Emperor Wu of Han (141-87 BC), it was reopened by the Tang in 639 when Hou Junji (d. 643) conquered the West, and remained open for almost four decades. It was closed after the Tibetans captured it in 678, but in 699, during Empress Wu's period, the Silk

Road reopened when the Tang reconquered the Four Garrisons of Anxi originally installed in 640, once again connecting China directly to the West for land-based trade. The Tang captured the vital route through the Gilgit Valley from Tibet in 722, lost it to the Tibetans in 737, and regained it under the command of the Goguryeo-Korean General Gao Xianzhi. After the An Shi Rebellion ended in 763, the Tang Empire had once again lost control over many of its outer western lands, as the Tibetan Empire largely cut off China's direct access to the Silk Road. An internal rebellion in 848 ousted the Tibetan rulers, while Tang China regained its western territories from Tibet in 851, which contained crucial grazing areas and pastures for raising horses that the Tang Dynasty desperately needed.

Despite the many western travelers coming into China to live and trade, many travelers, mainly religious monks, recorded the strict border laws that the Chinese enforced. As the monk Xuanzang and many other monk travelers attested to, there were many Chinese government checkpoints along the Silk Road that examined travel permits into the Tang Empire. Furthermore, banditry was a problem along the checkpoints and oasis towns, as Xuanzang also recorded that his group of travelers were assaulted by bandits on multiple occasions.

Seaports and Maritime Trade

Chinese envoys had been sailing through the Indian Ocean to India since perhaps the 2nd century BC, yet it was during the Tang Dynasty that a strong Chinese maritime presence could be found in the Persian Gulf and Red Sea, into Persia, Mesopotamia (sailing up the Euphrates River in modern-day Iraq), Arabia, Egypt, Aksum (Ethiopia), and Somalia in the Horn of Africa. From the same Quraysh tribe of Muhammad, Sa'd ibn Abi-Waqqas sailed from Ethiopia to China during the reign of Emperor Gaozu. He later traveled back to China with a copy of the Quran, establishing China's first mosque, the Mosque of Remembrance, during the reign of Emperor Gaozong. To this day he is still buried in a Muslim cemetery at Guangzhou.

During the Tang Dynasty, thousands of foreigners came and lived in numerous Chinese cities for trade and commercial ties with China, including Persians, Arabs, Hindu Indians, Malays, Sinhalese, Khmers, Chams, Jews and Nestorian Christians of the Near East, and many others. In 748, the Buddhist monk Jian Zhen described Guangzhou as a bustling mercantile center where many large and impressive foreign ships came to dock. He wrote that "many big ships came from Borneo, Persia, Qunglun (Indonesia/Java)...with...spices, pearls, and jade piled up mountain high", as written in the *Yue Jue Shu* (Lost Records of the State of Yue). After Arab and Persian pirates burned and looted Guangzhou in 758, the Tang government reacted by shutting the port down for roughly five decades, as foreign vessels docked at Hanoi instead. However, when the port reopened it continued to thrive. In 851 the Arab merchant Suleiman al-Tajir observed the manufacturing of Chinese porcelain in Guangzhou and admired its transparent quality. He also provided a description of Guangzhou's mosque, its granaries, its local government administration, some of its written records, the treatment of travellers, along with the use of ceramics, rice-wine, and tea. However, in another bloody episode at Guangzhou in 879, the Chinese rebel Huang Chao sacked the city, and purportedly slaughtered thousands of native Chinese, along with foreign Jews, Christians, and Muslims in the process. Huang's rebellion was eventually suppressed in 884.

Vessels from Korean Silla, Balhae and Hizen Province of Japan were all involved in the Yellow Sea trade, which Silla dominated. After Silla and Japan reopened renewed hostilities in the late 7th century, most Japanese maritime merchants chose to set sail from Nagasaki towards the mouth of the

Huai River, the Yangzi River, and even as far south as the Hangzhou Bay in order to avoid Korean ships in the Yellow Sea. In order to sail back to Japan in 838, the Japanese embassy to China procured nine ships and sixty Korean sailors from the Korean wards of Chuzhou and Lianshui cities along the Huai River. It is also known that Chinese trade ships traveling to Japan set sail from the various ports along the coasts of Zhejiang and Fujian provinces.

The Chinese engaged in large-scale production for overseas export by at least the time of the Tang. This was proven by the discovery of a silt-preserved shipwrecked Arab dhow in the Gaspar Strait near Belitung, which had 63,000 pieces of Tang gold, silver, and ceramics (including a Changsha bowl inscribed with a date: "16th day of the seventh month of the second year of the Baoli reign", or 826 AD, roughly confirmed by radiocarbon dating of star anise at the wreck). Beginning in 785, the Chinese began to call regularly at Sufala on the East African coast in order to cut out Arab middlemen, with various contemporary Chinese sources giving detailed descriptions of trade in Africa. The official and geographer Jia Dan (730-805) wrote of two common sea trade routes in his day: one from the coast of the Bohai Sea towards Korea and another from Guangzhou through Malacca towards the Nicobar Islands, Sri Lanka and India, the eastern and northern shores of the Arabian Sea to the Euphrates River. In 863 the Chinese author Duan Chengshi (d. 863) provided a detailed description of the slave trade, ivory trade, and ambergris trade in a country called Bobali, which historians suggest was Berbera in Somalia. In Fustat (old Cairo), Egypt, the fame of Chinese ceramics there led to an enormous demand for Chinese goods; hence Chinese often traveled there (this continued into later periods such as Fatimid Egypt). From this time period, the Arab merchant Shulama once wrote of his admiration for Chinese seafaring junks, but noted that their draft was too deep for them to enter the

Euphrates River, which forced them to ferry passengers and cargo in small boats. Shulama also noted that Chinese ships were often very large, with capacities up to 600-700 passengers.

Empress Wu and Emperor Xuanzong

Usurpation of Wu Zetian

Although she entered Emperor Gaozong's court as the lowly consort Wu Zhao, Wu Zetian would rise to the highest seat of power in 690, establishing the short-lived later Zhou Dynasty. Empress Wu's rise to power was achieved through cruel and calculating tactics. For example, she allegedly killed her own baby girl and blamed it on Gaozong's empress so that the empress would be demoted. Emperor Gaozong suffered a stroke in 655, and Wu began to make many of his court decisions for him, discussing affairs of state with his councilors that would take orders from her while she sat behind a screen. When Empress Wu's eldest son and crown prince began to assert his authority and announce his support for issues that were opposed to Empress Wu's ideas, he suddenly died in 675. Many suspected he was poisoned by Empress Wu. Although the next heir apparent kept a lower profile, in 680 he was accused by Wu of plotting a rebellion and was banished (and later forced to commit suicide). After only six weeks on the throne in 683, Emperor Zhongzong was deposed by Empress Wu after his attempt to appoint his wife's father as chancellor. Because she dominated the court of Emperor Ruizong (r. 684-690), a group of Tang princes and their allies staged a major rebellion against Empress Wu in 684; her armies suppressed their dissent within two months. Becoming China's first female emperor in 690 upon her son's forced abdication, she ruled until shortly before her death in 705, deposed by her own retainers while her designated heir became Emperor Zhongzong again.

In order to legitimize her rule, she circulated a document known as the *Great Cloud Sutra,* which predicted that a reincarnation of the Maitreya Buddha would be a female monarch who would dispel illness, worry, and disaster from the world. She even introduced numerous revised written characters to the written language, which reverted back to the originals after her death. Arguably the most important part of her legacy was diminishing the power of the northwest aristocracy, allowing people from other clans and regions of China to become more representative in Chinese politics and government.

Rise of Xuanzong

There were many prominent women at court during and after Wu's reign, including Shangguan Wan'er (664-710), a female poet, writer, and trusted official in charge of Wu's private office. In 706 the wife of Emperor Zhongzong of Tang, Empress Wei (d. 710), convinced her husband to staff government offices with his sister and her daughters, and in 709 requested that he grant women the right to bequeath hereditary privileges to their sons (which before was a male right only). Empress Wei eventually poisoned Zhongzong, whereupon she placed his fifteen year old son upon the throne in 710. Two weeks later, Li Longji (the later Emperor Xuanzong) entered the palace with a few followers and slew Empress Wei and her faction. He then installed his father Emperor Ruizong (r. 710-712) on the throne. Just as Emperor Zhongzong was dominated by Empress Wei, so too was Ruizong dominated by Princess Taiping. This was finally ended when Princess Taiping's coup failed in 712 (she later hanged herself in 713) and Emperor Ruizong abdicated to Emperor Xuanzong.

During the 44 year reign of Emperor Xuanzong, the Tang Dynasty was brought to its height, a golden age, a period of low economic inflation, as well as a toning down of the excessively lavish lifestyle of the imperial court. Seen as a progressive and benevolent ruler, Xuanzong even abolished the death penalty in the year 747, and all executions had to be approved beforehand by the emperor himself (which was relatively few, considering that there were only 24 executions in the year 730 alone). Xuanzong bowed to the consensus of his ministers on policy decisions and made efforts to fairly staff government ministries with different political factions. His staunch Confucian chancellor Zhang Jiuling (673-740) worked to reduce deflation and increase the money supply by upholding the use of private coinage, although his aristocratic and technocratic successor Li Linfu (d. 753) favored government monopoly over the issuance of coinage. After 737 most of Xuanzong's confidence rested in his long-standing chancellor Li Linfu, who championed a more aggressive foreign policy employing non-Chinese generals. This policy ultimately created the conditions for a massive rebellion against Xuanzong.

Decline

An Shi Rebellion and Catastrophe

The Tang Empire was at its height of power up until the middle of the 8th century, when the An Shi Rebellion (December 16, 755 - February 17, 763) destroyed the prosperity of the empire. An Lushan was a half-Sogdian, half-Turk Tang commander since 744, had experience fighting the Khitans of Manchuria with a victory in 744, yet most of his campaigns against the Khitans were unsuccessful. He was given great responsibility in Hebei, which allowed him to rebel with an army of more than one hundred thousand troops. After capturing Luoyang, he named himself emperor of a new, but short-lived, Yan Dynasty. Despite early victories scored by Tang General Guo Ziyi (697-781), the newly recruited troops of the army at the capital were no match for An Lushan's die-hard frontier veterans, so the court fled Chang'an. While the heir apparent raised troops in Shanxi and Xuanzong fled to Sichuan province, they called upon the help of the Uyghur

Turks in 756. The Uyghur khan Moyanchur was greatly excited at this prospect, and married his own daughter to the Chinese diplomatic envoy once he arrived, receiving in turn a Chinese princess as his bride. The Uyghurs helped recapture the Tang capital from the rebels, but they refused to leave until the Tang paid them an enormous sum of tribute in silk. Even Abbasid Arabs assisted the Tang in putting down An Lushan's rebellion. The Tibetans took hold of the opportunity and raided many areas under Chinese control, and even after the Tibetan Empire had fallen apart in 842 (and the Uyghurs soon after) the Tang were in no position to reconquer Central Asia after 763. So significant was this loss that half a century later *jinshi* examination candidates were required to write an essay on the causes of the Tang's decline. Although An Lushan was killed by one of his eunuchs in 757, this time of troubles and widespread insurrection continued until rebel Shi Siming was killed by his own son in 763.

One of the legacies that the Tang government left since 710 was the gradual rise of regional military governors, the jiedushi, who slowly came to challenge the power of the central government. After the An Shi Rebellion, the autonomous power and authority accumulated by the jiedushi in Hebei went beyond the central government's control. After a series of rebellions between 781 and 784 in today's Hebei, Shandong, Hubei and Henan provinces, the government had to officially acknowledge the jiedushi's hereditary ruling without accreditation. The Tang government relied on these governors and their armies for protection and to suppress locals that would take up arms against the government. In return, the central government would acknowledge the rights of these governors to maintain their army, collect taxes and even to pass on their title to heirs. As time passed, these military governors slowly phased out the prominence of civil officials drafted by exams, and became more autonomous from central authority. The rule of these powerful military governors lasted until 960, when a new civil order under the Song Dynasty was established. Also, the abandonment of the equal-field system meant that people could buy and sell land freely. Many poor fell into debt because of this, forced to sell their land to the wealthy, which led to the exponential growth of large estates. With the breakdown of the land allocation system after 755, the central Chinese state barely interfered in agricultural management and acted merely as tax collector for roughly a millennium, save a few instances such as the Song's failed land nationalization during the 13th century war with the Mongols.

With the central government collapsing in authority over the various regions of the empire, it was recorded in 845 that bandits and river pirates in parties of 100 or more began plundering settlements along the Yangtze River with little resistance. In 858, enormous floods along the Grand Canal inundated vast tracts of land and terrain of the North China Plain, which drowned tens of thousands of people in the process.

The Chinese belief in the Mandate of Heaven granted to the ailing Tang was also challenged when natural calamities occurred, forcing many to believe the Heavens were displeased and that the Tang had lost their right to rule. Then in 873 a disastrous harvest shook the foundations of the empire; in some areas only half of all agricultural produce was gathered, and tens of thousands faced famine and starvation. In the earlier period of the Tang, the central government was able to meet crises in the harvest, as it was recorded from 714-719 that the Tang government responded effectively to natural disasters by extending the price-regulation granary system throughout the country. The central government was able then to build a large surplus stock of foods to ward off the rising danger of famine and increased agricultural productivity through land reclamation. In the 9th century, however, the Tang government was nearly helpless in dealing with any calamity.

Rebuilding and Recovery

Although these natural calamities and rebellions stained the reputation and hampered the effectiveness of the central government, the early 9th century is nonetheless viewed as a period of recovery for the Tang Dynasty. The government's withdrawal from its role in managing the economy had the unintended effect of stimulating trade, as more markets with less bureaucratic restrictions were opened up. By 780, the old grain tax and labor service of the 7th century was replaced by a semiannual tax paid in cash, signifying the shift to a money economy bolstered by the merchant class. Cities in the Jiangnan region to the south, such as Yangzhou, Suzhou, and Hangzhou prospered the most economically during the late Tang period. Although weakened after the An Shi Rebellion, in 799 the Tang government's salt monopoly accounted for over half of the government's revenues, while the salt commission became one of the most powerful state agencies, run by capable ministers chosen as specialists in finance. S. A. M. Adshead writes that this salt tax represents "the first time that an indirect tax, rather than tribute, levies on land or people, or profit from state enterprises such as mines, had been the primary resource of a major state." Even after the power of the central government was in decline since the mid 8th century, it was still able to function and give out imperial orders on a massive scale. The *Tangshu* (Book of Tang) compiled in the year 945 recorded that in 828 the Tang government issued a decree that standardized irrigational square-pallet chain pumps in the country:

In the second year of the Taihe reign period [828 AD], in the second month...a standard model of the chain pump was issued from the palace, and the people of Jingzhao Fu (d footnote: the capital) were ordered by the emperor to make a considerable number of machines, for distribution to the people along the Zheng Bai Canal, for irrigation purposes.

The last great ambitious ruler of the Tang Dynasty was Emperor Xianzong of Tang (r. 805-820), his reign period aided by the fiscal reforms of the 780s, including the government monopoly on the salt industry. He also had an effective well trained imperial army stationed at the capital led by his court eunuchs; this was the Army of Divine Strategy, numbering 240,000 in strength as recorded in 798. Between the years 806 and 819, Emperor Xianzong conducted seven major military campaigns to quell the rebellious provinces that had claimed autonomy from central authority, managing to subdue all but two of them. Under his reign there was a brief end to the hereditary jiedushi, as Xianzong appointed his own military officers and staffed the regional bureaucracies once again with civil officials.

However, Xianzong's successors proved less capable and more interested in the leisure of hunting, feasting, and playing outdoor sports, allowing eunuchs to amass more power as drafted scholar-officials caused strife in the bureaucracy with factional parties. The eunuchs' power became unchallenged after Emperor Wenzong of Tang's (r. 826-840) failed plot to have them overthrown; instead the allies of Emperor Wenzong were publicly executed in the West Market of Chang'an, by the eunuchs' command.

Collapse

In addition to natural calamities and jiedushi amassing autonomous control, the Huang Chao Rebellion (874-884) resulted in the sacking of both Chang'an and Luoyang, and took an entire decade to suppress. Although the rebellion was defeated by the Tang, it never recovered from that crucial blow, weakening it for the future military powers to take over. There were also large groups of bandits, in the size of small armies, that ravaged the countryside in the last years of the Tang, who smuggled illicit salt, ambushed merchants and convoys, and even besieged several walled cities.

A certain Zhu Wen (originally a salt smuggler) who had served under the rebel Huang had later surrendered to Tang forces, his military merit in betraying and defeating Huang's forces meaning rapid military promotions for him. In 907, after almost 300 years in power, the dynasty was ended when this military governor, Zhu Wen (known soon after as Taizu of Later Liang), deposed the last emperor of Tang, Emperor Ai of Tang, and took the throne for himself. He established his Later Liang Dynasty, which thereby inaugurated the Five Dynasties and Ten Kingdoms Period. A year later, the deposed Emperor Ai was poisoned to death by Zhu Wen.

Although cast in a negative light by many for usurping power from the Tang, Zhu Wen turned out to be a skilled administrator. Emperor Taizu of Later Liang was also responsible for the building of a large seawall, new walls and roads for the burgeoning city of Hangzhou, which would later become the capital of the Southern Song Dynasty.

SOCIETY AND CULTURE

Both the Sui and Tang Dynasties had turned away from the more feudal culture of the preceding Northern Dynasties, in favor of staunch civil Confucianism. The governmental system was supported by a large class of Confucian intellectuals selected through either civil service examinations or recommendations. In the Tang period, Daoism and Buddhism reigned as core ideologies as well, and played a large role in people's daily lives. The Tang Chinese enjoyed feasting, drinking, holidays, sports, and all sorts of entertainment, while Chinese literature blossomed and was more widely accessible with new printing methods.

Leisure in the Tang

Much more than earlier periods, the Tang era was an era renowned for its time reserved for leisure activity, especially for those in the upper classes. Many outdoor sports and activities were enjoyed during the Tang, including archery, hunting, horse polo, cuju football, cockfighting, and even tug of war. Government officials were granted vacations during their tenure in office. Officials were granted 30 days off every three years to visit their parents if they lived 1,000 miles/ 1,600 kilometres away, or 15 days off if the parents lived more than 167 miles/269 kilometres away (travel time not included). Officials were granted nine days of vacation time for weddings of a son or daughter, and either five, three, or one days/day off for the nuptials of close relatives (travel time not included). Officials also received a total of three days off for their son's capping initiation rite into manhood, and one day off for the ceremony of initiation rite of a close relative's son.

Traditional Chinese holidays such as Chinese New Year, Lantern Festival, Cold Food Festival, and others were universal holidays. In the capital city of Chang'an there was always lively celebration, especially for the Lantern Festival since the city's nighttime curfew was lifted by the government for three days straight. Between the years 628 and 758, the imperial throne bestowed a total of sixty-nine grand carnivals nationwide, granted by the emperor in the case of special circumstances like important military victories, abundant harvests after a long drought or famine, the granting of amnesties, the installment of a new crown prince, etc. For special celebration in the Tang era, lavish and gargantuan-sized feasts were sometimes prepared, as the imperial court had staffed agencies to prepare the meals. This included a prepared feast for 1,100 elders of Chang'an in 664, a feast for 3,500 officers of the Divine Strategy Army in 768, and a feast for 1,200 women of the palace and members of the imperial family in the year 826. Drinking wine and alcoholic beverages was heavily ingrained into Chinese culture, as people drank for nearly every social event. A court official in the 8th century allegedly had a serpentine-shaped structure called the 'Ale Grotto' built with 50,000 bricks on the groundfloor that each featured a bowl from which his friends could drink.

Chang'an, the Tang Capital

Although Chang'an was the site for the capital of the earlier Han and Jin dynasties, after subsequent destruction in warfare, it was the Sui Dynasty model that comprised the Tang era capital. The roughly-square dimensions of the city had six miles (10 km) of outer walls running east to west, and more than five miles (8 km) of outer walls running north to south. From the large Mingde Gates located mid-center of the main southern wall, a wide city avenue stretched from there all the way north to the central administrative city, behind which was the Chentian Gate of the royal palace, or Imperial City. Intersecting this were fourteen main streets running east to west, while eleven main streets ran north to south. These main intersecting roads formed 108 rectangular wards with walls and four gates each, and each ward filled with multiple city blocks. The city was made famous for this checkerboard pattern of main roads with walled and gated districts, its layout even mentioned in one of Du Fu's poems. During the Heian period, the city of Heian kyô (present-day Kyoto) of Japan like many cities was arranged in the checkerboard street grid pattern of the Tang capital and in accordance with traditional geomancy following the model of Chang'an. Of these 108 wards in Chang'an, two of them (each the size of two regular city wards) were designated as government-supervised markets, and other space reserved for temples, gardens, ponds, etc. Throughout the entire city, there were 111 Buddhist monasteries, 41 Daoist abbeys, 38 family shrines, 2 official temples, 7 churches of foreign religions, 10 city wards with provincial transmission offices, 12 major inns, and 6 graveyards. Some city wards were literally filled with open public playing fields or the backyards of lavish mansions for playing horse polo and cuju football.

The Tang capital was the largest city in the world at its time, the population of the city wards and its suburban countryside reaching 2 million inhabitants. The Tang capital was very cosmopolitan, with ethnicities of Persia, Central Asia, Japan, Korea, Vietnam, Tibet, India, and many other places living within. Naturally, with this plethora of different ethnicities living in Chang'an, there were also many different practiced religions, such as Buddhism, Nestorian Christianity, Manichaeism, Zoroastrianism, Judaism, and Islam being practiced within. With widely open access to China that the Silk Road to the west facilitated, many foreign settlers were able to move east to China, while the city of Chang'an itself had about 25,000 foreigners living within. Exotic green-eyed, blond-haired Tocharian ladies serving wine in agate and amber cups, singing, and dancing at taverns attracted customers. If a foreigner in China pursued a Chinese woman for marriage, he was required to stay in China and was unable to take his bride back to his homeland, as stated in a law passed in 628 to protect women from temporary marriages with foreign envoys.

Chang'an was the center of the central government, the home of the imperial family, and was filled with splendor and wealth. However, incidentally it was not the economic hub during the Tang Dynasty. The city of Yangzhou along the Grand Canal and close to the Yangtze River was the greatest economic center during the Tang era.

Yangzhou was the headquarters for the Tang's government monopoly on salt, and the greatest industrial center of China; it acted as a midpoint in shipping of foreign goods that would be organized and distributed to the major cities of the north. Much like the seaport of Guangzhou in the south, Yangzhou boasted thousands of foreign traders from all across Asia.

There was also the secondary capital city of Luoyang, which was the favored capital of the two by Empress Wu. In the year 691 she had more than 100,000 families (more than 500,000 people) from around the region of Chang'an move to populate Luoyang instead. With a population of about a million, Luoyang became the second largest capital in the empire, and with its close proximity to the Luo River it benefited from southern agricultural fertility and trade traffic of the Grand Canal. However, the Tang court eventually demoted its capital status and did not visit Luoyang after the year 743, when Chang'an's problem of acquiring adequate supplies and stores for the year was solved. As early as 736, granaries were built at critical points along the route from Yangzhou to Chang'an, which eliminated shipment delays, spoilage, and pilfering. An artificial lake used as a transshipment pool was dredged east of Chang'an in 743, where curious northerners could finally see the array of boats found in southern China, delivering tax and tribute items to the imperial court.

Literature

The Tang period was a golden age of Chinese literature and art. There are over 48,900 poems penned by some 2,200 Tang authors that have survived until modern times. Perfecting one's skills in the composition of poetry became a required study for those wishing to pass imperial examinations, while poetry was also heavily competitive; poetry contests amongst esteemed guests at banquets and courtiers of elite social gatherings was common in the Tang period. Poetry styles that were popular in the Tang included gushi and jintishi, with the renowned Tang poet Li Bai (701-762) famous for the former style, and Tang poets like Wang Wei (701-761) and Cui Hao (704-754) famous for their use of the latter. Jintishi poetry, or regulated verse, is in the form of eight-line stanzas or seven characters per line with a fixed pattern of tones that required the second and third couplets to be antithetical (although the antithesis is often lost in translation to other languages). Tang poems in particular remain the most popular out of every historical era of China. This great emulation of Tang era poetry began in the Song Dynasty; in that period, Yan Yu (active 1194-1245) asserted that he was the first to designate the poetry of the High Tang (c. 713-766) era as the orthodox material with "canonical status within the classical poetic tradition." Yan Yu reserved the position of highest esteem among all Tang poets for Du Fu (712-770), who was not viewed as such in his own era, and was branded by his peers as an anti-traditional rebel.

There were other important literary forms besides poetry during the Tang period. There was Duan Chengshi's (d. 863) *Miscellaneous Morsels from Youyang*, an entertaining collection of foreign legends and hearsay, reports on natural phenomena, short anecdotes, mythical and mundane tales, as well as notes on various subjects. The exact literary category or classification that Duan's large informal narrative would fit into is still debated amongst scholars and historians.

Short story fiction and tales were also popular during the Tang, one of the more famous ones being *Yingying's Biography* by Yuan Zhen (779-831), which was widely circulated in his own time and by the Yuan Dynasty (1279-1368) became the basis for plays in Chinese opera. Timothy C. Wong places this story within the wider context of Tang love tales, which often share the plot designs of quick passion, inescapable societal pressure leading to the abandonment of romance, followed by a period of melancholy. Wong states that this scheme lacks the undying vows and total self-commitment to love found in Western romances such as *Romeo and Juliet*, but that underlying traditional Chinese values of inseparableness of self from one's environment (including human society) served to create the necessary fictional device of romantic tension.

There were large encyclopedias published in the Tang. The *Yiwen Leiju* encyclopedia was compiled in 624 by the chief editor Ouyang Xun (557-641) as well as Linghu Defen (582-666) and Chen Shuda (d. 635). The encyclopedia *Treatise on*

Astrology of the Kaiyuan Era was fully compiled in 729 by Gautama Siddha (fl. 8th century), an ethnic Indian astronomer, astrologer, and scholar born in the capital Chang'an.

Chinese geographers such as Jia Dan wrote accurate descriptions of places far abroad. In his work written between 785 and 805, he described the sea route going into the mouth of the Persian Gulf, and that the medieval Iranians (whom he called the people of Luo-He-Yi) had erected 'ornamental pillars' in the sea that acted as lighthouse beacons for ships that might go astray. Confirming Jia's reports about lighthouses in the Persian Gulf, Arabic writers a century after Jia wrote of the same structures, writers such as al-Mas'udi and al-Muqaddasi. The Tang Dynasty Chinese diplomat Wang Xuance traveled to Magadha (modern northeastern India) during the 7th century. Afterwards he wrote the book *Zhang Tianzhu Guotu* (Illustrated Accounts of Central India), which included a wealth of geographical information.

Many histories of previous dynasties were compiled between 636 and 659 by court officials during and shortly after the reign of Emperor Taizong of Tang. These included the *Book of Liang, Book of Chen, Book of Northern Qi, Book of Zhou, Book of Sui, Book of Jin, History of Northern Dynasties* and the *History of Southern Dynasties*. Although not included in the official *Twenty-Four Histories*, the *Tongdian* and *Tang Huiyao* were nonetheless valuable written historical works of the Tang period. The *Shitong* written by Liu Zhiji in 710 was a meta-history, as it covered the history of Chinese historiography in past centuries until his time. The *Great Tang Records on the Western Regions*, compiled by Bianji, recounted the journey of Xuanzang, the Tang era's most renowned Buddhist monk.

The Classical Prose Movement was spurred large in part by the writings of Tang authors Liu Zongyuan (773-819) and Han Yu (768-824). This new prose style broke away from the poetry tradition of the 'piantiwen' style begun in the ancient Han Dynasty. Although writers of the Classical Prose Movement imitated 'piantiwen', they criticized it for its often vague content and lack of colloquial language, focusing more on clarity and precision to make their writing more direct. This *guwen* (archaic prose) style can be traced back to Han Yu, and would become largely associated with orthodox Neo-Confucianism.

Religion and Philosophy

Since ancient times, the Chinese believed in a folk religion that incorporated many deities. The Chinese believed that the afterlife was a reality parallel to the living world, complete with its own bureaucracy and afterlife currency needed by dead ancestors. This is reflected in many short stories written in the Tang about people accidentally winding up in the realm of the dead, only to come back and report their experiences.

Buddhism, originating in India around the time of Confucius, continued to flourish during the Tang period and was adopted by the imperial family, becoming thoroughly sinicized and a permanent part of Chinese traditional culture. In an age before Neo-Confucianism and figures such as Zhu Xi (1130-1200), Buddhism had begun to flourish in China during the Southern and Northern Dynasties, and became the dominant ideology during the prosperous Tang. Buddhist monasteries played an integral role in Chinese society, offering lodging for travelers in remote areas, schools for children throughout the country, and a place for urban literati to stage social events and gatherings such as going-away parties. Buddhist monasteries were also engaged in the economy, since their land property and serfs gave them enough revenues to set up mills, oil presses, and other enterprises. Although the monasteries retained 'serfs', these monastery dependents could actually own property and employ others to help them in their work, including their own slaves.

The prominent status of Buddhism in Chinese culture began to decline as the dynasty and central government declined as well during the late 8th century to 9th century. Buddhist convents and temples that were exempt from state taxes beforehand were targeted by the state for taxation. In 845 Emperor Wuzong of Tang finally shut down 4,600 Buddhist monasteries along with 40,000 temples and shrines, forcing 260,000 Buddhist monks and nuns to return to secular life; this episode would later be dubbed one of the Four Buddhist Persecutions in China. Although the ban would be lifted just a few years after, Buddhism never regained its once dominant status in Chinese culture. This situation also came about through new revival of interest in native Chinese philosophies, such as Confucianism and Daoism. Han Yu (786-824)—who Arthur F. Wright stated was a "brilliant polemicist and ardent xenophobe"—was one of the first men of the Tang to denounce Buddhism. Although his contemporaries found him crude and obnoxious, he would foreshadow the later persecution of Buddhism in the Tang, as well as the revival of Confucian theory with the rise of Neo-Confucianism of the Song Dynasty. Nonetheless, Chán Buddhism gained popularity amongst the educated elite. There were also many famous Chan monks from the Tang era, such as Mazu Daoyi, Baizhang, and Huangbo Xiyun. The sect of Pure Land Buddhism initiated by the Chinese monk Huiyuan (334-416) was also just as popular as Chan Buddhism during the Tang.

Rivaling Buddhism was Daoism, a native Chinese philosophical and religious belief system that found its roots in the book of the *Daodejing* (attributed to Laozi in the 6th century BC) and the *Zhuangzi*. The ruling Li family of the Tang Dynasty actually claimed descent from the ancient Laozi. On numerous occasions where Tang princes would become crown prince or Tang princesses taking vows as Daoist priestesses, their lavish former mansions would be converted into Daoist abbeys and places of worship. Many Daoists were associated with alchemy in their pursuits to find an elixir of immortality and a means to create gold from concocted mixtures of many other elements. Although they never achieved their goals in either of these futile pursuits, they did contribute to the discovery of new metal alloys, porcelain products, and new dyes. The historian Joseph Needham labeled the work of the Daoist alchemists as "proto-science rather than pseudo-science." However, the close connection between Daoism and alchemy, which some sinologists have asserted, is refuted by Nathan Sivin, who states that alchemy was just as prominent (if not more so) in the secular sphere and practiced more often by laymen.

The Tang Dynasty also officially recognized various foreign religions. The Assyrian Church of the East, otherwise known as the Nestorian Christian Church, was given recognition by the Tang court. In 781, the Nestorian Stele was created in order to honor the achievements of their community in China. A Christian monastery was established in Shaanxi province where the Daqin Pagoda still stands, and inside the pagoda there is Christian-themed artwork. Although the religion largely died out after the Tang, it was revived in China following the Mongol invasions of the 13th century.

Tang Women

Women's social rights and social status during the Tang era were incredibly liberal-minded for the medieval period. However, this was largely reserved for urbane women of elite status, as men and women in the rural countryside labored hard in their different set of tasks; with wives and daughters responsible for more domestic tasks of weaving textiles and rearing of silk worms, while men tended to farming in the fields. There were many women in the Tang era who gained access to religious authority by taking vows as Daoist priestesses. The head mistresses of the bordellos in the North

Hamlet (also known as the Gay Quarters) of the capital Chang'an acquired large amounts of wealth and power. Their high-class courtesans, who very much resembled Japanese geishas, were well respected. These courtesans were known as great singers and poets, supervised banquets and feasts, knew the rules to all the drinking games, and were trained to have the utmost respectable table manners.

Although they were renowned for their polite behavior, the courtesans were known to dominate the conversation amongst elite men, and were not afraid to openly castigate or criticize prominent male guests who talked too much or too loudly, boasted too much of their accomplishments, or had in some way ruined dinner for everyone by rude behavior (on one occasion a courtesan even beat up a drunken man who had insulted her). When singing to entertain guests, courtesans not only composed the lyrics to their own songs, but they popularized a new form of lyrical verse by singing lines written by various renowned and famous men in Chinese history.

It was fashionable for women to be full-figured (or plump). Men enjoyed the presence of assertive, active women. The foreign horse-riding sport of polo from Persia became a wildly popular trend amongst the Chinese elite, and women often played the sport (as glazed earthenware figurines from the time period portray). The preferred hairstyle for women was to bunch their hair up like "an elaborate edifice above the forehead," while affluent ladies wore extravagant head ornaments, combs, pearl necklaces, face powders, and perfumes. A law was passed in 671 which attempted to force women to wear hats with veils again in order to promote decency, but these laws were ignored as some women started wearing caps and even no hats at all, as well as men's riding clothes and boots, and tight-sleeved bodices.

There were some prominent court women after the era of Empress Wu, such as Yang Guifei (719-756), who had

Emperor Xuanzong appoint many of her relatives and cronies to important ministerial and martial positions.

Tea, Food, and Necessities

During the earlier Southern and Northern Dynasties (420-589), and perhaps even earlier, the drinking of tea became popular in southern China. (Tea comes from the leaf buds of Camelia sinensis, native to southwestern China.) Tea was viewed then as a beverage of tasteful pleasure and with pharmacological purpose as well. During the Tang Dynasty, tea became synonymous with everything sophisticated in society. The Tang poet Lụ Tong (790-835) devoted most of his poetry to his love of tea. The 8th century author Lu Yu (known as the Sage of Tea) even wrote a treatise on the art of drinking tea, called the *Classic of Tea* (Chájîng). Tea was also enjoyed by Uyghur Turks; when riding into town, the first places they visited were the tea shops. Although wrapping paper had been used in China since the 2nd century BC, during the Tang Dynasty the Chinese were using wrapping paper as folded and sewn square bags to hold and preserve the flavor of tea leaves. Indeed, paper found many other uses besides writing and wrapping during the Tang era. Earlier, the first recorded use of toilet paper was made in 589 by the scholar-official Yan Zhitui (531-591), and in 851 an Arab Muslim traveler commented on how the Tang era Chinese were not careful about cleanliness because they did not wash with water when going to the bathroom; instead, he said, the Chinese simply used paper to wipe themselves.

In ancient times, the Chinese had outlined the five most basic foodstuffs known as the five grains: sesamum, legumes, wheat, panicled millet, and glutinous millet. The Ming Dynasty encyclopedist Song Yingxing (1587-1666) noted that rice was not counted amongst the five grains from the time of the legendary and deified Chinese sage Shennong (the existence of whom Yingxing wrote was "an uncertain matter") into the 2nd millenniums BC, because the properly wet and humid climate in southern China for growing rice was not yet fully settled or cultivated by the Chinese.

During the Tang, the many common foodstuffs and cooking ingredients in addition to those already listed were barley, garlic, salt, turnips, soybeans, pears, apricots, peaches, apples, pomegranates, jujubes, rhubarb, hazelnuts, pine nuts, chestnuts, walnuts, yams, taro, etc. The various meats that were consumed included pork, chicken, lamb (especially preferred in the north), sea otter, bear (which was hard to catch, but there were recipes for steamed, boiled, and marinated bear), and even Bactrian camels. In the south along the coast meat from seafood was by default the most common, as the Chinese enjoyed eating cooked jellyfish with cinnamon, Sichuan pepper, cardamom, and ginger, as well as oysters with wine, fried squid with ginger and vinegar, horseshoe crabs and red crabs, shrimp, and pufferfish, which the Chinese called 'river piglet'. Some foods were also off-limits, as the Tang court encouraged people not to eat beef (since the bull was a valuable draft animal), and from 831 to 833 Emperor Wenzong of Tang even banned the slaughter of cattle on the grounds of his religious convictions to Buddhism. From the trade overseas and over land, the Chinese acquired golden peaches from Samarkand, date palms, pistachios, and figs from Persia, pine seeds and ginseng roots from Korea, and mangoes from Southeast Asia. In China, there was a great demand for sugar; during the reign of Harsha (r. 606-647) over North India, Indian envoys to Tang China brought two makers of sugar who successfully taught the Chinese how to cultivate sugarcane. Cotton also came from India as a finished product from Bengal, although it was during the Tang that the Chinese began to grow and process cotton, and by the Yuan Dynasty it became the prime textile fabric in China.

Methods of food preservation were important and practiced throughout China. The common people used simple methods of preservation, such as digging deep ditches and trenches, brining, and salting their foods. The emperor had large ice pits located in the parks in and around Chang'an for preserving food, while the wealthy and elite had their own smaller ice pits. Each year the emperor had laborers carve 1000 blocks of ice from frozen creeks in mountain valleys, each block with the dimension of 0.91 m (3 ft) by 0.91 m by 1.06 m (3½ ft). There were many frozen delicacies enjoyed during the summer, especially chilled melon.

SCIENCE, TECHNOLOGY, AND MEDICINE

Woodblock Printing

Woodblock printing made the written word available to vastly greater audiences. One of the world's oldest surviving printed documents is a miniature Buddhist *dharani* sutra unearthed at Xi'an in 1974 and dated roughly from 650 to 670. The *Diamond Sutra* is the first full-length book printed at regular size, complete with illustrations embedded with the text and dated precisely to 868. Among the earliest documents to be printed were Buddhist texts as well as calendars, the latter essential for calculating and marking which days were auspicious and which days were not. With so many books coming into circulation for the general public, literacy rates could improve, along with the lower classes being able to obtain cheaper sources of study. Therefore, there was more lower class people seen entering the Imperial Examinations and passing them by the later Song Dynasty.

Although the later Bi Sheng's movable type printing in the 11th century was innovative for his period, woodblock printing that became widespread in the Tang would remain the dominant printing type in China until the more advanced printing press from Europe became widely accepted and used in East Asia. The first use of the playing card during the Tang Dynasty was an auxiliary invention of the new age of printing.

Clockworks and Timekeeping

Technology during the Tang period was built also upon the precedents of the past. The mechanical gear systems of Zhang Heng (78-139) and Ma Jun (fl. 3rd century) gave the Tang engineer, astronomer, and monk Yi Xing (683-727) inspiration when he invented the world's first clockwork escapement mechanism in 725. This was used alongside a clepsydra clock and waterwheel to power a rotating armillary sphere in representation of astronomical observation. Yi Xing's device also had a mechanically-timed bell that was struck automatically every hour, and a drum that was struck automatically every quarter hour; essentially, a striking clock. Yi Xing's astronomical clock and water-powered armillary sphere became well known throughout the country, since students attempting to pass the imperial examinations by 730 had to write an essay on the device as an exam requirement. However, the most common type of public and palace timekeeping device was the inflow clepsydra. Its design was improved *c.* 610 by the Sui-dynasty engineers Geng Xun and Yuwen Kai. They provided a steelyard balance that allowed seasonal adjustment in the pressure head of the compensating tank and could then control the rate of flow for different lengths of day and night.

Mechanical Delights and Automatons

There were many other mechanical inventions during the Tang era. This included a 0.91 m (3 ft) tall mechanical wine server of the early 8th century that was in the shape of an artificial mountain, carved out of iron and rested on a lacquered-wooden tortoise frame. This intricate device used a hydraulic pump that siphoned wine out of metal dragon-headed faucets, as well as tilting bowls that were timed to dip wine down, by force of gravity when filled, into an artificial lake that had intricate iron leaves popping up as trays for placing party treats. Furthermore, as the historian Charles Benn describes it:

> Midway up the southern side of the mountain was a dragon...the beast opened its mouth and spit brew into a goblet seated on a large [iron] lotus leaf beneath. When the cup was 80 percent full, the dragon ceased spewing ale, and a guest immediately seized the goblet. If he was slow in draining the cup and returning it to the leaf, the door of a pavilion at the top of the mountain opened and a mechanical wine server, dressed in a cap and gown, emerged with a wooden bat in his hand. As soon as the guest returned the goblet, the dragon refilled it, the wine server withdrew, and the doors of the pavilion closed...A pump siphoned the ale that flowed into the ale pool through a hidden hole and returned the brew to the reservoir [holding more than 16 quarts/15 liters of wine] inside the mountain.

Although the use of a teasing mechanical puppet in this wine-serving device was certainly ingenious, the use of mechanical puppets in China date back to the Qin Dynasty (221-207 BC) while Ma Jun in the 3rd century had an entire mechanical puppet theater operated by the rotation of a waterwheel. There was also an automatic wine-server known in the ancient Greco-Roman world, a design of Heron of Alexandria that employed an urn with an inner valve and a lever device similar to the one described above. There are many stories of automatons used in the Tang, including general Yang Wulian's wooden statue of a monk who stretched his hands out to collect contributions; when the amount of coins reached a certain weight, the mechanical figure moved his arms to deposit them in a satchel. This weight-and-lever mechanism was exactly like Heron's penny slot machine. Other devices included one by Wang Ju, whose "wooden otter" could allegedly catch fish; Needham suspects a spring trap of some kind was employed here.

Medicine

The Chinese of the Tang era were also very interested in the benefits of officially classifying all of the medicines used in pharmacology. In 657, Emperor Gaozong of Tang (r. 649-683) commissioned the literary project of publishing an official *materia medica,* complete with text and illustrated drawings for 833 different medicinal substances taken from different stones, minerals, metals, plants, herbs, animals, vegetables, fruits, and cereal crops. In addition to compiling pharmacopeias, the Tang fostered learning in medicine by upholding imperial medical colleges, state examinations for doctors, and publishing forensic manuals for physicians. Authors of medicine in the Tang include Zhen Qian (d. 643) and Sun Simiao (581-682), the former who first identified in writing that patients with diabetes had an excess of sugar in their urine, and the latter who was the first to recognize that diabetic patients should avoid consuming alcohol and starchy foods. As written by Zhen Qian and others in the Tang, the thyroid glands of sheep and pigs were successfully used to treat goiters; thyroid extracts were not used to treat patients with goiter in the West until 1890.

Structural Engineering

In the realm of technical Chinese architecture, there were also government standard building codes, outlined in the early Tang book of the *Yingshan Ling* (National Building Law). Fragments of this book have survived in the *Tang Lü* (The Tang Code), while the Song Dynasty architectural manual of the *Yingzao Fashi* (State Building Standards) by Li Jie (1065-1101) in 1103 is the oldest existing technical treatise on Chinese architecture that has survived in full. During the reign of Emperor Xuanzong of Tang (712-756) there were 34,850 registered craftsmen serving the state, managed by the Agency of Palace Buildings (Jingzuo Jian).

Cartography

In the realm of cartography, there were further advances beyond the map-makers of the Han Dynasty. When the Tang chancellor Pei Ju (547-627) was working for the Sui Dynasty as a Commercial Commissioner in 605, he created a well-known gridded map with a graduated scale in the tradition of Pei Xiu (224-271). The Tang chancellor Xu Jingzong (592-672) was also known for his map of China drawn in the year 658. In the year 785 the Emperor Dezong had the geographer and cartographer Jia Dan (730-805) complete a map of China and her former colonies in Central Asia. Upon its completion in 801, the map was 9.1 m (30 ft) in length and 10 m (33 ft) in height, mapped out on a grid scale of one inch equaling one hundred *li* (Chinese unit of measuring distance). A Chinese map of 1137 is similar in complexity to the one made by Jia Dan, carved on a stone stele with a grid scale of 100 li. However, the only type of map that has survived from the Tang period are star charts. Despite this, the earliest extant terrain maps of China come from the ancient State of Qin; maps from the 4th century BC that were excavated in 1986.

Alchemy, Gas Cylinders, and Air Conditioning

The Chinese of the Tang period employed complex chemical formulas for an array of different purposes, often found through experiments of alchemy. These included a waterproof and dust-repelling cream or varnish for clothes and weapons, fireproof cement for glass and porcelain wares, a waterproof cream applied to silk clothes of underwater divers, a cream designated for polishing bronze mirrors, and many other useful formulas. The vitrified, translucent ceramic known as porcelain was invented in China during the Tang, although many types of glazed ceramics preceded it.

Ever since the Han Dynasty (202 BC - 220 AD), the Chinese had drilled deep boreholes to transport natural gas from bamboo pipelines to stoves where cast iron evaporation pans boiled brine to extract salt. During the Tang Dynasty, a gazetteer of Sichuan province stated that at one of these 182 m (600 ft) 'fire wells', men collected natural gas into portable bamboo tubes which could be carried around for dozens of km (mi) and still produce a flame. These were essentially the first gas cylinders; Robert Temple assumes some sort of tap was used for this device.

The inventor Ding Huan (fl. 180 AD) of the Han Dynasty invented a rotary fan for air conditioning, with seven wheels 3 m (10 ft) in diameter and manually powered. In 747, Emperor Xuanzong had a "Cool Hall" built in the imperial palace, which the *Tang Yulin* describes as having water-powered fan wheels for air conditioning as well as rising jet streams of water from fountains. During the subsequent Song Dynasty, written sources mentioned the air conditioning rotary fan as even more widely used.

Historiography

The first classic work about the Tang is the *Book of Tang* by Liu Xu (887-946) et al. of the Later Jin, who redacted it during the last years of his life. This was edited into another history (labelled the *New Book of Tang*) in order to distinguish it, which was a work by the Song historians Ouyang Xiu (1007-1072), Song Qi (998-1061), et al. of the Song Dynasty (between the years 1044 and 1060). Both of them were based upon earlier annals, yet those are now lost. Both of them also rank among the *Twenty-Four Histories* of China. One of the surviving sources of the *Book of Tang,* primarily covering up to 756, is the *Tongdian,* which Du You presented to the emperor in 801. The Tang period was again placed into the enormous universal history text of the *Zizhi Tongjian,* edited, compiled, and completed in 1084 by a team of scholars under the Song Dynasty Chancellor Sima Guang (1019-1086). This historical text, written with 3 million Chinese characters in 294 volumes, covered the history of China from the beginning of the Warring States (403 BC) until the beginning of the Song Dynasty (960).

●●

8
Roman Empire

The **Roman Empire** was the post-Republican phase of the ancient Roman civilization, characterised by an autocratic form of government and large territorial holdings in Europe and around the Mediterranean. The term is used to describe the Roman state during and after the time of the first emperor, Augustus. The nearly 500-year-old Roman Republic, which preceded it, had been weakened by several civil wars. Several events are commonly proposed to mark the transition from Republic to Empire, including Julius Caesar's appointment as perpetual dictator (44 BC), the victory of Octavian at the Battle of Actium (2 September 31 BC), and the Roman Senate's granting to Octavian the honorific *Augustus* (4 January 27 BC).

The Latin term *Imperium Romanum* (Roman Empire), probably the best-known Latin expression where the word *imperium* denotes the sphere of human life (for example some countries - lands with people) subdued to military commander - imperator, under Roman rule. Roman expansion began in the days of the Republic, but reached its zenith under Emperor Trajan. At this territorial peak, the Roman Empire controlled approximately 6,500,000 km^2 of land surface. Because of the Empire's vast extent and long endurance, Roman influence upon the language, religion, architecture, philosophy, law, and government of nations around the world lasts to this day.

In the late 3rd century AD, Diocletian established the practice of dividing authority between four co-emperors, in order to better administer the vast territory. In 330 AD, the first Christian Emperor Constantine I, founded Constantinople as new capital of the Empire.. In 392 AD, Emperor Theodosius appointed as co-emperors, his elder son Arcadius for the east part of the Empire and his younger son Honorius for the west part of the Empire. After the death of Theodosius in 395 AD, the empire was finally divided to its east part having Constantinople as capital, and to its west part having Mediolanum (since 402) then Ravenna as capital.

The Western Roman Empire collapsed in 476 as Romulus Augustus was forced to abdicate by Odoacer. The Eastern Roman or Byzantine Empire endured until 1453 with the death of the last de jure Roman Emperor Constantine XI and the capture of Constantinople by the Ottoman Turks led by Mehmed II.

Government

Emperor

The powers of an emperor, (his *imperium*) existed, in theory at least, by virtue of his "tribunician powers" (*potestas tribunicia*) and his "proconsular powers" (*imperium proconsulare*). In theory, the tribunician powers (which were similar to those of the Plebeian Tribunes under the old republic) made the emperor's person and office sacrosanct, and gave the emperor authority over Rome's civil government, including the power to preside over and to control the Senate.

The proconsular powers (similar to those of military governors, or Proconsuls, under the old republic) gave him authority over the Roman army. He was also given powers that, under the republic, had been reserved for the Senate and the assemblies, including the right to declare war, to ratify treaties, and to negotiate with foreign leaders.

The emperor also had the authority to carry out a range of duties that had been performed by the censors, including the power to control senate membership. In addition, the emperor controlled the religious institutions, since, as emperor, he was always *Pontifex Maximus* and a member of each of the four major priesthoods. While these distinctions were clearly defined during the early empire, eventually they were lost, and the emperor's powers became less constitutional and more monarchical.

Realistically, the main support of an emperor's power and authority was the military. Being paid by the imperial treasury, the legionaries also swore an annual military oath of loyalty towards him, called the Sacramentum.

The death of an emperor led to a crucial period of uncertainty and crisis. In theory the senate was entitled to choose the new emperor, but most emperors chose their own successors, usually a close family member. The new emperor had to seek a swift acknowledgement of his new status and authority in order to stabilize the political landscape. No emperor could hope to survive, much less to reign, without the allegiance and loyalty of the Praetorian Guard and of the legions. To secure their loyalty, several emperors paid the *donativum*, a monetary reward.

Senate

While the Roman assemblies continued to meet after the founding of the empire, their powers were all transferred to the Roman Senate, and so senatorial decrees (*senatus consulta*) acquired the full force of law.

In theory, the emperor and the senate were two equal branches of government, but the actual authority of the senate was negligible and it was largely a vehicle through which the emperor disguised his autocratic powers under a cloak of republicanism. Still prestigious and respected, the Senate was largely a glorified rubber stamp institution which had been stripped of most of its powers, and was largely at the emperor's mercy.

Many emperors showed a certain degree of respect towards this ancient institution, while others were notorious for ridiculing it. During senate meetings, the emperor sat between the two consuls, and usually acted as the presiding officer. Higher ranking senators spoke before lower ranking senators, although the emperor could speak at any time. By the third century, the senate had been reduced to a glorified municipal body.

Senators and Equestrians

No emperor could rule the empire without the Senatorial order and the Equestrian order. Most of the more important posts and offices of the government were reserved for the members of these two aristocratic orders. It was from among their ranks that the provincial governors, legion commanders, and similar officials were chosen.

These two classes were hereditary and mostly closed to outsiders. Very successful and favoured individuals could enter, but this was a rare occurrence. The careers of the young aristocrats was influenced by their family connections and the favour of patrons. As important as ability, knowledge, skill, or competence; patronage was considered vital for a successful career and the highest posts and offices required the emperor's favour and trust.

Senatorial Order

The son of a senator was expected to follow the *Cursus honorum*, a career ladder, and the more prestigious positions were restricted to senators only. A senator also had to be wealthy; one of the basic requirements was the wealth of 12,000 gold aurei (about 100 kg of gold), a figure which would later be raised with the passing of centuries.

Equestrian Order

Below the Senatorial order was the Equestrian order. The requirements and posts reserved for this class, while perhaps not so prestigious, were still very important. Some of the more vital posts, like the governorship of Aegyptus, were even forbidden to the members of the Senatorial order and available only to equestrians.

MILITARY

Legions

During and after the civil war, Octavian reduced the huge number of the legions (over 60) to a much more manageable and affordable size (28). Several legions, particularly those with doubtful loyalties, were simply disbanded. Other legions were amalgamated, a fact suggested by the title *Gemina* (Twin).

In AD 9, Germanic tribes wiped out three full legions in the Battle of the Teutoburg Forest. This disastrous event reduced the number of the legions to 25. The total of the legions would later be increased again and for the next 300 years always be a little above or below 30.

Augustus also created the Praetorian Guard: nine cohorts ostensibly to maintain the public peace which were garrisoned in Italy. Better paid than the legionaries, the Praetorians also served less time; instead of serving the standard 25 years of the legionaries, they retired after 16 years of service.

Auxillia

While the Auxillia (Latin: *auxilia* = supports) are not as famous as the legionaries, they were of major importance. Unlike the legionaries, the auxilia were recruited from among the non-citizens. Organized in smaller units of roughly cohort strength, they were paid less than the legionaries, and after 25 years of service were rewarded with Roman citizenship, also extended to their sons. According to Tacitus there were roughly as many auxiliaries as there were legionaries. Since at this time there were 25 legions of around 5,000 men each, the auxilia thus amounted to around 125,000 men, implying approximately 250 auxiliary regiments.

Navy

The Roman Navy (Latin: *Classis*, lit. "fleet") not only aided in the supply and transport of the legions, but also helped in the protection of the frontiers in the rivers Rhine and Danube. Another of its duties was the protection of the very important maritime trade routes against the threat of pirates. Therefore it patrolled the whole of the Mediterranean Sea, parts of the North Atlantic (coasts of Hispania, Gaul, and Britannia), and had also a naval presence in the Black Sea. Nevertheless the army was considered the senior and more prestigious branch.

Provinces

In the old days of the Republic the governorships of the provinces were traditionally awarded to members of the Senatorial Order. Augustus' reforms changed this policy.

Imperial Provinces

Augustus created the Imperial provinces. Most, but not all, of the Imperial provinces were relatively recent conquests and located at the borders. Thereby the overwhelming majority of legions, which were stationed at the frontiers, were under direct Imperial control. Very important was the Imperial province of Aegyptus (modern Egypt), the major breadbasket of the empire, whose grain supply was vital to feed the masses in Rome. It was considered the personal fiefdom of the emperor, and Senators were forbidden to even visit this province.

The governor of Aegyptus and the commanders of any legion stationed there were not from the Senatorial Order, but were chosen by the emperor from among the members of the lower Equestrian Order.

Senatorial Provinces

The old traditional policy continued largely unchanged in the Senatorial provinces. Due to their location, away from the borders, and to the fact that they were under longer Roman sovereignty and control, these provinces were largely peaceful and stable. Only a single legion was based in a Senatorial province: Legio III Augusta, stationed in the Senatorial province of Africa (modern northern Algeria).

The status of a province was subject to change; it could change from Senatorial towards Imperial, or vice-versa. This happened several times during Augustus' reign. Another trend was to create new provinces, mostly by dividing older ones, or by expanding the empire.

Religion

As the empire expanded, and came to include people from a variety of cultures, the worship of an ever increasing number of deities was tolerated and accepted. The imperial government, and the Romans in general, tended to be very tolerant towards most religions and cults, so long as they did not cause trouble. This could easily be accepted by other faiths as Roman liturgy and ceremonies were frequently tailored to fit local culture and identity.

An individual could attend to both the Roman Gods representing his Roman identity and his own personal faith, which was considered part of his personal identity. There were periodic persecutions of various religions at various points in time, most notably that of Christians. As the historian Edward Gibbon noted, however, most of the recorded histories of Christian persecutions come to us through the Christian church, which had an incentive to exaggerate the degree to which the persecutions occurred. The non-Christian contemporary sources only mention the persecutions passingly and without assigning great importance to them.

Imperial Cult

In an effort to enhance loyalty, the inhabitants of the empire were called to participate in the Imperial cult to revere (usually deceased) emperors as demigods. Few emperors claimed to be Gods while living, with the few exceptions being emperors who were widely regarded at the time to be insane (such as Caligula). Doing so in the early empire would have risked revealing the shallowness of what the emperor Augustus called the "restored republic" and would have had a decidedly eastern quality to it. It was, for example, his attempt to make himself a god (in the mold of the kings of the Achaemenid Persian Empire, which he had conquered) that helped to turn Alexander the Great's troops against him. Since the tool was mostly one the emperor used to control his subjects, its usefulness was greatest in the chaotic later empire, when the emperors were often Christians and unwilling to participate in the practice.

Usually, an emperor was deified after his death by his successor in an attempt by that successor to enhance his own prestige. This practice can be misunderstood, however, since "deification" was to the ancient world what canonization is to the Christian world. Likewise, the term "God" had a different context in the ancient world. This could be seen during the years of the Roman Republic with religio-political practices such as the disbanding of a senate session if it was believed the Gods disapproved of the session or wished a particular vote. Deification was one of the many honors a dead emperor was entitled to, as the Romans (more than modern societies) placed great prestige on honors and national recognitions.

The importance of the Imperial cult slowly grew, reaching its peak during the Crisis of the Third Century. Especially in the eastern half of the empire imperial cults grew very popular. As such it was one of the major agents of romanization. The central elements of the cult complex were next to a temple; a theatre or amphitheatre for gladiator displays and other games and a public bath complex. Sometimes the imperial cult was added to the cults of an existing temple or celebrated in a special hall in the bath complex.

The seriousness of this belief is unclear. Some Romans ridiculed the notion that a Roman emperor was to be considered a living god, or would even make fun of the deification of an emperor after his death. Seneca the Younger parodied the notion of apotheosis in his only known satire *The Pumpkinification of Claudius,* in which the clumsy and ill-spoken Claudius is not transformed into a god, but into a pumpkin. In fact, bitter sarcasm was already effected at Claudius' funeral in 54.

Absorption of Foreign Cults

Since Roman religion did not have a core belief that excluded other religions several foreign gods and cults became popular.

The worship of Cybele was the earliest, introduced from around BC 200. Isis and Osiris were introduced from Egypt a century later. Bacchus and Sol Invictus were quite important and Mithras became very popular with the military. Several of these were Mystery cults. In the first century BC Julius Caesar granted Jews the freedom to worship in Rome as a reward for their help in Alexandria.

CONTROVERSIAL RELIGIONS

Druids

Druids were seen as essentially non-Roman: a prescript of Augustus forbade Roman citizens to practice "druidical" rites. Pliny reports that under Tiberius the druids were suppressed—along with diviners and physicians—by a decree of the Senate, and Claudius forbade their rites completely in AD 54.

Judaism

While Judaism was largely accepted, it was on occasion subject to (mostly) local persecution.

Until the rebellion in Judea in AD 66, Jews were generally protected. To get around Roman laws banning secret societies and to allow their freedom of worship, Julius Caesar declared Synagogues were colleges. Tiberius forbade Judaism in Rome but they quickly returned to their former protected status. Claudius expelled Jews from the city however the passage of Suetonius is ambiguous: *"Because the Jews at Rome caused continuous disturbances at the instigation of Chrestus he [Claudius] expelled them from the city"* . *Chrestus* has been identified as another form of *Christus*; the disturbances may have been related to the arrival of the first Christians, and that the Roman authorities, failing to distinguish between the Jews and the early Christians, simply decided to expel them all.

Christianity

Christianity, originally a Jewish religious sect, emerged in Roman Judea in the first century AD. The religion gradually spread out of Judea, initially establishing major bases in first Antioch, then Alexandria, and over time throughout the Empire. For the first two centuries, the imperial authorities largely viewed Christianity simply as a Jewish sect rather than a distinct religion. Suetonius mentions passingly that: *"[during Nero's reign] Punishments were also inflicted on the Christians, a sect professing a new and mischievous religious belief"* but he does not explain for what they were punished.

Tacitus reports that after the Great Fire of Rome in AD 64 some in the population held Nero responsible and that to diffuse blame, he targeted and blamed the Christians. The war against the Jews during Nero's reign, which so destabilized the empire that it led to the first civil war since the days of Julius Caesar and Mark Antony, as well as Nero's suicide, plausibly provided an additional rationale for persecutions against this 'Jewish' sect.

Persecution of Christians would be a recurring theme in the Empire for the next two centuries. Eusebius and Lactantius document the last great persecution of the Christians under Diocletian at the beginning of the 4th century at the urging of Galerius. This was the most vicious persecution of Christians in the Empire's history. After Diocletian, however, the fact that emperors were often Christians themselves lessened whatever persecutions may have still been occurring.

As the 4th century progressed, Christianity had become so widespread that it became officially tolerated, then promoted (Constantine I), and in 380 established as the Empire's official religion (Theodosius I). By the 5th century Christianity had become the Empire's predominant religion rapidly changing the Empire's identity even as the Western provinces collapsed. This would lead to the persecution of the traditional polytheistic religions that had previously characterized most of the Empire.

Languages

The language of Rome before its expansion was Latin, and this became the empire's official language. By the time of the imperial period Latin began evolving into two languages: the 'high' written Classical Latin and the 'low' spoken Vulgar Latin. While Classical Latin remained relatively stable, even through the Middle Ages, Vulgar Latin as with any spoken language was fluid and evolving. Vulgar Latin became the lingua franca in the western provinces, later evolving into the modern Romance languages: Italian, French, Portuguese, Spanish, Romanian, etc. Greek and Classical Latin were considered the languages of literature, scholarship, and education.

Although Latin remained the official and most widely spoken language through to the fall of Rome and for some centuries after in the East, the Greek language was the literary language and sometimes the lingua franca in the Eastern Provinces. With the exception of Carthage, the Romans generally did not attempt to supplant local cultures and languages. It is to their credit that they generally left established customs in place and only gradually supplemented with the typical Roman-style improvements.. Along with Greek, many other languages of different tribes were used but almost without expression in writing.

Greek was already widely spoken in many cities in the east, and as such, the Romans were quite content to retain it as an administrative language there rather than impede bureaucratic efficiency. Hence, two official secretaries served in the Roman Imperial court, one charged with correspondence in Latin and the other with correspondence in Greek for the East. Thus in the Eastern Province, as with all provinces, original languages were retained.

Moreover, the process of hellenisation continued more extensively during the Roman period, for the Romans perpetuated "Hellenistic" culture, but with all the trappings of Roman improvements. This further spreading of "Hellenistic" culture (and therefore language) was largely due to the extensive infrastructure (in the form of entertainment, health, and education amenities, and extensive transportation networks, etc.) put in place by the Romans and their tolerance of, and inclusion of, other cultures, a characteristic which set them apart from the xenophobic nature of the Greeks preceding them.

Since the Roman annexation of Greece in 146 BC, the Greek language gradually obtained a unique place in the Roman world, owing initially to the large number of Greek slaves in Roman households. In Rome itself Greek became the second language of the educated elite. It became the common language in the early Church (as its major centers in the early

Christian period were in the East), and the language of scholarship and the arts.

However, due to the presence of other widely spoken languages in the densely populated east, such as Coptic, Syriac, Armenian, Aramaic and Phoenician (which was also extensively spoken in North Africa), Greek never took as strong a hold beyond Asia Minor (some urban enclaves notwithstanding) as Latin eventually did in the west. This is partly evident in the extent to which the derivative languages are spoken today. Like Latin, the language gained a dual nature with the literary language, an Attic Greek variant, existing alongside spoken language, Koine Greek, which evolved into Medieval or Byzantine Greek (Romaic).

By the 4th century AD, Greek no longer held such dominance over Latin in the Church, arts and sciences as it had previously, resulting to a great extent from the growth of the western provinces (reflected, for example, in the publication in the early 5th century AD of the Vulgate Bible, the first officially accepted Latin Bible; before this only Greek translations were accepted). As the Western Empire declined, the number of people who spoke both Greek and Latin declined as well, contributing greatly to the future East–West / Orthodox–Catholic cultural divide in Europe.

Important as both languages were, today the descendants of Latin are widely spoken in many parts of the world, while the Greek dialects are limited mostly to Greece, Cyprus, and small enclaves in Turkey and southern Italy. To some degree this can be attributed to the fact that the western provinces fell mainly to "Latinised" Christian tribes whereas the eastern provinces fell to Muslim Arabs and Turks for whom Greek held less cultural significance.

Culture

Life in the Roman Empire revolved around the city of Rome, and its famed seven hills. The city also had several theatres. gymnasiums, and many taverns, baths and brothels. Throughout the territory under Rome's control, residential architecture ranged from very modest houses to country villas, and in the capital city of Rome, to the residences on the elegant Palatine Hill, from which the word "*palace*" is derived. The vast majority of the population lived in the city centre, packed into apartment blocks.

Most Roman towns and cities had a forum and temples, as did the city of Rome itself. Aqueducts were built to bring water to urban centres and wine and oil were imported from abroad. Landlords generally resided in cities and their estates were left in the care of farm managers. To stimulate a higher labour productivity, many landlords freed a large numbers of slaves. By the time of Augustus, cultured Greek household slaves taught the Roman young (sometimes even the girls). Greek sculptures adorned Hellenistic landscape gardening on the Palatine or in the villas.

Many aspects of Roman culture were taken from the Greeks. In architecture and sculpture, the difference between Greek models and Roman paintings are apparent. The chief Roman contributions to architecture were the arch and the dome.

The centre of the early social structure was the family, which was not only marked by blood relations but also by the legally constructed relation of patria potestas. The Pater familias was the absolute head of the family; he was the master over his wife, his children, the wives of his sons, the nephews, the slaves and the freedmen, disposing of them and of their goods at will, even putting them to death. Originally, only patrician aristocracy enjoyed the privilege of forming familial clans, or *gens*, as legal entities; later, in the wake of political struggles and warfare, clients were also enlisted. Thus, such plebian *gentes* were the first formed, imitating their patrician counterparts.

Slavery and slaves were part of the social order; there were slave markets where they could be bought and sold. Many slaves were freed by the masters for services rendered; some slaves could save money to buy their freedom. Generally mutilation and murder of slaves was prohibited by legislation. It is estimated that over 25% of the Roman population was enslaved. Professor Gerhard Rempel from the Western New England College claims that in the city of Rome alone, during the Empire, there were about 400,000 slaves.

The city of Rome had a place called the Campus Martius ("Field of Mars"), which was a sort of drill ground for Roman soldiers. Later, the Campus became Rome's track and field playground. In the campus, the youth assembled to play and exercise, which included jumping, wrestling, boxing and racing. Riding, throwing, and swimming were also preferred physical activities.

In the countryside, pastime also included fishing and hunting. Board games played in Rome included Dice (Tesserae or Tali), Roman Chess (Latrunculi), Roman Checkers (Calculi), Tic-tac-toe (Terni Lapilli), and Ludus duodecim scriptorum and Tabula, predecessors of backgammon. There were several other activities to keep people engaged like chariot races, musical and theatrical performances,

Clothing, Dining, and the Arts

The cloth and the dress distinguished one class of people from the other class. The tunic worn by plebeians (common people) like shepherds and slaves was made from coarse and dark material, whereas the tunic worn by patricians was of linen or white wool. A magistrate would wear the tunic augusticlavi; senators wore a tunic with broad stripes, called tunica laticlavi. Military tunics were shorter than the ones worn by civilians. Boys, up until the festival of Liberalia, wore the *toga praetexta*, which was a toga with a crimson or purple border. The *toga virilis*, (or *toga pura*) was worn by men over the age of 16 to signify their citizenship in Rome.

The *toga picta* was worn by triumphant generals and had embroidery of their skill on the battlefield. The *toga pulla* was worn when in mourning. Even footwear indicated a person's social status. Patricians wore red and orange sandal, senators had brown footwear, consuls had white shoes, and soldiers wore heavy boots. Men typically wore a toga, and women a stola. The woman's *stola* looked different than a toga, and was usually brightly coloured. The Romans also invented socks for those soldiers required to fight on the northern frontiers, sometimes worn in sandals.

Romans had simple food habits. Staple food was simple, generally consumed at around 11 o'clock, and consisted of bread, salad, cheese, fruits, nuts, and cold meat left over from the dinner the night before. The Roman poet, Horace mentions another Roman favourite, the olive, in reference to his own diet, which he describes as very simple: "As for me, olives, endives, and smooth mallows provide sustenance." The family ate together, sitting on stools around a table. Fingers were used to eat solid foods and spoons were used for soups.

Wine was considered a staple drink, consumed at all meals and occasions by all classes and was quite cheap. Many types of drinks involving grapes and honey were consumed as well. Drinking on an empty stomach was regarded as boorish and a sure sign for alcoholism, whose debilitating physical and psychological effects were known to the Romans. An accurate accusation of being an alcoholic was an effective way to discredit political rivals.

Roman literature was from its very inception influenced heavily by Greek authors. Some of the earliest works we possess are of historical epics telling the early military history of Rome. As the empire expanded, authors began to produce poetry, comedy, history, and tragedy. Virgil represents the pinnacle of Roman epic poetry. His *Aeneid* tells the story of flight of Aeneas from Troy and his settlement of the city that would become Rome. Lucretius, in his *On the Nature of Things*, attempted to explicate science in an epic poem. The genre of satire was common in Rome, and satires were written by, among others, Juvenal and Persius. Many Roman homes were decorated with landscapes by Greek artists. Portrait sculpture during the period utilized youthful and classical proportions, evolving later into a mixture of realism and idealism. Advancements were also made in relief sculptures, often depicting Roman victories.

Music was a major part of everyday life. The word itself derives from Greek ìïõóéêÞ (*mousike*), "(art) of the Muses". Many private and public events were accompanied by music, ranging from nightly dining to military parades and manoeuvres. In a discussion of any ancient music, however, non-specialists and even many musicians have to be reminded that much of what makes our modern music familiar to us is the result of developments only within the last 1,000 years; thus, our ideas of melody, scales, harmony, and even the instruments we use would not be familiar to Romans who made and listened to music many centuries earlier.

Over time, Roman architecture was modified as their urban requirements changed, and the civil engineering and building construction technology became developed and refined. The Roman concrete has remained a riddle, and even after more than 2,000 years some Roman structures still stand magnificently. The architectural style of the capital city was emulated by other urban centres under Roman control and influence.

Education

Following various military conquests in the Greek East, Romans adapted a number of Greek educational precepts to their own fledgling system. Home was often the learning centre, where children were taught Roman law, customs, and physical training to prepare the boys to grow as Roman citizens and for eventual recruitment into the army. Conforming to discipline was a point of great emphasis. Girls generally received instruction from their mothers in the art of spinning, weaving, and sewing.

Education began at the age of around six, and in the next six to seven years, boys and girls were expected to learn the basics of reading, writing and counting. By the age of twelve, they would be learning Latin, Greek, grammar and literature, followed by training for public speaking. Oratory was an art to be practised and learnt, and good orators commanded respect. To become an effective orator was one of the objectives of education and learning. In some cases, services of gifted slaves were utilized for imparting education.

Economy

The imperial government was, as all governments, interested in the issue and control of the currency in circulation. To mint coins was a political act: the image of the ruling emperor appeared on most issues, and coins were a means of showing his image throughout the empire. Also featured were predecessors, empresses, other family members, and heirs apparent. By issuing coins with the image of an heir his legitimacy and future succession was proclaimed and reinforced. Political messages and imperial propaganda such as proclamations of victory and acknowledgements of loyalty also appeared in certain issues.

Legally only the emperor and the Senate had the authority to mint coins inside the empire. However the authority of the Senate was mainly in name only. In general, the imperial government issued gold and silver coins while the Senate issued bronze coins marked by the legend *"SC"*, short for *Senatus Consulto* "by decree of the Senate". However, bronze coinage could be struck without this legend. Some Greek cities were allowed to mint bronze and certain silver coins, which today are known as *Greek Imperials* (also *Roman Colonials* or *Roman Provincials*). The imperial mints were under the control of a chief financial minister, and the provincial mints were under the control of the imperial provincial procurators. The Senatorial mints were governed by officials of the Senatorial treasury.

Demography

In recent years, question relating to ancient demographics have received increasingly more scholarly attention, with estimates of the population size of the Roman empire at its demographic peak now varying between 60-70 million ("low count") and over 100 million ("high count"). Even by adhering to the more traditional value of 55 million inhabitants, the Roman Empire constituted the most populous Western political unity until the mid-19th century and on a global scale probably until around AD 1000.

HISTORY

Augustus (27 BC–AD 14)

The Battle of Actium resulted in the defeat and subsequent suicides of Mark Antony and Cleopatra. Octavian, now sole ruler of Rome, began a full-scale reformation of military, fiscal and political matters. The powers that he secured for himself were identical in form, if not in name, to those that his predecessor Julius Caesar had secured years earlier as Roman Dictator.

In 36 BC, he was given the power of a Plebeian Tribune, which gave him veto power over the senate, the ability to control the principle legislative assembly (the Plebeian Council), and made his person and office sacrosanct. Up until 32 BC, his status as a Triumvir gave him the powers of an autocrat, but when he deposed Mark Antony that year, he resigned from the Triumvirate, and was then given powers identical to those that he had given up. In 29 BC, Octavian was given the authority of a Roman Censor, and thus the power to appoint new senators.

The senate granted Octavian a unique grade of Proconsular *imperium,* which gave him authority over all Proconsuls (military governors). The unruly provinces at the borders, where the vast majority of the legions were stationed, were under the control of Augustus. These provinces were classified as imperial provinces. The peaceful senatorial provinces were under the control of the Senate. The Roman legions, which had reached an unprecedented number (around 50) because of the civil wars, were reduced to 28.

Augustus also created nine special cohorts, ostensibly to maintain the peace in Italy, keeping at least three of them stationed at Rome. These cohorts became known as the Praetorian Guard. In 27 BC, Octavian transferred control of the state back to the Senate and the People of Rome. The Senate refused the offer, which, in effect, functioned as a popular ratification of his position within the state. Octavian was also granted the title of "Augustus" by the senate, and took the title of *Princeps,* or "first citizen".

As the adopted heir of Caesar, Augustus preferred to be called by this name. *Caesar* was a component of his family name. Julio-Claudian rule lasted for almost a century (from Julius Caesar in the mid-1st century BC to the emperor Nero in the mid-1st century AD). By the time of the Flavian Dynasty, and the reign of Vespasian, and that of his two sons, Titus and Domitian, the term *Caesar* had evolved, almost *de facto,* from a family name into a formal title.

Augustus' final goal was to figure out a method to ensure an orderly succession. In 6 BC Augustus granted tribunician powers to his stepson Tiberius, and before long Augustus realized that he had no choice but to recognize

Tiberius as his heir. In AD 13, the point was settled beyond question. A law was passed which linked Augustus' powers over the provinces to those of Tiberius, so that now Tiberius' legal powers were equivalent to, and independent from, those of Augustus. Within a year, Augustus was dead.

Tiberius to Alexander Severus (14–235)

Augustus was succeeded by his stepson Tiberius, the son of his wife Livia from her first marriage. Augustus was a scion of the *gens* Julia (the Julian family), one of the most ancient patrician clans of Rome, while Tiberius was a scion of the *gens* Claudia, only slightly less ancient than the Julians. Their three immediate successors were all descended both from the *gens* Claudia, through Tiberius's brother Nero Claudius Drusus, and from *gens* Julia, either through Julia the Elder, Augustus's daughter from his first marriage (Caligula and Nero), or through Augustus's sister Octavia Minor (Claudius). Historians thus refer to their dynasty as "Julio-Claudian Dynasty".

The early years of Tiberius's reign were peaceful and relatively benign. However, Tiberius's reign soon became characterised by paranoia and slander. He began a series of treason trials and executions, which continued until his death in 37. The logical successor to the hated Tiberius was his grandnephew, Gaius (better known as "Caligula" or "little boots"). Caligula started out well, but quickly became insane. In 41 Caligula was assassinated, and for two days following his assassination, the senate debated the merits of restoring the republic.

Due to the demands of the army, however, Claudius was ultimately declared emperor. Claudius was neither paranoid like his uncle Tiberius, nor insane like his nephew Caligula, and was therefore able to administer the empire with reasonable ability. In his own family life he was less successful, as he married his niece, who may very well have poisoned him in 54. Nero, who succeeded Claudius, focused much of his attention on diplomacy, trade, and increasing the cultural capital of the empire. Nero, though, is remembered as a tyrant, and committed suicide in 68.

The forced suicide of Nero was followed by a brief period of civil war, known as the "Year of the Four Emperors". Augustus had established a standing army, where individual soldiers served under the same military governors over an extended period of time. The consequence was that the soldiers in the provinces developed a degree of loyalty to their commanders, which they did not have for the emperor. Thus the empire was, in a sense, a union of inchoate principalities, which could have disintegrated at any time. Between June 68 and December 69, Rome witnessed the successive rise and fall of Galba, Otho and Vitellius until the final accession of Vespasian, first ruler of the Flavian dynasty. These events showed that any successful general could legitimately claim a right to the throne.

Vespasian, though a successful emperor, continued the weakening of the Senate which had been going on since the reign of Tiberius. Through his sound fiscal policy, he was able to build up a surplus in the treasury, and began construction on the Colosseum. Titus, Vespasian's successor, quickly proved his merit, although his short reign was marked by disaster, including the eruption of Mount Vesuvius in Pompeii. He held the opening ceremonies in the still unfinished Colosseum, but died in 81. He was succeeded by his brother, Domitian, who had exceedingly poor relations with the senate. Domitian, ultimately, was a tyrant with the character which always makes tyranny repulsive, and this derived in part from the fact that he had no son, and thus was constantly in danger of being overthrown. In September of 96, he was murdered.

The next century came to be known as the period of the "Five Good Emperors", in which the successions were peaceful and the Empire was prosperous. Each emperor of this period was adopted by his predecessor. The last 2 of the "Five Good Emperors" and Commodus are also called Antonines. After his accession, Nerva, who succeeded Domitian, set a new tone: he restored much confiscated property and involved the Roman Senate in his rule.

In 112, Trajan marched on Armenia and annexed it to the Roman Empire. Then he turned south into Parthia, taking several cities before declaring Mesopotamia a new province of the empire, and lamenting that he was too old to follow in the steps of Alexander the Great. During his rule, the Roman Empire was to its largest extent, and would never again advance so far to the east. Hadrian's reign was marked by a general lack of major military conflicts, but he had to defend the vast territories that Trajan had acquired.

Antoninus Pius's reign was comparatively peaceful. During the reign of Marcus Aurelius, Germanic tribes launched many raids along the northern border. The period of the "Five Good Emperors" also commonly described as the Pax Romana, or "Roman Peace" was brought to an end by the reign of Commodus. Commodus was the son of Marcus Aurelius, breaking the scheme of adoptive successors that had turned out so well. Commodus became paranoid and slipped into insanity before being murdered in 192.

The Severan Dynasty, which lasted from 193 until 235, included several increasingly troubled reigns. A generally successful ruler, Septimius Severus, the first of the dynasty, cultivated the army's support and substituted equestrian officers for senators in key administrative positions. His son, Caracalla, extended full Roman citizenship to all free inhabitants of the empire. Increasingly unstable and autocratic, Caracalla was assassinated by Macrinus, who succeeded him, before being assassinated and succeeded by Elagabalus. Alexander Severus, the last of the dynasty, was increasing unable to control the army, and was assassinated in 235.

Crisis of the Third Century and the Later Emperors (235–395)

The Crisis of the Third Century is a commonly applied name for the crumbling and near collapse of the Roman Empire between 235 and 284. During this time, 25 emperors reigned, and the empire experienced extreme military, political, and economic crises. Additionally, in 251, the Plague of Cyprian broke out, causing large-scale mortality which may have seriously affected the ability of the Empire to defend itself. This period ended with the accession of Diocletian, who reigned from 284 until 305, and who solved many of the acute problems experienced during this crisis.

However, the core problems would remain and cause the eventual destruction of the western empire. Diocletian saw the vast empire as ungovernable, and therefore split the empire in half and created two equal emperors to rule under the title of *Augustus*. In doing so, he effectively created what would become the Western Roman Empire and the Eastern Roman Empire. In 293 authority was further divided, as each *Augustus* took a junior Emperor called a *Caesar* to provide a line of succession. This constituted what is now known as the Tetrarchy ("rule of four"). The transitions of this period mark the beginnings of Late Antiquity.

The Tetrarchy would effectively collapse with the death of Constantius Chlorus, the first of the Constantinian dynasty, in 306. Constantius's troops immediately proclaimed his son Constantine the Great as *Augustus*. A series of civil wars broke, which ended with the entire empire being united under Constantine, who legalised Christianity definitively in 313 through the *Edict of Milan*.

In 361, after decades of further civil war, Julian became emperor. His edict of toleration in 362 ordered the reopening of pagan temples, and, more problematically for the Christian Church, the recalling of previously exiled Christian bishops. Julian eventually resumed the war against Shapur II of Persia, although he received a mortal wound in battle and died in 363. His officers then elected Jovian emperor. Jovian is remembered for ceding terrorities won from the Persians, dating back to Trajan, and for restoring the privileges of Christianity, before dying in 364.

Upon Jovian's death, Valentinian I, the first of the Valentinian dynasty, was elected Augustus, and chose his brother Valens to serve as his co-emperor. In 365, Procopius managed to bribe two legions, who then proclaimed him Augustus. War between the two rival Eastern Roman Emperors continued until Procopius was defeated, although in 367, eight-year-old Gratian was proclaimed emperor by the other two. In 375 Valentinian I led his army in a campaign against a Germanic tribe, but died shortly thereafter. Succession did not go as planned. Gratian was then a 16-year-old and arguably ready to act as Emperor, but the troops proclaimed his infant half-brother emperor under the title Valentinian II, and Gratian acquiesced.

Meanwhile, the Eastern Roman Empire faced its own problems with Germanic tribes. One tribe fled their former lands and sought refuge in the Eastern Roman Empire. Valens let them settle on the southern bank of the Danube in 376, but they soon revolted against their Roman hosts. Valens personally led a campaign against them in 378. However this campaign proved disastrous for the Romans. The two armies approached each other near Adrianople, but Valens was apparently overconfident of the numerical superiority of his own forces over the enemy. Valens, eager to have all of the glory for himself, rushed into battle, and on 9 August 378, the

Battle of Adrianople resulted in a crushing defeat for the Romans, and the death of Valens.

Contemporary historian Ammianus Marcellinus estimated that two thirds of the Roman army were lost in the battle. The battle had far-reaching consequences, as veteran soldiers and valuable administrators were among the heavy casualties, which left the Empire with the problem of finding suitable leadership. Gratian was now effectively responsible for the whole of the Empire. He sought however a replacement Augustus for the Eastern Roman Empire, and in 379 choose Theodosius I.

Theodosius, the founder of the Theodosian dynasty, proclaimed his five year old son Arcadius an Augustus in 383 in an attempt to secure succession. Hispanic Celt general Magnus Maximus, stationed in Roman Britain, was proclaimed Augustus by his troops in 383 and rebelled against Gratian when he invaded Gaul. Gratian fled, but was assassinated. Following Gratian's death, Maximus had to deal with Valentinian II, at the time only twelve years old, as the senior Augustus. Maximus soon entered negotiations with Valentinian II and Theodosius, attempting to gain their official recognition, although Negotiations were unfruitful. Theodosius campaigned west in 388 and was victorious against Maximus, who was then captured and executed. In 392 Valentinian II was murdered, and shortly thereafter Arbogast arranged for the appointment of Eugenius as emperor.

However, the eastern emperor Theodosius I refused to recognise Eugenius as emperor and invaded the West, defeating and killing Arbogast and Eugenius. He thus reunited the entire Roman Empire under his rule. Theodosius was the last Emperor who ruled over the whole Empire. As emperor, he made Christianity the official religion of the Roman Empire. After his death in 395, he gave the two halves of the Empire to his two sons Arcadius and Honorius. The Roman state would continue to have two different emperors with different seats of power throughout the 5th century, though the Eastern Romans considered themselves Roman in full. The two halves were nominally, culturally and historically, if not politically, the same state.

Decline of the Western Roman Empire (395–476)

After 395, the emperors in the Western Roman Empire were usually figureheads, while the actual rulers were military strongmen. The year 476 is generally accepted as the formal end of the Western Roman Empire. That year, Orestes refused the request of Germanic mercenaries in his service for lands in Italy. The dissatisfied mercenaries, led by Odoacer, revolted, and deposed the last western emperor, Romulus Augustus. This event has traditionally been considered the fall of the Western Roman Empire.

Odoacer quickly conquered the remaining provinces of Italy, and then sent the Imperial Regalia back to the Eastern Roman Emperor Zeno. Zeno soon received two deputations. One was from Odoacer, requesting that his control of Italy be formally recognised by the Empire, in which case he would acknowledge Zeno's supremacy. The other deputation was from Nepos, the emperor before Romulus Augustus, asking for support to regain the throne. Zeno granted Odoacer's request. Upon Nepos's death in 480, Zeno claimed Dalmatia for the East. Odoacer attacked Dalmatia, and the ensuing war ended with Theodoric the Great, King of the Ostrogoths, conquering Italy.

The Empire became gradually less Romanised and increasingly Germanic in nature: although the Empire buckled under Visigothic assault, the overthrow of the last Emperor Romulus Augustus was carried out by federated Germanic troops from within the Roman army rather than by foreign troops. In this sense had Odoacer not renounced the title of Emperor and named himself "King of Italy" instead, the

Empire might have continued in name. Its identity, however, was no longer Roman—it was increasingly populated and governed by Germanic peoples long before 476.

The Roman people were by the fifth century *"bereft of their military ethos"* and the Roman army itself a mere supplement to federated troops of Goths, Huns, Franks and others fighting on their behalf. Many theories have been advanced in explanation of the decline of the Roman Empire, and many dates given for its fall, from the onset of its decline in the third century to the fall of Constantinople in 1453.

Militarily, however, the Empire finally fell after first being overrun by various non-Roman peoples and then having its heart in Italy seized by Germanic troops in a revolt. The historicity and exact dates are uncertain, and some historians do not consider that the Empire fell at this point. Disagreement persists since the decline of the Empire had been a long and gradual process rather than a single event.

Eastern Roman Empire (476–1453)

As the Western Roman Empire declined during the 5th century, the richer Eastern Roman Empire would be relieved of much destruction, and in the mid 6th century the Eastern Roman Empire (known also as the Byzantine Empire) under the emperor Justinian I reconquered Italy and parts of Illyria from the Ostrogoths, North Africa from the Vandals, and southern Hispania from the Visigoths. The reconquest of southern Hispania was somewhat ephemeral, but North Africa served the Byzantines for another century, parts of Italy for another 5 centuries, and parts Illyria even longer.

Of the many accepted dates for the end of the classical Roman state, the latest is 610. This is when the Emperor Heraclius made sweeping reforms, forever changing the face of the empire. Greek was readopted as the language of government and Latin influence waned. By 610, the Eastern

Roman Empire had come under definite Greek influence, and could be considered to have become what many modern historians now call the Byzantine Empire; however, the Empire was never called thus by its inhabitants, who used terms such as *Romania, Basileia Romaion* or *Pragmata Romaion,* meaning "Land of the Romans", "Kingdom of the Romans", and who still saw themselves as Romans, and their state as the rightful successor to the ancient empire of Rome.

The sack of Constantinople at the hands of the Fourth Crusade in 1204 is sometimes used to date the end of Eastern Roman Empire: the destruction of Constantinople and most of its ancient treasures, total discontinuity of leadership, and the division of its lands into rival states with a Catholic-controlled "Emperor" in Constantinople itself was a blow from which the Empire never fully recovered. Nevertheless, the Byzantines continued to call themselves Romans until their fall to Ottoman Turks in 1453. That year the eastern part of the Roman Empire was ultimately ended by the Fall of Constantinople. Even though Mehmed II, the conqueror of Constantinople, declared himself the Emperor of the Roman Empire (*Caesar of Rome / Kayser-i Rum*) in 1453, Constantine XI is usually considered the last Roman Emperor. The Greek ethnic self-descriptive name "Rhomios" (*Roman*) survives to this day.

MILITARY HISTORY

Principate (27 BC–AD 235)

Between the reigns of the emperors Augustus and Trajan, the Roman Empire achieved great territorial gains in both the East and the West. In the West, following several defeats in 16 BC, Roman armies pushed north and east out of Gaul to subdue much of Germania. Despite the loss of a large army almost to the man in Varus' famous defeat in the Battle of the Teutoburg Forest in AD 9, Rome recovered and continued its expansion up to and beyond the borders of the known world. The Romans invaded Britain in AD 43, forcing their way inland, and building two military bases to protect against rebellion and incursions from the north, from which Roman troops built and manned Hadrian's Wall.

Emperor Claudius ordered the suspension of further attacks across the Rhine, setting what was to become the permanent limit of the Empire's expansion in this direction. Further east, Trajan turned his attention to Dacia. Following an uncertain number of battles, Trajan marched into Dacia, besieged the Dacian capital and razed it to the ground. With Dacia quelled, Trajan subsequently invaded the Parthian empire to the east, his conquests taking the Roman Empire to its greatest extent.

In AD 69, Marcus Salvius Otho had the Emperor Galba murdered and claimed the throne for himself, but Vitellius had also claimed the throne. Otho left Rome, and met Vitellius at the First Battle of Bedriacum, after which the Othonian troops fled back to their camp, and the next day surrendered to the Vitellian forces. Meanwhile, the forces stationed in the Middle East provinces of Judaea and Syria had acclaimed Vespasian as emperor. Vespasians' and Vitellius' armies met in the Second Battle of Bedriacum, after which the Vitellian troops were driven back into their camp. Vespasian, having successfully ended the civil war, was declared emperor.

The First Jewish-Roman War, sometimes called The Great Revolt, was the first of three major rebellions by the Jews of Judaea Province against the Roman Empire. Earlier Jewish successes against Rome only attracted greater attention from Emperor Nero, who appointed general Vespasian to crush the rebellion. By the year 68, Jewish resistance in the North had been crushed. In 115, revolt broke out again in the province, leading to the second Jewish-Roman war known as the Kitos

War, and again in 132 in what is known as Bar Kokhba's revolt. Both were brutally crushed.

Due in large part to their employment of powerful heavy cavalry and mobile horse-archers, the Parthian Empire was the most formidable enemy of the Roman Empire in the east. Trajan had campaigned against the Parthians and briefly captured their capital, putting a puppet ruler on the throne, but the territories were abandoned. A revitalised Parthian Empire renewed its assault in 161, and defeated two Roman armies. General Gaius Avidius Cassius was sent in 162 to counter the resurgent Parthia. The Parthian city of Seleucia on the Tigris was destroyed, and the Parthians made peace but were forced to cede western Mesopotamia to the Romans.

In 197, Emperor Septimius Severus waged a brief and successful war against the Parthian Empire, during which time the Parthian capital was sacked, and the northern half of Mesopotamia was restored to Rome. Emperor Caracalla marched on Parthia in 217 from Edessa to begin a war against them, but he was assassinated while on the march. In 224, the Parthian Empire was crushed not by the Romans but by the rebellious Persian vassal king Ardashir, who revolted, leading to the establishment of Sassanid Empire of Persia, which replaced Parthia as Rome's major rival in the East.

Barracks and Illyrian Emperors (235-284) and Dominate (284–395)

Although the exact historicity is unclear, some mix of Germanic peoples, Celts, and tribes of mixed Celto-Germanic ethnicity were settled in the lands of Germania from the first century onwards. The essential problem of large tribal groups on the frontier remained much the same as the situation Rome faced in earlier centuries, the third century saw a marked increase in the overall threat.

The assembled warbands of the Alamanni frequently crossed the border, attacking Germania Superior such that they were almost continually engaged in conflicts with the Roman Empire. However, their first major assault deep into Roman territory did not come until 268. In that year the Romans were forced to denude much of their German frontier of troops in response to a massive invasion by another new Germanic tribal confederacy, the Goths, from the east. The pressure of tribal groups pushing into the Empire was the end result of a chain of migrations with its roots far to the east.

The Alamanni seized the opportunity to launch a major invasion of Gaul and northern Italy. However, the Visigoths were defeated in battle that summer and then routed in the Battle of Naissus. The Goths remained a major threat to the Empire but directed their attacks away from Italy itself for several years after their defeat.

The Alamanni on the other hand resumed their drive towards Italy almost immediately. They defeated Aurelian at the Battle of Placentia in 271 but were beaten back for a short time, only to reemerge fifty years later. In 378 the Goths inflicted a crushing defeat on the Eastern Empire at the Battle of Adrianople.

At the same time, Franks raided through the North Sea and the English Channel, Vandals pressed across the Rhine, Iuthungi against the Danube, Iazyges, Carpi and Taifali harassed Dacia, and Gepids joined the Goths and Heruli in attacks round the Black Sea. At the start of the fifth century AD, the pressure on Rome's western borders was growing intense.

A military that was often willing to support its commander over its emperor meant that commanders could establish sole control of the army they were responsible for and usurp the imperial throne. The so-called Crisis of the Third Century describes the turmoil of murder, usurpation and in-fighting that is traditionally seen as developing with the murder of the Emperor Alexander Severus in 235.

Emperor Septimius Severus was forced to deal with two rivals for the throne: Pescennius Niger and then Clodius Albinus. Severus' successor Caracalla passed uninterrupted for a while until he was murdered by Macrinus, who proclaimed himsef emperor in his place. The troops of Elagabalus declared him to be emperor instead, and the two met in battle at the Battle of Antioch in AD 218, in which Macrinus was defeated.

However, Elagabalus was murdered shortly afterwards and Alexander Severus was proclaimed emperor, who at the end of his reign was murdered in turn. His murderers raised in his place Maximinus Thrax. However, just as he had been raised by the army, Maximinus was also brought down by them and was murdered when it appeared to his forces as though he would not be able to best the senatorial candidate for the throne, Gordian III.

Gordian III's fate is not certain, although he may have been murdered by his own successor, Philip the Arab, who ruled for only a few years before the army again raised a general to proclaimed emperor, this time Decius, who defeated Philip in the Battle of Verona to seize the throne. Gallienus, emperor from AD 260 to 268, saw a remarkable array of usurpers. Diocletian, a usurper himself, defeated Carinus to become emperor. Some small measure of stability again returned at this point, with the empire split into a Tetrarchy of two greater and two lesser emperors, a system that staved off civil wars for a short time until AD 312. In that year, relations between the tetrarchy collapsed for good. From AD 314 onwards, Constantine the Great defeated Licinius in a series of battles. Constantine then turned to Maxentius, beating him in the Battle of Verona and the Battle of Milvian Bridge.

After overthrowing the Parthian confederacy, the Sassanid Empire that arose from its remains pursued a more aggressive expansionist policy than their predecessors and continued to make war against Rome. In 230, the first Sassanid emperor attacked Roman territory, and in 243, Emperor Gordian III's army defeated the Sassanids at the Battle of Resaena.

In 253 the Sassanids under Shapur I penetrated deeply into Roman territory, defeating a Roman force at the Battle of Barbalissos and conquering and plundering Antiochia. In 260 at the Battle of Edessa the Sassanids defeated the Roman army and captured the Roman Emperor Valerian.

There was a lasting peace between Rome and the Sassanid Empire between 297 and 337 following a treaty between Narseh and Emperor Diocletian. However, just before the death of Constantine I in 337, Shapur II broke the peace and began a twenty-six year conflict, attempting with little success to conquer Roman fortresses in the region. Emperor Julian met Shapur in 363 in the Battle of Ctesiphon outside the walls of the Persian capital. The Romans were victorious but were unable to take the city and were forced to retreat. There were several later wars.

Collapse of the Western Empire (395–476)

After the death of Theodosius I in 395, the Visigoths renounced their treaty with the Empire and invaded northern Italy under their new king Alaric, but were repeatedly repulsed by the Western commander-in-chief Stilicho. However, the *limes* on the Rhine had been depleted of Roman troops, and in early 407 Vandals, Alans, and Suevi invaded Gaul *en masse* and, meeting little resistance, proceeded to cross the Pyrenees, entering Spain in 409.

Stilicho became a victim of court intrigues in Ravenna (where the imperial court resided since 402) and was executed for high treason in 408. After his death, the government became increasingly ineffective in dealing with the barbarians, and in 410 Rome was sacked by the Visigoths.

Under Alaric's successors, the Goths then settled in Gaul (412-418) as *foederati* and for a while were successfully employed against the Vandals, Alans, and Suevi in Spain. Meanwhile, in the turmoil of the preceding years, Roman Britain had been abandoned.

After Honorius' death in 423, the Eastern empire installed the weak Valentinian III as Western Emperor in Ravenna. After a violent struggle with several rivals, Aetius rose to the rank of *magister militum*. Aetius was able to stabilize the empire's military situation somewhat, relying heavily on his Hunnic allies. With their help he defeated the Burgundians, who had occupied part of southern Gaul after 407, and settled them as Roman allies in the Savoy (433). Later that century, as Roman power faded away, the Burgundians extended their rule to the Rhone valley.

Meanwhile, pressure from the Visigoths and a rebellion by the governor of Africa, Bonifacius, had induced the Vandals under their king Gaiseric to cross over from Spain in 429. After capturing Carthage, they established an independent state with a powerful navy (439), which was officially recognised by the Empire in 442. The Vandal fleet from then on formed a constant danger to Roman seafare and the coasts and islands of the Western and Central Mediterranean.

In 444, the Huns, who had been employed as Roman allies by Aetius, were united under their king Attila, who invaded Gaul and was only stopped with great effort by a combined Roman-Germanic force led by Aetius in the Battle of Chalons (451). The next year, Attila invaded Italy and proceeded to march upon Rome, but he halted his campaign and died a year later in 453.

Aetius was murdered by Valentinian in 454, who was then himself murdered by the dead general's supporters a year later. With the end of the Theodosian dynasty, a new period of dynastic struggle ensued. The Vandals took advantage of the unrest, sailed up to Rome, and plundered the city in 455. As the barbarians settled in the former provinces, nominally as allies but *de facto* operating as independent polities, the territory of the Western Empire was effectively reduced to Italy and parts of Gaul.

From 455 onward, several emperors were installed in the West by the government of Constantinople, but their authority only reached as far as the barbarian commanders of the army and their troops (Ricimer (456-472), Gundobad (473-475)) allowed it to. In 475, Orestes, a former secretary of Attila, drove Emperor Julius Nepos out of Ravenna and proclaimed his own son Romulus Augustus as emperor.

In 476, Orestes refused to grant Odoacer and the Heruli federated status, prompting the latter to kill him, depose his son and send the imperial insignia to Constantinople, installing himself as king over Italy. Although isolated pockets of Roman rule continued even after 476, the city of Rome itself was under the rule of the barbarians, and the control of Rome over the West had effectively ended. The Eastern Roman or Byzantine Empire endured until 1453 with the capture of Constantinople by the Ottoman Turks led by Mehmed II.

Legacy

The American magazine *National Geographic* described the legacy of the Roman Empire in *The World According to Rome*:

The enduring Roman influence is reflected pervasively in contemporary language, literature, legal codes, government, architecture, engineering, medicine, sports, arts, etc. Much of it is so deeply inbedded that we barely notice our debt to ancient Rome. Consider language, for example. Fewer and fewer people today claim to know Latin – and yet, go back to the first sentence in this paragraph. If we removed all the words drawn directly from Latin, that sentence would read; "The."

Several states claimed to be the Roman Empire's successors after the fall of the Western Roman Empire. The Holy Roman Empire, an attempt to resurrect the Empire in the West, was established in 800 when Pope Leo III crowned Frankish King Charlemagne as Roman Emperor on Christmas Day, though the empire and the imperial office did not become formalised for some decades. After the fall of Constantinople, the Russian Tsardom, as inheritor of the Byzantine Empire's Orthodox Christian tradition, counted itself the third Rome (with Constantinople having been the second).

When the Ottomans, who based their state on the Byzantine model, took Constantinople in 1453, Mehmed II established his capital there and claimed to sit on the throne of the Roman Empire, and he even went so far as to launch an invasion of Italy with the purpose of "re-uniting the Empire", although Papal and Neapolitan armies stopped his march on Rome at Otranto in 1480. Constantinople was not officially renamed Istanbul until 28 March 1930.

Excluding these states claiming its heritage, if the traditional date for the founding of Rome is accepted as fact, the Roman state can be said to have lasted in some form from 753 BC to the fall in 1461 of the Empire of Trebizond (a successor state and fragment of the Byzantine Empire which escaped conquest by the Ottomans in 1453), for a total of 2,214 years. The Roman impact on Western and Eastern civilisations lives on. In time most of the Roman achievements were duplicated by later civilisations. For example, the technology for cement was rediscovered 1755–1759 by John Smeaton.

The Empire contributed many things to the world, such as a calendar with leap years, the institutions of Christianity and aspects of modern neo-classicistic and Byzantine architecture. The extensive system of roads that was constructed by the Roman Army lasts to this day. Because of this network of roads, the time necessary to travel between destinations in Europe did not decrease until the 19th century, when steam power was invented. Even modern astrology comes to us directly from the Romans.

The Roman Empire also contributed its form of government, which influences various constitutions including those of most European countries and many former European colonies. In the United States, for example, the framers of the Constitution remarked, in creating the Presidency, that they wanted to inaugurate an "Augustan Age". The modern world also inherited legal thinking from Roman law, fully codified in Late Antiquity. Governing a vast territory, the Romans developed the science of public administration to an extent never before conceived or necessary, creating an extensive civil service and formalised methods of tax collection.

While in the West the term "Roman" acquired a new meaning in connection with the church and the Pope of Rome the Greek form Romaioi remained attached to the Greek-speaking Christian population of the Eastern Roman Empire and is still used by Greeks in addition to their common appellation.

The Roman Empire's territorial legacy of controlling the Italian peninsula would serve as an influence to Italian nationalism and the unification (*Risorgimento*) of Italy in 1861.

●●

Index

H

I

J

K

L

M

N

P

Q

R

S

T

V

W

Y

Z